POLITICAL REPRESENTATION

Cultural Memory
in
the
Present

Mieke Bal and Hent de Vries, Editors

POLITICAL
REPRESENTATION

F. R. Ankersmit

STANFORD UNIVERSITY PRESS

STANFORD, CALIFORNIA

2002

Stanford University Press
Stanford, California

© 2002 by the Board of Trustees of the
Leland Stanford Junior University

Printed in the United States of America
on acid-free, archival-quality paper.

Library of Congress Cataloging-in-Publication Data

Ankersmit, F. R.
    Political representation / F.R. Ankersmit.
        p.   cm. — (Cultural memory in the present)
    Includes bibliographical references and index.
    ISBN 0-8047-3981-1 (alk. paper) — ISBN 0-8047-3982-X (pbk. : alk.paper)
    1. Political science.   2. Democracy.   3. History.   I. Title.   II. Series.
JA78 .A55   2002
321.8—dc21   2001048430

Original Printing 2002
Last figure below indicates year of this printing:
11   10   09   08   07   06   05   04   03   02

Typeset by James P. Brommer in 11/13.5 Garamond

CONTENTS

ACKNOWLEDGMENTS

A Dutch version of Chapter 2, "Edmund Burke: Natuurrecht en geschiedenis," was published in my *Macht door representatie*, vol. 3 of *Exploraties: Politieke filosofie* (Kampen, Neth.: Kok/Agora, 1997). Some of the views expounded in chapters 6 to 9 have their origins in this book. This essay first appeared in Wil Verhoeven, ed., *Revolutionary Histories: Cultural Crossings, 1775–1875* (London: Palgrave, 2001) and is reproduced by permission of Palgrave Publishers.

Chapter 3 was published, with the same title, in W. Wrzoska, ed., *Swiat historii* (Poznan, Pol.: Instytut Historii UAM, 1998), 9–35.

Parts of Chapter 4 were previously published as "Political and Historical Representation," in A. C. Sukla, ed., *Art and Representation. Contributions to Contemporary Aesthetics* (Westport: Praeger Press, 2001), 69–90.

A Dutch version of Chapter 5, "Politieke stijl: Schumann en Schiller," was published in D. Pels and H. te Velde, eds., *Politieke stijl: Over representatie en optreden in de politiek* (Amsterdam: Amsterdam University Press, 2000), 15–43.

I would like to thank the publishers mentioned above for their gracious permission to reprint these essays in this book.

POLITICAL REPRESENTATION

INTRODUCTION

This book is about the relationship between history and politics. The history of this relationship is as old and variegated as politics and the writing of history themselves. As soon as the writing of history came into being, and as soon as politics came to be recognized as a separate domain of human endeavor, the nature of their relationship became a topic of intellectual speculation. A first milestone in the history of their relationship is Thucydides' insight into the purpose of his account of the war between Athens and Sparta:

> The absence of romance in my history will, I fear, detract somewhat from its interest; but if it be judged useful by those inquirers who desire an exact knowledge of the past as an aid to interpretation of the future, which in the course of human things must resemble if it does not reflect it, I shall be content. In fine, I have written my work, not as an essay which is to win the applause of the moment, but as a possession for all time.[1]

And countless other authors down to the present—Polybius, Tacitus, Machiavelli, and others—would follow Thucydides' conceptualization of historical writing. Hence, since Cicero, the topos of *historia magistra vitae*.[2]

This topos—or, in Machiavelli's words, the view that "it is an easy thing for whoever examines past things diligently to foresee future things in every republic"[3]—is all the more plausible since most historical writing is, or at least until recently has been, the history of past politics. Certainly one may expect illumination of the nature of politics from a discipline that has politics as its main topic, but a similar argument could be made for the history of art. We need only recall Vasari's *Le vite de più eccellenti architetti, pittori, et scultori italiani* (1550), which was written to promote Florentine art, to see that a history of *x* has, and is often intended to have, its implications for the future practice of *x*. And the same approach can be observed in philosophy: the most influential rewritings of the history of philosophy drew their inspiration from new developments in philosophical thought; and, inversely, each new philosophical system found in a reinterpretation of the history of philosophy part of its intellectual justification. But the relationship between history and politics is an even more intimate one than that between history and art or philosophy. For history and politics not only have a shared subject matter, but there is also considerable overlap in how the historian or the politician attempt to make sense of the world. Two elements in this overlap require our special attention here.

In the first place, political action is by its very nature exclusivist: doing one thing automatically means not doing another. Put differently, on the one hand we have the chaotic context within which political action is to occur, and on the other there is one specific political action that is, in the end, considered to be the most appropriate one. Hence, when moving from chaotic manifold to action, somewhere and somehow a step toward synthesis and unification has to be made. *This* action, and no alternative, is in the end recognized as the proper reaction to or intervention in a complex social and political reality—a reduction or synthesis that is shared by the writing of history and the practice of politics. In the companion volume to this book, *Historical Representation*, I discuss the nature of this synthesizing operation, establishing that the notion of representation is crucial for a proper understanding of it. Furthermore, I show there that representation— either the historical representation of the past or the representation of political reality that is the basis of all meaningful political action—is essentially aesthetic. That is to say, no one can or will doubt for a moment that all of the instruments discovered and refined by (social) scientists and by epistemologists discussing the relationship between knowledge (or language) and the world may be immensely valuable for our knowledge of the past and for political action. But whatever help is offered to us from these specialists, in the end an act of aesthetic synthesis will have to round off the process; and this final move cannot be reduced to these specialists' tools. This is the point at which the politician and the historian meet.

In the second place, political action demands not only an adequate assessment of the context of action: it will often, though not necessarily always, also aim at the realization of certain political or ethical ideals. For two reasons, the logic of the writing of history should be of help here as well. To begin with, there is the problem of the application of a political ideal to the situation in which the politician has to act. How should a context-independent, well-specified aim be tied to a given complex social reality? It is as if one had to find the right words after having heard a performance of, say, Bach's *Mass in B Minor*; no rules can be given that will solve the problem under all circumstances. But we cannot fail to be struck by the parallel with the practice of history, insofar as the historian approaches the past with certain specific questions—for example, what the cause of a certain historical phenomenon has been, how it can best be characterized, what has been its nature, and so on. Both the politician having to realize *tant bien que mal* a political ideal *and* the historian having to answer such questions about the past must consider how an abstract principle (either political ideal or historical question) makes its way into the complexities of a social and political reality. Obviously then, an acquaintance with how the historian approaches this problem may be of help in the practice of politics.

Equally obviously, much will depend on the nature of the political ideals in question. As we saw in Chapter 2 of *Historical Representation*, the criteria of plausibility to which we appeal in order to assess the merits of historical representations are themselves value-independent—and therefore aesthetics takes precedence here over ethics. And this fact justifies the conclusion that the writing of history can be read as an implicit judgment of the pros and cons of political ideals and values. *The best political ideals and values are those that inspire and permeate the most convincing historical writing.* It is true that our own political ideals and values will often predispose us in favor of or against certain historical representations. But the history of historical writing provides an objective standard and reliable measuring instrument for finding out which historical representations have commanded greater respect than others. And this discernment of what values are predominant in the apparently more plausible historical representations will be our best guide in the world of value. Thus, when we enter this world of value we do not enter a domain where, in the end, only subjective preference can be decisive. Not some ultimate or final political or ethical system, but the writing of history will permit us to make an objective decision about political values and ideals.

Of course, one may decide against or in favor of some political value contrary to one's better knowledge and judgment. This has happened only too often: our love of some political ideal often outrivals our love of historical reason, and our political or ethical idealism comes into conflict with the mundane and sobering results of historical debate. Moreover, we need to think only of Marxist historical writing to recognize that it will not always be easy to disentangle ethical preferences from preferences that are aesthetically, representationally based. In cases like these we shall often have to wait until all the dust has settled before we can distinguish one from the other. These facts should not make us forget, however, that in the writing of history aesthetic criteria are, from a logical point of view, stronger than ethical criteria, and hence, that the right political ideals will be found in what has in the long run proven to be the best historical writing. And if it is now objected that the history of historical writing will present us with many examples of how the basest self-interest, ideological prejudice, or even censorship have distorted the judgment of what is good and bad historical representation, my answer is that this merely indicates what should be our supreme political ideals: freedom of thought and the press and the willingness to risk oneself in historical debate. But as soon as these two preliminary conditions of open-minded historical discussion have been fulfilled, one can safely leave the rest to the course and outcome of historical debate.

In sum, we had best rely upon history both for an adequate appraisal of the situation in which the politician has to act and for the selection of the best and most rational political ideals. Obviously, this will have its implications for the place of ethics in politics (and in political theory). It should be noted that the foregoing considerations do not in the least exclude ethics from political action or deny that ethics is an indispensable ingredient in political decision making. What has been argued thus far is merely that the writing of history may show us what kind of ethics we should prefer; when clarity has been reached about this, however, we have no good reason to therefore take ethics less seriously. To repeat: the priority of history to ethics is certainly not to be interpreted as an implicit exhortation to discard ethics and to doubt its value as a guide for ethical and political action.

ETHICS

But, as we all know, this is not the real problem. The real problem only presents itself when the context within which the statesman has to act seems to oblige him to sin against what ethics requires us to do; or, to formulate the problem as it paradigmatically presents itself, when the obligations that the statesman has with regard to a public good come into conflict with his obligation to respect the rights of one or more separate individuals. The former type of obligation is then (often) identified with history and the latter with ethics. Instead of just two gods in our discussion—the gods of history and of politics—there are three: history, politics, *and* ethics. And unlike the happy situation in the Christian pantheon, where God, the Son, and the Holy Ghost form together the Holy Trinity, this pantheon is divided against itself. This disunion in our political heaven forces the politician to decide between an alliance with history or one with ethics.

One preliminary remark is due here. It should be observed that the politician's conflict could also be reformulated exclusively in either "historical" or "ethical" terms. It is important to insist on this since we should not commit the mistake of identifying a politician's actual dilemma with the dilemma between history and ethics. A politician's judgment about the latter dilemma does not automatically resolve all the problems with which he or she may be confronted. And sometimes the "historical" decision may look surprisingly like the "ethical" one, or vice versa. For even though politicians may decide to appeal to historical expediency or prudence (to use the most appropriate term in this context), precisely this may require them to prefer the respect of individual rights to the public good. A politician may realize, for example, that doing the opposite would result in some disastrous social conflict, a conflict that might even escalate into civil war or revolution. On the other hand, ethics may sometimes require politicians to prefer the public good to the rights of individuals. For example, a politician may come to see that the property rights of rich individuals have to be overridden since a more just distribution of wealth and income will, in the end, be in the nation's interest. So we should not caricaturize the opposition between history and ethics by believing that politicians' dilemmas have all been solved once they have made up their minds about the conflict between history and ethics. Though both history and ethics suggest their own way of dealing with political dilemmas, in neither case is it automatically clear what has to be done and in each case a careful and responsible deliberation, weighing the two alternatives, will still be necessary.

But if history and ethics provide different ways of dealing with political dilemmas, we may well ask what the nature of the difference is. Surely, this is the point at which Machiavelli comes in with his notorious observation that the prince should *entrare nel malo, necessitato.* That is, sometimes historical necessity will require the prince to sin against the requirements of (Christian) ethics. Though we all immediately recognize what Machiavelli had in mind, it is not so easy to define the nature of the conflict between historical prudence and ethics. For it might now be pointed out, in agreement with what was said in the previous paragraph, that the conflict could, in principle, be reformulated in exclusively ethical terms. For if the politician is confronted with the dilemma between furthering the public good and the respect of the right of individuals, a consequentionalist or utilitarian ethics could be conceived that would require a preference of the former over the latter. And this would transform the (then only apparent) conflict between history and ethics into what proves to be, in the end, a civil war between different ethical systems.

Nevertheless, if the politician has to decide between, on the one hand, having to cheat and murder in order to realize the public good and, on the other hand, decent behavior, we feel an invincible need to phrase this dilemma in terms of the opposition between history and ethics. The five-centuries-long scandal of Machiavellianism has only been possible because we unhesitatingly reject any attempt to admit the "historical option" to the domain of ethics. Why is this so? Admittedly, although most ethical systems would leave no room for the this option, it is not a priori clear that this necessarily would be true for *all* ethical systems. Whence, then, our firm decision to see here only a conflict between history and ethics?

My hunch would be that we are inclined not to see the "historical option" as a solution to the dilemma. It simply is a *choice,* a choice that may well have contributed to the realization of the public good, but that, on the other hand, has also made politicians commit the grossest injustices toward many individual people. It is a choice that has not solved our problem at all. For a *real solution* to the dilemma would have given us both the realization of the public good *and* the respect of the rights of individual persons. And this is what we always expect from ethics. If we see in dilemmas like these a conflict between history and ethics rather than the sign of a civil war going on in ethics itself, this probably is because we like to believe that, like scientific problems, ethical problems can always be solved if only we think long and hard enough. We think that the realm of ethics is that within which all human actions can be made commensurable with each other: for does not the rationality of ethical discussion and deliberation automatically "secrete," create, or suggest an atmosphere of commensurability? If ethical problems can be discussed rationally—and who would wish to doubt this? —is reason then not the *tertia comparationis* of *all* our moral options, however much they may differ or may seem to lack a common ground? Therefore, if ethics runs into intractable paradoxes we will feel an irrepressible urge to believe that the real malefactor should be looked for elsewhere—for example, in history.

This, then, is in the end the nature of the problem that Machiavelli put on the agenda of political philosophy. That is to say, can all our moral dilemmas be stated in such a way as to make them commensurable? As Isaiah Berlin has demonstrated,[4] Machiavelli answered this question with a firm and unambiguous "no" by making his readers aware of the *in*commensurability of our moral ideals—in his case the incommensurability of Christian ethics and the pagan morality from which his acceptance of historical prudence originated. We live in a world in which one moral good may be the mortal enemy of another moral good. Undoubtedly Berlin was correct in saying that we find this most regrettable aspect of the *condition humaine* extremely difficult to accept, and that we therefore tend to forget it; and that, by doing so, we create this unbridgeable gap between what history on the one hand and ethics on the other seem to require us to do. Or, to be more precise, there are two gaps instead of just one: there is the gap between historical reason and ethical reason *and* the gap between what each of them may recommend us to do in case of a political dilemma.

The example of Machiavelli may explain, next, why the gap is so deep and unbridgeable. We should recall here that Machiavelli should be placed in the republican tradition that goes back to Roman historians and political theorists, in which the citizen is required to prefer the public good to personal well-being. *Iustum et dulce est pro patria mori.* On the other hand, Machiavelli's prince is very much a product of the Renaissance, that is, an individual who is left to his own devices in a hostile world ruled by chance and (mis)fortune. The reassuring all-encompassing Stoic or Christian order had fallen away, and the domains of the private and the public, hitherto in an intimate union, had now been polarized to an unprecedented degree. The human individual (and, especially, the politician), then, was henceforward the citizen of two domains, the gap between which is truly unbridgeable. So, to the extent that the distinction between the private and the public (each domain being the natural biotope for a specific set of ethical systems) will appear necessary to us, the conflict between history and ethics will be as inevitable as it is insoluble. Half a millennium of vain intellectual struggle with Machiavelli's problem testifies to this. Indeed, as long as we believe the distinction between the private and the public makes sense, everyone courageously diving into this murky slough of stubborn paradoxes is bound to come to the surface again with mud on his or her face.

PROSPECT

The first three chapters of this book are a historical investigation of the conflict between history and ethics. The first chapter deals with the relationship between Machiavellianism and natural law philosophy. It is argued that we should distinguish between two variants of Machiavellianism: the *arcanum imperii* tradition, which avoids any concession in the conflict between history and ethics (or natural law), and the *raison d'état* tradition, which aims at a reconciliation between the two. The former tradition was a historical curiosity that was destined to die off before the middle of the seventeenth century; the other tradition flourished mainly in Germany and, as was shown already by Friedrich Meinecke, has substantially contributed to the rise of historism and thus to the birth of the writing of history as we know it down to the present day.

The second chapter also deals with the problem of historism; specifically, why Burke's political philosophy prevented him from reaching historist conclusions. This question is an obvious one, since Burke's insistence that the politician should take into account actual historical fact brought him quite close to historism. I argue that Burke's Aristotelianism differed from the one that was current in eighteenth-century Germany. German Aristotelianism justified the formulation of political goals on the basis of history, whereas within Burke's Aristotelianism history was only a reality that should not be overlooked. History could become a *guide* for politicians in Germany, whereas history was for Burke merely an indispensable *companion*.

Freud is presented in the third chapter as a natural law philosopher whose state of nature is the primeval horde dominated by the powerful father. The murder of the father by the sons is, for Freud, the beginning of human society as we still know it. Just as in seventeenth- and eighteenth-century natural law speculations, Freud derives all the essential features of human society from the circumstances under which this transition from the state of nature to human society took place. But whereas earlier natural law philosophy often used these speculations to defend suggestions for the improvement of the existing social and political order, Freud leaves little room for such improvement. This is not primarily because of Freud's political pessimism (though this undoubtedly is part of the explanation as well) but mainly is a result of the tension between psychologism and sociologism that is inherent in all natural law speculation. To the extent that the psychological component is stronger (as also is the case with, for example, Rousseau), pessimism is the more likely outcome; but if the picture of the human psyche is poor and sketchy (as in Hobbes or Locke) and the emphasis is on social interaction, optimistic conclusions are more likely. The result is either a satisfactory natural law philosophy that is founded on a poor psychology or a satisfactory psychology that results in a poor natural law philosophy. One cannot help but suspect, therefore, that an irreparable mismatch between psychology and politics is one of the fatal weaknesses of all natural law philosophy.

The subject of Chapter 4, which is the most important chapter of the book, is representative democracy—at first sight, a completely different topic from those of the previous chapters. Nevertheless there is continuity. In Chapters 1 to 3, natural law philosophy is discussed mainly in relation to its resistance to history, a resistance that has its parallel in our seeing democracy as a timeless truth, just as natural law was for seventeenth- and eighteenth-century theorists. Of course, I do not wish to say that the historical and intellectual origins of democracy have not been eagerly and exhaustively explored. On the contrary, few aspects of the past have been more intensively investigated by historians, philosophers, sociologists, and other thinkers. But since we are all democrats (or so one may hope!), we tend to see democracy as the fulfillment of our political destiny and as the political system that will remain with us for the rest of human history. For what alternative is there to democracy? In other words, we tend to dehistoricize democracy in spite of all the research that has been done on the his-

torical antecedents of democracy—thus, though unwittingly, repeating natural law philosophy patterns of thought. More specifically, we tend to see
our political history antedating the advent of democracy in much the same
way as natural law theorists saw the state of nature, and we see the advent
of democracy the way they saw the phase of the social contract. Finally,
now that democracy is (fortunately) triumphant all over the globe, we tend
to believe with Francis Fukuyama that we have entered a historical period
that will not allow for any more fundamental political change. For what
could possibly come after democracy? We tend to view those who take this
question seriously as having forfeited their credentials as democrats.

Recognizing these parallels between the mentality of natural law philosophy and our own counterproductive attitude toward democracy may
invite us to attempt a radical historicization of democracy. Such a historicization is effected in Chapter 4 by the proposal to see democracy as the
(time-bound) answer to solve a (time-bound) specific type of political problem, namely, the problem of how to avoid civil war in a politically, sociologically, and economically strongly polarized society. The consequences of
such a historicization of democracy are in two respects at odds with how we
ordinarily think of democracy. On the one hand, it obviously entails a rel-
ativization of democracy: we should not see it as the epiphany of the ultimate political Truth, as we so often tend to do. On the other hand, such
thinking may stimulate a more realistic attitude toward democracy than
customarily is the case, an attitude that may be more beneficial to the cause
of democracy than ahistorist adoration and blind glorification. For if we
recognize under which contingent historical circumstances democracy came
into being, we will be obliged to investigate how the present differs from
those circumstances; and this may enable us to deal with the question of
how we should adapt democracy to these changed circumstances. Specifically, we will recognize that the crucial difference in this regard is that in
democracy's past political problems typically opposed one set of the electorate to another, while political problems are now more or less the same
for all of the electorate. Recognizing this shift (or changes like these) are the
conditio sine qua non if we wish to keep our democracies alive and vigorous.

A first step toward a reorientation of our conception of democracy is
proposed in Chapter 5. The main idea is that political *content* agrees with
the functioning of original democracy, hence with democracy aiming at the
juste milieu between the extremes in a politically polarized society. How-

ever, the new kind of political problem, hence the kind of problem that confronts all of the electorate in a more-or-less similar way, can best be defined (and solved) in terms of *form* or *style*. A politically polarized civil society needs a politics of ideological content; our depolarized societies are in need of a politics of style. Characteristic is the shift from material legislation to procedural legislation that can be observed in most Western democracies over the last two to three decades: legislation in modern democracies focuses more and more on how, and by means of which procedures, an outcome is to be reached, rather than on the outcome of public decision making itself. The objection that, in politics, the outcome is in the end all that counts, and that therefore the sacrifice of a politics of content for a politics of style is an irresponsible forfeiture of democracy, can be answered with the argument that there is a continuum between form and content. Contents have forms proper to them, and form determines content. Hence a politics of form or style will also generate political content.

Chapters 6 to 9 form together one continuous argument. In Chapter 6, Rorty's arguments in favor of the antifoundationalism of democracy are discussed and, where necessary, improved. Rawls's ideas about how consensus is reached in democracy had been Rorty's main source of inspiration. The foundationalist reminiscences in Rawls's (and Rorty's) argument are identified and criticized. Chapter 7 deals with developments in contemporary democracies that are threatening democracy's antifoundationalism; these threats can be grouped under the rubric of the birth of the network. Within the complex web of our contemporary societies, networks are like calculations in a text: they may be necessary, but they are nevertheless a stylistic violation of the greater whole of which they are a part. Scientific, technological, and financial networks increasingly make their presence felt make in contemporary public decision making. I argue, first, that this is a challenge for democracy's well-being; and second, that by its very nature the *regime of the network* can never replace democracy. *Quis custodiet ipsos custodes?* For there is no "network of all the networks"; hence, democratic decision making will always remain indispensable if one wishes to keep control of how all the networks interact (or should interact) with each other. The last two chapters elaborate the implications of the antifoundationalism of democracy for both the functioning of that political system (Chapter 8) and for the political rights of the individual (Chapter 9). In Chapter 8, Rawls's notion of "overlapping consensus" is contrasted with political compromise. The foundationalist presuppositions of the notion of consensus are exposed, and it is argued that the notion of compromise better fits the practice of democracy and can, also, explain the surprising political creativity of democracy. This creativity has its main source in the fact that it requires the politician to adopt the mentality of the historian in political practice. Lastly, Chapter 9 addresses the frequent criticism of historism and a historist approach to politics for endangering the rights of individuals. It is shown, however, that historism suggests a more powerful argument in favor of human rights than rival, antihistorist traditions can provide. And all this will enable us to assess what we stand to gain by heeding Machiavelli's advice and by looking at politics and political theory from the perspective of history.

PART I

HISTORY AND POLITICS

1

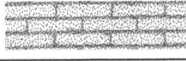

HISTORY AND POLITICAL THEORY

Political theory is the discipline that focuses on the political order in which we human beings live. It may attempt to justify or to attack this order by means of philosophical or historical argument, or it may take any one of a number of other approaches. Hence the nature of the discipline is difficult to define. This is why, for a discussion such as the present one, it is most advisable to take into account the history of political theory: the history of a notion often presents us with the best means for grasping its nature. This history we will find in the textbooks on the history of political thought from "Plato to Nato," as one of them is actually entitled.[1]

The tables of contents of these textbooks show that much agreement apparently exists as to who were the most important political philosophers in the period before 1800. Whether one lets classical political theory begin with the politician Pericles, the historian Herodotus, or the architect Hippodamus of Milete, all textbooks present Plato, Aristotle, Cicero, and perhaps Polybius as the most important classical theorists. Agreement is even more unanimous for the period between the Middle Ages and the nineteenth century, which one may well see as the golden age in the history of political thought. All of the textbooks deal with roughly the same set of theorists, authors such as Machiavelli, Bodin, Althusius, Grotius, Hobbes, Spinoza, Locke, Montesquieu, Hume, Bentham, and Kant.

However, far less consensus seems to exist among the textbook writers as to who are the most important theorists of the period after 1800;

there is no universally accepted canon for this postclassical period in the history of political thought. Surely, Hegel and Marx will never fail to be discussed. But apart from these most obvious names, historians of political theory make their own way through the vicissitudes of nineteenth- and twentieth-century political theory. Thus, George Sabine's book (after fifty years, probably still the best and most widely used textbook) does not discuss Tocqueville, whereas others often see in Tocqueville the most perspicuous analyst of (early-nineteenth-century) democracy. Ulrich Steinvorth does not discuss the utilitarians such as Bentham, James, and John Stuart Mill; perhaps too English for him. He does have, on the other hand, a lengthy chapter on Weber, who is ordinarily not on the top-ten list of the Anglo-Saxon textbook writers. And much the same unclarity exists with regard to the historical significance of people like Friedrich Nietzsche, Sigmund Freud, Benedetto Croce, Maurice Barrès, Ferdinand Tönnies, Vilfredo Pareto, Joseph A. Schumpeter, Friedrich von Hayek, or Hannah Arendt. Even whole movements whose historical importance can impossibly be doubted, such as nationalism, are dealt with in some textbooks but not in others.

Several explanations could be given of this state of affairs, but I shall restrict myself here to the conventional one, since that is also the best introduction to this chapter. The explanation proceeds in two steps. It is pointed out, in the first place, that history began to play an ever more prominent role in political thought at the beginning of the nineteenth century. Admittedly, the most fruitful political thought in the preceding period was also inspired by concrete historical problems (think of Hobbes's *Leviathan* as a reaction to the Puritan revolution, or of Locke as reacting to the autocracy of James II), but these very concrete and time-bound political problems were always immediately translated into the ahistorical idiom of natural law philosophy. Nineteenth-century political theory, on the other hand, consistently refused to abandon and ignore the historical dimension of the political issues investigated by it: it always respected the concrete historical context of the kind of political issues with which it attempted to deal. One need only think here of theoreticians such as Hegel, Marx, Comte, Spencer, Tocqueville, or Weber. History no longer merely was the context, but became the very essence of political thought.

The second step concerns the tension or even outright animosity of the apriorism of philosophy in general and of political thought in particular, on the one hand, and the respect of the refractory complexity of the given implied by a historical approach, on the other. Because of this animosity, the disorientation of postclassical political thought is easy to explain: a historicized political thought apparently is a *contradiction in adiectis.* Since any statement can be derived from a logical contradiction, a discipline with a contradiction in its very heart can be expected to move in almost any direction. Needless to say, this has been the background of the crisis of historism occasioned by the alleged incompatibility of timeless values and historical change.

The issue has been most succinctly formulated by the German American political theorist Leo Strauss, whose ideas are still quite influential in contemporary American political thought.[2] In his *Natural Right and History* (1950), Strauss argued how history and historism can result even in the death of political theory and of all political speculation. "There cannot be natural right," he writes, "if there are no immutable principles of justice, but history shows that all principles of justice are mutable."[3] For Strauss— as for the neo-Kantians who became entangled in the crisis of historism— political theory is precisely this search for immutable moral and political truths. Natural law philosophy, which claimed to derive such immutable political truths from the nature of the human individual, was for Strauss therefore the only reliable model for all political thought. History in this view had to be eliminated from political thought. Even Hegel, who attempted to transcend history and historical change by presenting history as moving toward a moment of absolute and transhistorical truth, was rejected by Strauss. Strauss's objection was that Hegel does not offer a legitimation of these transhistorical or absolute moral and political truths, which present themselves at the end of history, that is independent of history itself: "One cannot simply assume that one lives or thinks in the absolute moment [i.e., Hegel's end of history]; one must show, somehow, how the absolute moment can be recognized as such."[4] As long as we do not possess ahistorical criteria of what is morally and politically right, we will be unable to come to a moral and political assessment of what we may find, with Hegel, at the end of history. In sum, truth in history and in political theory are incompatible, and to found political theory on history is like building on quicksand.[5]

This, then, will be the topic of this chapter. First, is Strauss right when he argues that a historical or historicist political theory is a contradiction in terms? And, second, we had best focus our thinking about this issue on the relationship between history and natural law philosophy. For if Strauss is right, the conflict between history and political theory will most clearly manifest itself there. And that means that we shall have to focus on the period before 1800.

HISTORY AND NATURAL LAW PHILOSOPHY

If we wish to grasp the relationship between history and political philosophy for this period, it will be necessary, before all, to obtain clarity about their status as disciplines or forms of knowledge. With regard to history, one had best start with Arno Seifert's erudite *Cognitio historica: Die Geschichte als Namengeberin der frühneuzeitlichen Empirie* (Historical knowledge: Early modern conceptions of history as empirical knowledge), which demonstrates that during this period the word "history" could have two meanings. In the first place, it could refer to the events of human history and the historian's account of these events. This obviously is how we use the word and how it was used also in Greek and Roman antiquity. It should be added, though, that when the word was used in this customary sense in the sixteenth to the eighteenth centuries, one primarily associated it with classical history. It took some time before the word was generally used for the history of nations, wars, or illustrious persons of later periods. In the second place, the word could refer to the "experiential knowledge" that one might have in any domain of human experience and knowledge. This use is in accordance with the original meaning of the Greek word *historein,* "investigation," "research," or "information" in general. Even nowadays one sometimes still speaks of "natural history" instead of "biology"—and this is a legacy of the use of the word "history" intended here. Characteristic is how Kant still wrote about experimental physics: "Experimental physics is historical since it had to do with singular facts. Only thanks to general laws does it become truly rational. History merely presents us with material for rational knowledge."[6] Till Kant, historical knowledge primarily was a *cognitio singularum,* a knowledge of individual facts, and thus had the character of all "prescientific knowing remaining close to reality itself."[7] Historical events in our sense of the word were only a subclass of the totality of this knowledge. The result was that the more general properties of this kind of knowledge tended to rub off on history in our sense of the word.[8]

Hence, at first sight one might observe here an anticipation of the neo-Kantian distinction between the idiographic historical sciences and the nomothetic natural sciences. But this would imply the projection of a modern notion of the relationship between the individual and the general onto an older conception of the relationship between what is historical and what is scientific. The difference is that, in the modern view, knowledge of individuals—even though lacking generality—may still be certain knowledge. Think of statements like "The cat lies on the mat." As Seifert makes clear, early modern use of the notion of history is expressed by the fact that "historical knowledge" in the period in question was ordinarily believed to be knowledge that is only "probable." To which it should immediately be added that the word "probable" must not be related to the modern notion of what is "statistically probable." Instead, this is an instance of the Aristotelian use of the word "probable," where it has the connotation of beliefs that are inevitably and irrevocably unreliable, uncertain, and incomplete. Or, as Notker Hammerstein put it: "The incomplete knowledge of alien experiences is the domain of the probable."[9] Some seventeenth-century authors, such as Vossius, even went as far as to refuse to "the historical" not only the status of being a science but even that of being an art or a discipline.[10]

In sum, in the sense discussed here, "history" opens up a domain of an insuperable epistemological uncertainty, where we can move only gropingly and where a successful contact with reality, in the form of knowledge or in any other way, can never be assured. Probable knowledge belongs to the domain of the *doxai*, of what is mere public opinion and where in open and public debate one view and its opposite may peacefully coexist together without the possibility of identifying which is right and which is wrong. It follows from this that the only way to historical truth left to the historian is to assert in his work *doxai* that are part of just anybody's stock of knowledge. A book like Voltaire's *Essai sur mes moeurs*, presenting a new and fascinating panorama of the past but without mentioning new, unknown, and therefore doubtful historical facts could therefore command a far greater respect than the works by the Cartesian *érudits*. Whereas since historism the presentation of new historical facts is welcomed, perhaps even seen as the essence of historical writing, the Aristotelian paradigm of historical knowledge requires the historian to capitalize on what is common knowledge already. From this perspective we should admire not only Gibbon's genius but even more so his courage for audaciously introducing in his *De-cline and Fall* so many historical facts that were unknown to his audience. And, arguably, Gibbon's revolutionary mix of an Aristotelian and a Carte-sian conception of historical fact was only acceptable to his audience, and could only become so immensely successful, thanks to the majestic rhetor-ical flow of his prose. His rhetoric transformed new facts into *doxai*; and without the indispensable support of his rhetoric he would have been a mere pitiable pedant in the eyes of his readers.

However, philosophy—and the same is true of moral and political philosophy—was considered to be a discipline that presents us with certain knowledge, like the sciences. Thus physics was often referred to as "the philosophy of nature." It follows from this that history could not possibly be of any help to us if we are looking for a science of society. Such a sci-ence of society—as natural law philosophy attempted to develop—could only have its foundations in the indubitable certainties that would be as-sociated later on with those achieved by the Cartesian cognitive self. Such was the suggestion of Grotius—no Cartesian, of course—in the method-ological prolegomena of his *De iure belli ac pacis*:

> It has been my first care to relate those things having to do with natural law to no-tions that are so certain, that nobody could possibly deny them, unless he would do violence to himself. The principles of natural law are, if only the mind per-ceives them correctly, almost as obvious and self-evident as the things that we per-ceive with our senses.[11]

And elsewhere he even equates argument in mathematics with argument in natural law philosophy.[12] Hence, though Grotius was by no means hostile to historical argument (one may think of how he used [or, rather, abused] history in his *De antiquitate reipublicae Batavicae* in order to prove that the sovereignty of Holland had always resided with the Estates General and not with its rulers and their heirs [such as Philip II of Spain]), history had no role to play in his natural law philosophy. Similarly, most contract theories that were proposed since Grotius in the seventeenth and eighteenth cen-turies reduced history to the all-decisive event of the prehistorical founda-tion of society. One and a half centuries later the same was still true with Rousseau. Even if one agrees with Lionel Gossman, or with Horowitz in his seminal book on Rousseau of some ten years ago,[13] that history is more prominent in Rousseau's political thought than contemporary scholarship on Rousseau was ever prepared to recognize, one must still concede that history remained for Rousseau an abstract category never comprising the fullness and concrete detail of, for example, a nation's history.

Against this background, Hegel's position is of specific interest. Hegel broke through this traditional disciplinary hierarchy of history and philosophy with his effort to develop a *philosophia* of *historia*. He wanted to bring the light of philosophical truth into this domain of what is merely "probable," the domain of historical truth; or, as he put it himself, "The philosophical approach has no other purpose than to remove the mere contingency of historical knowledge." And he hoped to attain this purpose by attributing to philosophical reason a role in history itself. "The only idea that the philosophy of history introduces," writes Hegel in his lectures on philosophy of history, "is the simple idea of Reason, that Reason rules the world and that history is a rational process."[14] And reason suffices since it is active in the past itself and therefore will recognize and become aware of itself if it is applied to what is, in fact, its own past.

As is well known, historist historians accused Hegel of "discovering" in the past no other historical or political truths than he had already hidden in it himself. For people like Ranke or Humboldt, the Truth about the past could only be found out by an investigation of *historical facts* and not by idle philosophical speculation.[15] In fact, this well-known and apparently so humble claim is a most momentous one if placed against the background of this history of the relationship of disciplines that we have been discussing here. For it amounts to a complete revolution of this hierarchy: to the historical fact is now attributed the absolute certainty that one had previously attributed to philosophy; philosophy was now degraded to the domain of the merely "probable." Hegel's philosophy of history embodies, therefore, a crucial moment in the history of the relationship between the two disciplines in question: history's rank had always been immeasurably lower than that of philosophy; then, Hegel elevated history to the status of philosophy and for a short moment the two held each other in a precarious equilibrium in his philosophy of history. But after Hegel their roles were reversed; philosophy was reduced to history's former humble status, whereas history became the sure basis for philosophy, especially for political philosophy. Within such a scenario Hegel's system could be seen as the result, exponent, or exemplification of this movement of the disciplines rather than its cause. Probably, therefore, one would be well advised to see in this movement of the disciplines a kind of *longue durée* in intellectual history that may generate developments on the "surface"—such as Hegel's philosophy of history—rather than being dependent on them. This is, of course, how the Foucault of *Les Mots et les choses* would have required us to look at the matter.

MACHIAVELLI

Nevertheless, the above Strauss-like picture of an irreconcilable conflict between history and natural law philosophy is too simple, and must be corrected by taking into account the deep and pervasive influence of Machiavelli on almost all of natural law philosophy. Needless to say, Machiavelli had always required the politician and the political theorist to be aware of the concrete historical context within which all political action has to take place. In the preface to the *Discourses on Livy*, he states that "the knowledge of histories" is the primary source of all useful political insight, and the book amply demonstrates what political insight can be gained from Livy's *Ab urbe condita*. Elsewhere Machiavelli writes that "it is an easy thing for whoever examines past things diligently to foresee future things in every republic"[16]—a clear identification of history and the experience taught by it as the only sound basis for successful political thought and action.

So much is clear, then. But it is less obviously clear in what way Machiavelli's use of history necessarily clashes with natural law philosophy, if it does. Machiavelli himself never dealt with that question. Of course, if it wasn't anachronistic and pointless, one might now start rereading Machiavelli in order to discover in his writings a theory on history that can meaningfully be contrasted with natural law philosophy as it would develop in the seventeenth and eighteenth centuries. But if we wish to find out about the nature of the conflict between Machiavellianism and natural law philosophy, we had far better look at how this conflict did, in actual historical fact, develop. Put differently, we had far better look at what was done with Machiavelli's heritage between, roughly, 1600 and 1800, and at how later theorists mediated between natural law philosophy and Machiavelli's insistence on the necessity of history. This is a vast topic on which whole libraries have been written already. In order to keep the issue within manageable proportions here—and this inevitably forces me to ignore many important details—it will be helpful to distinguish between two variants of Machiavellianism.

Arcana Imperii

The first variant remained closest to the immediate impact that Machiavelli's writings had on his contemporaries; no attempt was made in it to soften the moral outrage caused by Machiavelli's recommendations to the prince. On the contrary, within this tradition, as recently described by Peter Donaldson in a profoundly interesting study, it is argued that the prince has to live and act in a world different from our own and that our moral outrage merely demonstrates how little we understand of this different world. The world of the prince is, for us ordinary citizens, a secret, and all the possibilities of Baroque political thought were in this tradition applied in order to try to explain these secrets of the government or of the prince.

These secrets were known under the name of the *arcana imperii*, a term that is derived from the Latin verb *arcere*, which means "to shut up" or "to prohibit access to,"[17] and could best be translated, as was suggested already by Ernst Kantorowicz, as "the mystery of state."[18] The notion of the *arcana imperii* has a long and venerable tradition going back to Tacitus, who used the term himself, and to what Aristotle described as the *sophismata* or *kryphia* of the government. Though the notion did play a role during the Middle Ages,[19] it was intensively discussed again in the sixteenth and seventeenth centuries. The explanation is that Machiavelli's writings gave a new and far more dramatic content to the notion of the *arcana*; Machiavelli's open recognition that the prince might be forced to do what is evil—that he must *entrare nel malo, necessitato* in his well-known formulation—now became the paradigmatic content of the *arcana*. Jean Bodin already recognized as much when he observed in his *Methodus ad facilem historiarum cognitionem* (1566) that Machiavelli was the first to write again about the *arcana*: "after about 1200 years during which barbarism buried everything."[20]

The most striking and, for our present purpose, most illuminating claims with regard to the *arcana imperii* were made by Gabriel Naudé and by Louis Machon. Naudé (1600–1653) expounded his view of the *arcana* in his *Considérations sur les coups d'état* (1639). He emphasized that these *coups d'état*—his term for the actions by the prince to be related to the *arcana*—are not merely such admittedly regrettable, but generally accepted, practices such as the killing of prisoners of war when there are too many of them, espionage, or the prince's personal misbehavior. All this, he says, can be rationalized and legitimized in advance. This is different, however, with the coups that are defined by Naudé as:

audacious and extraordinary actions that princes are forced to execute under difficult and desperate circumstances, that go against common law and even against any form of justice and where the interest of the individual is sacrificed to the common good. In order to properly distinguish them from maxims of action we should add that in the latter causes, reasons, manifestos, declarations and all what might legitimate an action, always precede action and how one sets about it. Whereas with the coup d'etat one sees the thunderbolt before one hears it groaning in the clouds, it strikes before the flame shines forth, there matins are said before the bells have rung, the execution precedes the sentence, everything is done *à la Judaique*—one receives the stroke who thought to give it, he dies who thought himself quite safe, one suffers what one never expected, all is done at night, in obscurity, in fog and darkness, the goddess Laverna [the goddess of thieves] presides.

"Make people mistake themselves so that I seem to be just and holy / Cover my sins by night and my frauds by a cloud."[21]

The coup is a sudden disruption of, or infraction upon, the natural social and political order; effects precede their causes; everything takes place in darkness and obscurity and belies our natural expectations. In this way the coups d'etat curiously seem to anticipate in the domain of history and politics the speculations of eighteenth-century philosophers on the sublime. We need only recall here how Kant related the sublime to what transcends the imagination's application of the categories of the understanding. For in a similar manner the coup d'etat transgresses all our moral expectations; the moral world we are living in is shattered to dust, although a great collective good may have been served by the prince's immoral behavior.[22] As the sublime transcends the apparently insurmountable opposition between pain and pleasure or delight,[23] so do the *arcana* transcend the opposition between the moral and the immoral. This is the sublime moral paradox to which no one can remain insensitive when Machiavelli proclaims that it is better to be feared than loved, or that "experience shows that princes who have achieved great things have been those who have given their word lightly."[24] Prudence sometimes requires immorality, and the well-being of society can sometimes only be achieved by crime; or, as Naudé put it:

These coups d'etat are like a sword that one can use or abuse, like the lance of Telephus that can wound and heal, like the Diana of Ephesus that had two faces, the one sorrowful and the other joyous, in brief like those medallions devised by heretics that carry the face of a pope and a devil under the same contours and lineaments, or like those tableaux that represent life or death depending upon from what side one looks at them.[25]

Such alternations between good and evil, such sudden reversions between the highest demands of ethics and religion, do not seem to be permissible to ordinary human beings. Just as we ordinary human beings are incapable of seeing a rabbit and a duck at one and the same time in the Jastrow-Wittgenstein drawing, so only a god or a prince may be able to grasp and weigh the sublime paradox of "the morality of immorality." And it need not surprise us therefore that Naudé related the *arcana* to the topos of the prince's action as an *imitatio dei*:

Naudé does not shrink from the idea that *imitatio dei* makes the prince a partaker, with deity, in the paradoxes and the complexities of the relation between good and evil; rather his use of the imagery of mystery and cultic secrecy reinforces it. The Naudean prince is a sacred ruler, and his use of the *arcana* and of Machiavellian methods are part of the mystery of the state.[26]

Whereas Naudé still sees a conflict between morals and what the Bible teaches us, on the one hand, and the prince's coups d'état, Louis Machon (1600–ca. 1672) goes one step further and presents to his appalled readers the Bible as the most important source for the secrets of the state.[27] This was not without its precedents, since it had been pointed already, for example by both Naudé and by Antonio Mirandola (in his book of 1630 on reason of state), that there is something Machiavellian about God's decision to allow Christ to suffer on the Cross for the salvation of mankind. We see here, by the way, how reason, no longer allowing itself to be dulled by theological speculation, becomes sensitive to God's sublime immorality.[28] In the tradition of the *imitatio dei*, this sometimes led to the perverse argument that the prince deserves our moral praise when committing Machiavellian crimes because he then appears to be prepared to sacrifice his own salvation for that of his people. But Machon goes much further and discovers in the Bible a great number of Machiavellianisms, such as "Moses's deception of the pharaoh, the Israelites' plunder of the Egyptian jewels, military trickery in the campaign for Canaan, Abraham's pretense that Sarah was his sister, not his wife; Joseph's pretending not to know his brothers, Jacob's deception of both Laban and Esau etc."[29] And even Christ can be argued to have been guilty of deception when hiding his divine nature under a human appearance.

The crucial idea here is that the prince—and in Machon's case even God Himself—has to act in an imperfect, unpredictable, and inscrutable world, and that this necessitates actions clashing with moral perfection. The thought-provoking intuition is that moral perfection is only possible in and for a perfect world; morality is inevitably tainted, so to speak, by the imperfection of the world where its rules must be applied. More specifically, since our knowledge of the world is imperfect, or, to put it in the right Machiavellian words, since half of what happens in the world is in the hands of the goddess Fortuna, the right, prudential, or correct Machiavellian action will often seem to us to be like an irruption from the outside into the cognitive and moral domain that is known and familiar to us. Hence the peculiarly sublime character of the *arcana* that we observed a moment ago, or, as Naudé put it with a most ingenious metaphor:

I shall note in passing that one can draw a good parallel between this River Nile and the secrets of state for, just as the people who live near its power draw from it a thousand commodities without having any knowledge of its origin, so it is needful that the people admire the happy effects of these master strokes, without, however, understanding anything of their causes and diverse origins.[30]

Hence also the surprising discrepancy that we may often discern between huge political revolutions and the insignificant means that the prince has artfully applied for effecting them.[31] Cause and effect seem permanently out of tune in the prince's actions.

It also follows that the prince's actions ordinarily will be mysterious to the populace, to the ordinary people who are his subjects. This is why the *arcana* are a secret; not so much because they are kept secret, but because the context within which the prince has to act is unknown and inaccessible to ordinary people. This posed quite a problem for authors like Naudé or Machon, for they themselves were such ordinary people. Machiavelli was already sensitive to this problem when he tried to explain in the dedicatory letter of *The Prince* why he, as an ordinary citizen, believed he was able to say something of value for princes. Naudé solved the problem in a most peculiar way. After he had written the book for his master, Cardinal Nicholas Bagni, only twelve copies (not coincidentally the number of the Apostles) of it were made by the printer. Though the book was reprinted all through the seventeenth and eighteenth centuries, even the editions of these reprints were restricted, so that still now the book is very hard to obtain. And surely it makes sense to ensure that a book on the secret mysteries of the state cannot fall into the hands of just anybody. Though published posthumously, Machiavelli did not seem to have had such qualms with *The Prince* and *Discourses of Livy*. This is why some sixteenth- and seventeenth-century writers, such as Cardinal Reginald Pole, not implausibly argued that Machiavelli must, in fact, have been an enemy of princes and tyrants since he apparently had intended to betray their horrible secrets to their subjects.[32]

A sudden and unexpected end came to this stream of treatises on the *arcana imperii* somewhere around the 1660s. In as far as it survived, it now tended to move from the actions of the prince to that of the sphere of social life in general. For this transition one may think of Baltasar Graciàn's *The Hero* (1637), whose Machiavellianism has often been pointed out,[33] and which indeed reads like a kind of mixture of Machiavelli's *The Prince* and Castiglione's *The Courtier*, or like the collections of cynical maxims composed by La Rochefoucauld (1665) or the memoir of Cardinal de Retz (1717). Machiavellianism thus traveled from the domain of politics to that of social interaction and "the presentation of the self in everyday life," to use the title of Erving Goffman's well-known book. During this journey it managed to infect with its cynicism the conception of the human individual as presented in modern natural law philosophies.[34] In this way much of modern natural law philosophy has its foundations in Machiavellianism, which is in other respects so completely different from it.[35]

Naudé's *Considérations politiques sur les coups d'etat* is of no less interest here. For at the end of this truly amazing book, Naudé enumerates the tasks of the prince's advisor (probably having himself in mind when writing this). And then we are presented with a completely different picture, for the advisor is required to observe all the traditional Christian duties, such as to be just and honest, to love God and his fellow human beings, and even to desire *plustost le bien que le mal à ses ennemis* ("good rather than evil to his enemies"). The anticlimax is no less stunning than the end of Mozart's *Don Giovanni*, when the quartet of honest people contentedly sings the terrible fate of false villains, at which point we have only barely recovered from the sublime confrontation of Don Giovanni with the Commendatore's statue. All Machiavellist evil and immorality are apparently exclusively reserved for the prince by Naudé: even those who are closest to him are never allowed to enter the dark and sublime realm of the *arcana imperii*. So, the development since Naudé mentioned at the end of the previous paragraph could be seen as a "democratization" of Machiavellism for which Naudé himself was not yet prepared.

But the irony is that the end of Naudé's book could be differently interpreted as well, that is, as its ultimate *peroratio* rather than as its anticlimax. For is the observance of Christian morality not in the advisor's own Machiavellist interest? The political life of Machiavellian advisors may well be expected to be desperately short. If this interpretation makes sense, it would follow that Naudé was no less aware of the often surprising parallelism of Machiavellism and moral decency than the theorists to be discussed in the next section. And this interpretation is all the more likely to be the correct one since Naudé was quite capable of objectifying ethics and of recognizing what Machiavellian selfish aims can be served by observing Christian ethics.[36] For one of the further requirements that the prince's advisor should be able to satisfy is "that he should live in the world as if he were outside it; and under heaven as if he were above it."[37] Obviously, this puts the advisor in a sublime position that is "beyond good and evil" and that will allow him to calculate the costs and the benefits of the observation of Christian ethics. If seen from this perspective, Naudé's amazing book is not only the culmination of Machiavellism but its transcendence as well.

Raison d'État

In order to understand the disappearance of the *arcana imperii* from the political scene, it is necessary first to recognize the two Machiavellian traditions that I referred to above. The first tradition is the *arcana imperii* just described. But a second, more relaxed form of Machiavellianism had already come into being around 1600 with Giovanni Botero, Traiano Boccalini, and Scipione Ammirato in Italy, and Christoph Besold, Christoph von Forstner, Johann Elias Kessler, and especially, Arnold Clapmarius in Germany (who still used the term *arcana*). This second form of Machiavellianism was destined to have a longer and far more fruitful future, since it aimed at the realization of the state's interests by permissible, or at least acceptable, means. It rejected what Tacitus had called the *flagitia*, where the personal interests of the prince, instead of or not necessarily those of the state, are the source of Machiavellian policies. Only because of the state's interests, only "for reasons of state," was a certain amount of Machiavellianism allowed to the statesman—this is why one speaks of the *raison d'état* school. Though the transition from the *arcana imperii* tradition to that of the *raison d'état* school took place rather noiselessly (if compared to the amount of noise provoked by Machiavelli's writings), though no great and well-known names are to be associated with it, the transition was of the greatest significance from the perspective of the relationship between history and political theory. For it resulted in what one might call a desublimization of the *arcana imperii* tradition and—as we shall see in a moment—created the basis for an integration of history and natural law philosophy.

Paradigmatic here is Hermann Conring (1606–1681), who was fascinated by Hobbes's system, introduced it into Germany, and then tried to reconcile it with the requirements of *raison d'état*. Conring attempted such a reconciliation by claiming that what is "right" (*iustum*) from the point of view of natural law philosophy is not necessarily at odds with what is the "respectable" (*honestum*) thing to do from the point of view of *raison d'état*. Precisely Hobbes's system enabled him to effect such a reconciliation. For self-preservation was the (Machiavellianist) foundation of Hobbes's argument. Conring pointed out, then, that we can best serve the aim of self-preservation by behaving in a predictably and morally responsible way. So it is in our own Machiavellian self-interest not to commit the *flagitia* and to avoid Machiavelli's more radical recommendations as counterproductive. And the same is true for states: a state that respects the requirements of *pacta sunt servanda* and that is not at the throat of its neighbor's as soon as a suitable occasion for doing so arises, will survive more easily in the Hobbesian *bellum omnium contra omnes* of European states than one behaving like a mafia gangster. In sum, a large part of the trajectory of political action can be traveled together by the disciple of natural law philosophy and the adept of the doctrine of *raison d'état*. Nevertheless, at some point on this trajectory the two will part. Conring was well aware of this and tried to identify the point at which *raison d'état* passes into the *flagitia*. To the extent that he was successful in doing this, we may agree with Stolleis

that Conring defined the classical *limits* of *raison d'état*. This makes clear once again that for Conring *raison d'état* is a normative concept respecting the requirements of ethics and of natural law philosophy. These limits are necessary in order to prevent that the prince might be tempted to abuse *raison d'état*—*ultimam subditorum finem* (the ultimate aim of a state's subjects) and *salutem et egregium publicum* (the common welfare)—as an excuse for injustice and deceit.[38]

It is doubtful, however, whether Conring really succeeded in identifying these limits of *raison d'état*. For in his analyses he tended to restrict himself to where ethical norms and the interest of the state are still in harmony with each other—but he carefully avoided the domain where the two come into conflict. And obviously this is where the real difficulties will present themselves.

With the notion of *raison d'état*, history was introduced into German natural law philosophy. For Conring—and here he is a faithful disciple of Machiavelli—history is the statesmen's best guide for knowing how best to serve his country in agreement with the requirements of *raison d'état*. He only need compare his own situation to that of statesmen from the past; such a comparison will instruct his own course of action. History is a compendium of past experience that the statesman should assimilate in order to refine his knowledge of the theory and the practice of politics.[39] "Est enim illa historia reapse quasi civilis ipsa philosophia sed in exemplis"[40]—history is a philosophy of the state presented in the form of examples. We may observe here already an anticipation of the fusion of philosophy and history that would take place in Hegel, and it should be added that the Hegel of the "cunning of reason" was just as optimistic about the possibility of avoiding the clash between *raison d'état* and the *flagitia* as was Conring.

Conring has been praised as "the founder of German history of law," as "the father of statistics or descriptions of the state" and as "teacher of *raison d'état*."[41] These qualifications indicate the three ways this German natural law philosopher has served the cause of history. First of all, Conring contributed more to the study of German history of law than any of his contemporaries; the students who were following his courses and who would become public servants afterward ought, in his view, to be well acquainted with German institutions and their juridical history. But no less important is his reputation to have been the father of statistics. Statistics was a discipline where history and politics met in the eighteenth century and was developed in that century by people like Gottfried Achenwall and August Ludwich von Schloezer (and even Frederick II himself) on the basis of suggestions from previous writers such as Christian Thomasius and, especially, Conring. When we hear the word "statistics," we immediately think of tables and ciphers, whereas actually the term was derived from the word "state" as used in *raison d'état*.[42] Statistics is the cognitive apparatus serving *raison d'état* politics. For Achenwall and Schloezer, statistics gave an accurate, often even quantified description of the state, information about its constitutional and juridical organization, about the country's wealth, its population's religious preferences, its crafts and industries, its exact size and geographical nature, and so on. It is only on the basis of such data that the statesman could be a good Machiavellian in the *raison d'état* tradition. And this statistical knowledge was historical in the two senses of the word current before the nineteenth century: it was historical by giving an accurate description of a singular composite fact (Seifert), and it was historical in the more traditional sense that history would be needed in order to obtain and correctly interpret the relevant data. As such, statistics had an intermediary position between history and politics. Or, as Achenwall put it, "Statistics is a kind of stalled history and history a statistics moving on continuously."[43] In sum, statistics is of the greatest value for politics because the results of its research can be used for a political purpose, namely, how the interest of the state can best be furthered, if necessary, or, even preferably, at the cost of other nations. *Raison d'état* requires the statesman and the prince to get the better of their rivals and of other states by means that will not be counterproductive—as will often be the case when one would apply the more offensive lessons of Machiavelli. This, then is how in the course of the development of seventeenth- and eighteenth-century political philosophy a bridge was built between natural law and Machiavelli: natural law defined what moral and political rules one should adopt in one's transactions with others as long as it would serve no rational purpose to risk their ill will; history taught the politician under what circumstances this risk should nevertheless be taken. Natural law and history thus balanced each other; and each of them should always be taken as the background for the proper use of the other. Natural law functioned as a break on a counterproductive application of the lessons of Machiavelli, whereas historical knowledge of the state's history, of its nature, and of its political and economic interests will show the politician when the application of natural law philosophy would hurt the common good. In this way *raison d'état* thinking attempted to reconcile the teachings of natural law philosophy with those of history.

But it is even more important in the present context, as Friedrich Meinecke had already suggested in his impressive *Idee der Staatsräson in der neueren Geschichte* (1924; The idea of reason of state in early modern history), how the tradition of *raison d'état* contributed to the birth of historicism and, hence, of modern historical writing. The two are linked by an awareness of the specific individual nature of a state, nation, or institution. Political action as dictated by *raison d'état* required of the statesman a recognition of the historical, statistical facts under which he has to act. And the historicist's demand that the action of historical agents must be understood against the background of existing historical realities is based on a similar argument. "Not free choice but the necessity of things governed the movement of states"; thus Ranke echoes Machiavelli's insistence on necessity.[44] The Machiavellianist doctrine that objective historical circumstances necessitate the statesman to act in a certain way underlies both *raison d'état* thinking and historicism. Meinecke gives several examples of how this resulted in Ranke's writings in a Machiavellianist understanding of the past. And he comments that Ranke tended to come to terms with the many violations of treaties in the past with a certain "elastic dialectics" that did not completely do away with the personal moral responsibilities of the historical agent but nevertheless gave priority to the explanatory force of circumstances and of power politics—that is, the *raison d'état* philosophy that lay behind the breaking of the treaties.[45]

It is likely that Ranke was himself aware of his closeness to Machiavelli. In the first place, we may think here of his inaugural address of 1836, in which he argued that "it is History's task to reveal the state's nature on the basis of events from the past; it is the task of politics to develop further the mind of insight that has thus been gained."[46] With Machiavelli he recognizes that historical necessity is the statesman's most reliable compass. In the second place, we should consider the strangely elusive comment on Machiavelli that Ranke wrote at the end of his long career as a historian, in which he tried to reconcile an indignant rejection of Machiavelli's dissimulation with a forgiveness of it, considering how difficult it would be to unite Italy. Ranke had deep respect for Machiavelli's worldly shrewdness and attempted to mitigate Machiavelli's unpleasant message by emphasizing how close Machiavelli had remained, in fact, to such a generally respected philosopher as Aristotle.[47] All the problems and issues to be associated with the relativism inherent in historical writing are foreshadowed in this curious piece of self-deconstruction.

I began this chapter with an exposition of Strauss's argument about the incompatibility of natural right and history; I hope that the foregoing may have made clear what is wrong with this traditional approach. From a historical point of view, we should realize that this opposition never actually existed. Natural law philosophy, for all its apriorism, has never been insensitive to the demands of history. It is true that several seventeenth-century theorists, especially, wanted to argue *more geometrico* and to transcend the vicissitudes of history—I mentioned Grotius in this context—but their arguments always proved in the end to be remarkably hospitable to historical considerations. Indeed, the closer one comes to the nineteenth century the more natural philosophy becomes saturated with history. Think of Conring, of Bernard de Mandeville's *The Fable of the Bees* and the de-sacralization of natural law philosophy by history in the course of the eighteenth century, culminating in the Scottish Enlightenment. We may therefore see seventeenth- and eighteenth-century natural law philosophy as a most interesting experiment that tried to exclude history from political thought. But the experiment of a pure and ahistorical natural law philosophy failed, as in contemporary political philosophy, historical reality refuses to remain hidden under Rawls's "veil of ignorance."

Second, and more importantly, when history made its entrance through the back door in political philosophy it did so under the guise of Machiavellism. Hence, it was not just some kind of neutral, innocuous, or edifying historical consciousness that then made its entrance; rather, it was history in its most threatening and immoralist form. History made itself felt where it really hurt most—and the conventional neo-Kantian and Straussian opposition of natural right and history may still remind us of the shock effected thereby.

Third, we have seen that Machiavellianism manifested itself in a more virulent and benign variant. The more virulent variant was the *arcana imperii* tradition, which lost its appeal before the second half of the seventeenth century and disappeared from the public to the private domain. And since secrecy was its hallmark, it is appropriate that it vanished thus, for private secrets can have no lasting impact on the public domain. The other, more benign variant of Machiavellism truly was benign because it gave us all kinds of sociopolitical disciplines that gather knowledge that can be used for the public interest and that may further public welfare.

But, as we have seen with Meinecke, it also gave us modern, "historist," historical writing. And I would not hesitate to attribute to history a certain priority if compared to the sociopolitical disciplines that I referred to just now. For what distinguishes history from those disciplines is its public accessibility. If there is anything to be learned from the history of the two variants of Machiavellism, it is that secrecy is a great evil in forms of knowledge having a public function. And it cannot be doubted that several of those sociopolitical disciplines tend more than history toward abstraction, aloofness, and secrecy. Public debate is, to a large extent, a discussion of what is good and evil for a democratic society. Thanks to its incompatibility with secrecy, history offers a better platform for such a discussion than any other discipline. However, it will never give us certainty; history will always give us mere opinions, *doxai* that are only "probable" in the Aristotelian sense. Certainty in this domain can be achieved only at the price of abandoning publicity for secrecy, hence of good Machiavellism for bad Machiavellism. And the paradox is that good Machiavellism implies openly allowing some scope to evil: the greatest evil will inevitably be the result when we relentlessly want to drive out all evil from our world. In this way, part of the sublimity of the *arcana imperii* will always be with us.

2

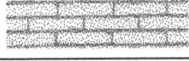

EDMUND BURKE: NATURAL RIGHT AND HISTORY

Tritt man vom Humeschen Bild des Staatslebens und der es tragenden
geschichtlichen Kräfte zu dem von Burke geschauten Bilde herüber, so ist
es alsob genau dieselbe Landschaft, die eben im Morgengrauen kalt und
nüchtern vor uns lag, in der warmen Sonne zo leuchten beginnt.

If one moves from Hume's picture of the state and of the historical forces
supporting it to that of Burke, it is as if one and the same landscape lying
cold and colorless in the morning twilight suddenly begins to shine under
the rays of the warm sun.

—F. Meinecke, *Die Entstehung des Historismus*

BURKE VERSUS ROUSSEAU

Historians nowadays tend to be democratic with regard to causality,
no longer believing in an "aristocratic causalism" that claims only "big"
causes can produce "big" consequences. Contemporary historians are ready
to recognize that small events can have big events as their legitimate off-
spring.[1] A perfect illustration of this new, democratic regime governing
cause and effect in history is Rousseau's psychology. Obviously, Rousseau's
psychology is a mere trifle if compared to those majestic social forces that
used to fascinate Marxist historians—and not only them. Yet we all know,
and are prepared to accept as fact, that what went on in Rousseau's mind
powerfully contributed to the downfall of a proud and thousand-year-old
monarchy.

And there is more. For the regime governing causes and effects in
human psychology is even more democratic. As we all know, psychoana-
lysts preferably discover the causes of human behavior in the most banal
and insignificant events of human life. The most trivial of events in our

childhood may deeply influence the rest of our whole life. Once again, Rousseau presents us with a striking illustration of this truth. Jean Starobinski begins his brilliant *La Transparence et l'obstacle* with the account of a most trivial event in Rousseau's youth. In his *Confessions*, Rousseau tells us that, when staying with the family Lambercier as a young boy, he was unjustly accused of having deliberately broken the teeth of Mademoiselle Lambercier's comb.[2] This completely trivial event proved to be utterly traumatic to the young and oversensitive child, who experienced it as the opening up of an unbridgeable gap between the social world and himself. And Rousseau was well aware, says Starobinski, that the event and the way he experienced it formed the ultimate basis of most of his social and political thought. "Dès ce moment je cessai de jouir d'un bonheur pur,"[3] commented Rousseau himself. And he goes on to explain that from that moment onward he was permanently aware of having been excluded from all meaningful and satisfactory human contact by an intrinsically alien, uncomprehending, and hostile social world. In sum, the young boy's most crucial experience was, as Starobinski so well put it, "l'opposition bouleversante de *l'être innocent* et du *paraître coupable*" (the overwhelming conflict between innocent being and guilty appearance).[4] The experience instilled in him a traumatic intensity the opposition between the world of his innermost self and a social reality supremely indifferent to authenticity and private conviction. Appearances may be completely at odds with how things really are—and nobody seems to care. This is what Rousseau could never accept or endure.

This is why Rousseau hated history and why his political thought can well be seen as a permanent effort to undo, in one way or another, the workings of history. History is for him the history of how layer upon layer of appearances precipitated upon the pure crystal of human nature and succeeded in hiding that pure crystal below the sediments of spurious appearance. To use Starobinski's terminology, history is the obstacle that is primarily responsible for our exchanging the original transparency of human nature for the murky, obscure and impure world of chaos, injustice and struggle. History gives us the perversion and destruction of human nature. To be more exact, what Rousseau condemns in history is not so much the obstruction of natural goodness—for like most of his contemporaries Rousseau held a fairly cynical view of human nature—as history's concealment of what is the true foundation of the just political order. The real opposition in Rousseau's thought is that between unclarity and transparency; and the opposition between good and evil is a mere corollary of this more fundamental, essentially Cartesian opposition.

Because Rousseau and Burke agreed in condemning the triumphant and self-congratulatory complacency of the Enlightenment,[5] it is all the more striking that they assigned completely different roles to history in their attack on the Enlightenment. Rousseau condemned the Enlightenment's for being blind to how history had tainted man's certainties about the true and the good; Burke attacked the Enlightenment's for being blind to how history can reveal to us what are the truly significant facts about social life. In one sentence: in opposition to the Enlightenment's dissociation of history and human nature, Rousseau claimed that history *conceals* human nature, whereas for Burke human nature *reveals* itself only in history.

As if attempting to refute Rousseau, Burke wrote in his *Appeal from the New to the Old Whigs* (1791) the famous and often quoted words: "For man is by nature reasonable; and he is never perfectly in his natural state, but when he is placed where reason may be best cultivated and most predominates. Art is man's nature."[6] In the first place we should observe with how little reluctance Burke avails himself here of natural law terminology; he has no hesitation in speaking about "human nature" and is no less in agreement with the traditional natural law theory by identifying human nature with reason. Even more so, Burke graciously subscribes to the tired naturalist metaphor of the covenant founding society: "Now, though civil society might be at first a voluntary act (which, in many cases, it undoubtedly was), its continuance is under a permanent standing covenant, coexisting with society."[7]

Hence, the idiom of Burke's political philosophy does not differ from the one that was used by Rousseau (and by most natural law theorists at the end of the eighteenth century). But precisely this shared background enables us to see where Rousseau and Burke fundamentally differ with regard to the relationship between nature and history. For where Rousseau sees an irreconcilable opposition between history and nature, it is for Burke only in history that human nature can articulate itself. "Art is man's nature," that is, human nature requires the "artificiality" of human history to express itself. So in fact Burke is no less a natural law theorist than Rousseau,[8] with the all-important qualification that he *historicizes* man's nature: we are what we are, because history has made us into what we are.

PREJUDICE, WISDOM, AND FOLLY

If history is the most powerful generator of prejudice, we no longer need to be amazed by Burke's utterly un-Enlightened eulogy of prejudice: "You see, Sir, that in this enlightened age I am bold enough to confess that we are generally men of untaught feelings: that, instead of casting away all our old prejudices, we cherish them to a very considerable degree; and the longer they have lasted, and the more generally they have prevailed, the more we cherish them."[9] Burke defends prejudice not, as Hans-Georg Gadamer would much later defend it, with the argument that only prejudice may provide us with a point of view that gives us a handle on the world in which we are living.[10] No prejudice, no point of view; and no point of view, no understanding of the world, either. For according to Gadamer, it is only thanks to the prejudices separating the historian from the people investigated by him that the historian becomes aware of being confronted by a historical problem in the true sense of that word; and it is only then that the whole machine of *Verstehen* (as analyzed by Gadamer) can be set in motion. Differences in prejudice(s) are, so to speak, the stuff of which history is made. Put differently, for Gadamer prejudice places the historian *opposite* to historical reality; even more, it is only thanks to this opposition that historical reality comes into being.

This is where we may observe the transcendentalist residue in Gadamer's own argument—however much Gadamer may have hoped to have defeated transcendentalism by means of a Heideggerian ontological analysis of what it is to be a human being.[11] In this way we could see Gadamer's rehabilitation of prejudice as a *historicization* of that pure, ahistorical Kantian cognitive self. But by historicizing the transcendental self, we have not, as Gadamer so liked to believe, gotten rid of it. On the contrary, by so doing we have protected transcendentalism against the accusation of being naively ahistoricist; hence, we have now (unwittingly) given to transcendentalism precisely its strongest form instead of removing it from the philosopher's agenda. Transcendentalism can only be avoided after we have recognized that the problems that hermeneutics (Gadamerian or not) attempts to solve are all themselves a spin-off from transcendentalism. No transcendentalism, no hermeneutics, to put it succinctly; and as soon as one takes the hermeneuticist's problems seriously, one has already accepted transcendentalism, whether one likes it or not.

Since Gadamer's dealings with prejudice have been so unsuccessful (though we must praise Gadamer for avoiding the all too easy condemnation of prejudice and for properly recognizing its value and significance), it becomes all the more interesting to consider Burke's views on prejudice. Most importantly, Burke's rehabilitation of prejudice, unlike Gadamer's, is free from transcendentalist reminiscences. The explanation is that for Burke the human individual must always be thought of as being *absorbed* by sociohistorical reality, whereas transcendentalism always construes an *opposition* between the self and reality. This opposition is still present in Gadamer's view (in spite of his attempt to exchange epistemology for [Heideggerian] ontology) of the historian's unceasing, Tantalus-like efforts to reach the ever unattainable meaning of the text.

However, for Burke prejudice does not place us *opposite* to sociohistorical reality—according to him it is only thanks to prejudice that we truly become *part* of it. Prejudice does not place us *outside* sociohistorical reality (transforming reality into an enigma challenging all our cognitive powers to the utmost), but *inside* it (which makes the world essentially *un*problematic). Burke's Aristotelianism (to which we shall return later on in this chapter) safeguarded him against all transcendentalist temptations, though it must be admitted that he was probably little aware of why and where his own Aristotelian mental map differed so fundamentally from that of so many of his contemporaries (and of later theorists, such as Gadamer).

Anyway, this is what, according to Burke, the French revolutionaries with all their striving for clarity, for "transparency" and for a political Cartesianism, were never able to comprehend.[12] Those revolutionaries longed for that clarity, and even thought that it was within their reach, that insofar as this clarity was realizable, everything in sociopolitical reality could now be manipulated by them at will. By forgetting the extent to which even they were *absorbed* by sociopolitical reality, they could believe that they had the possibility of placing themselves *opposite* to it—in the way that physicists are placed *opposite* to their experimental setup. The revolutionaries now believed that they could experiment with sociopolitical reality just as freely as biologists use their mice; thus Burke accuses them of seeing the citizen "as they do mice in an airpump, or in a recipient of mephitic gas."[13] But this kind of scientific objectivity and Rousseauistic transparency is a foolish and unrealistic ideal in politics—and where Rousseau, and with him, the French revolutionaries, discern the alpha and omega of all meaningful politics, Burke could only see a denial of all that belongs to the essence of politics. One might well define politics as that domain of human activity where *eo ipso* clarity and transparency are unattainable; we need politics for no other reason than to deal in a most responsible and careful way with the sort of intractable problems that arise in a reality without clarity and transparency. It follows, therefore, that an approach to politics such as that recommended by Rousseau and practiced by the French revolutionaries is utterly inappropriate.

Rousseau and the French revolutionaries would undoubtedly retort now that it is precisely prejudice that continuously blurs political reality, and that it is therefore prejudice that stands in the way of the desired clarity and precision of the right political view. In harmony with the *sapere aude* of the Enlightenment, they would conclude that a relentless war on prejudice is therefore the basis and presupposition of all rational politics; for as long as prejudice can successfully sow confusion in the hearts of citizens, a rational politics will be distracted from its proper course. Burke's reaction to this declaration of war on prejudice and tradition by the French revolutionaries is this: "In this you think you are combating prejudice, but you are at war with nature."[14] For it is human nature, as acquired in history, to allow ourselves to be led by prejudice, and it is in prejudice that our nature announces itself. For example, why do we respect our princes and parliaments: "Why? Because, when such ideas are brought before our minds, it is *natural* [Burke's emphasis] to be so affected."[15]

And, once again, "natural" does not refer here to an inclination toward traditionalism that is part of human psychology, but to the fact that we never could completely objectify such "ideas" and never could completely isolate them from other such "ideas"—as is the case with the variables in a scientific law. Such a "thinking away" of the prince or of parliament in order to find out what the world would look like without them— that is, the kind of thought experiment that is the presupposition of the possibility of the sciences—is an almost impossible task in sociopolitical reality. For that sort of "idea" has its ramifications all over sociopolitical reality and cannot be isolated from others. And prejudice is at hand when— as will almost always be the case—these ramifications indeed reach further than rationalist, apriorist schemes seem to suggest. Burke's view of prejudice is, therefore, even more ontological than Gadamer's, whose thought is still seduced by epistemology, as evident when he emphasizes the cognitive, hermeneutic advantages of prejudice.[16]

It is here that one discovers what is, arguably, most profound in Burke's political philosophy. He recognizes that the transcendentalist, epistemological regime of the true versus the false, the Enlightenment's trusted compass, is helpless in the sphere of politics, where our only help can be found in the regime of wisdom versus folly. The distinction between these two regimes is that the second does not presuppose that opposition between the world and the cognitive self characteristic of all (even of Gadamer's) transcendentalism. The world is not the exclusive and decisive criterion for distinguishing wisdom from folly—as it undoubtedly it is in the case of truth and falsity—for the distinction between wisdom and folly is, no less, a distinction between subjects—that is, between *persons* and all that contributes to their *personality*. The regime of wisdom and folly does not oppose chunks of reality to certain chunks of language—as is the case with the regime of truth and falsity—but opposes *combinations* of certain chunks of reality together with certain chunks of language to other such *combinations*.[17] For wisdom and folly relate to the kind of patterns we may discern in how people act; and human action always gives us this combination of language (or thought) and the world. Both regimes are fundamentally different: under certain circumstances it may be foolish to utter a certain truth, and wisdom is not incompatible with falsity. For example, who would speak the truth if a German *Feldwebel* were to ask us whether we have Jewish persons hiding in our house? And we should note that Kant, whose respect for the regime of truth and falsity was greater than that of any other, would have required us to speak the truth even under such circumstances: think of Kant's *fiat iustitia, pereat mundus* and of his categorical claim "that everything which is correct in ethics from a theoretical perspective, is also valid for practice."[18]

An important implication follows from this: we can only decide about wisdom and folly if we are in the position to *compare* several such combinations of reality and language (belief, thought, and action) to another such combination. So a plurality of combinations that we can label as either "wise" or "foolish" must be available; for, if no meaningful comparison between combinations is possible, nothing can properly be said about what is wise or foolish. The situation is different, of course, in the regime of true and false statements: we need no false statements in order to find out which statements are true. Such a comparison between true and false statements is not required to that end (though, in practice, the possibility of such a comparison may prove to be helpful). The explanation of this asymmetry of the two regimes is that the clear line demarcating reality from language has its counterpart in the distinction between truth and falsity.[19] And this means that, in opposition to the notion of truth and falsity, the notions of wisdom and folly mutually presuppose each other. Obviously, we can without contradiction imagine a world in which no false statement has ever been made (or no true one, for that matter); whereas wisdom and folly can only be recognized thanks to the actual existence of instances of the other. A world of only wise people or of only fools is inconceivable by the very logic of these words (in contrast to persons who only speak the truth, or who only pronounce falsities).

It follows that such clear-cut and unambiguous delimitations as between truth and falsehood can never be expected for wisdom and folly, and that each of the latter two can only be discerned thanks to the presence of the other. Therefore it is a true sign of the greatest wisdom—namely of insight into the nature of wisdom itself—to recognize the inevitability of acquiescing in the existence of human folly (without which human wisdom would paradoxically be impossible). True wisdom will therefore never be lured into the Enlightenment's nonwisdom of a total warfare upon folly— or as Burke puts it himself in a very wise wisecrack: "Wisdom is not the most severe corrector of human folly."[20] Burke expresses here the profound Erasmian insight that wisdom and folly do not mutually exclude each other and that it is, in fact, the highest achievement of wisdom to acknowledge this necessity of folly[21]—not because wisdom would never be able to distinguish between itself and folly (we have not been discussing *definitions* of wisdom and folly here but these things themselves), nor because folly is just as much part of reality as houses or trees are, but because folly truly is part of wisdom, and because both folly and wisdom presuppose the existence of the other.

Foucault discovered an illuminating paradox in the history of folly from the High Middle Ages down to Erasmus. Paradox arises since there appear to have been two intimately related, yet opposite movements in this history. In the first place, Foucault observes a movement of secularization or of domestication resulting in the transformation of folly from an alien and threatening power into that depressing, but not really very alarming list of all too familiar human weaknesses, such as impiety, pride, avarice, licentiousness, gluttony, jealousy, and so on. Insanity became ordinary vice and human weakness. But this movement of familiarization is counteracted by a second movement of estrangement: for, as Erasmus argues, if we would look at our world, as Menippos liked to do, from the point of view of the moon, all human effort and all human struggle would seem to us as insignificant as the futile interaction between swarms of flies or mosquitoes. Surely, from that point of view all human endeavor is mere folly. And it is wisdom that effects such a disillusioned view of the human condition. Or, as Erasmus metaphorically expressed it himself, it is only under the escort of folly that we can get access to the stronghold of wisdom and happiness and, though less surprisingly, vice versa.[22] It is, once again, the recurring message of the *Praise of Folly* that wisdom and folly presuppose the presence of each other and that the greatest fools are therefore precisely those who think themselves to be the purest incarnations of wisdom. However, as such a wise man as Erasmus, himself impersonating folly in his book, enjoins again and again upon his readers, without folly there can be no wisdom that recognizes folly for what it is—and vice versa.[23]

When Erasmus brought late medieval speculation on wisdom and folly to its ultimate perfection, then, he did so by situating the regime of wisdom and folly within the gap that he had deliberately created between what is most familiar to us (our permanent follies, or weaknesses) and what is most remote from us (the Olympian or Menippean point of view from which we may look, with wisdom, at those weaknesses and at their unintended effects). To put it differently, both wisdom and folly only come into being in the logical space where they can be presented as *representations* of each other and where they can define each other by means of the mutual representational relationship between them. For it is the privilege of the wise man to be able to recognize or to "represent" folly for what it is; and it is the sad characteristic of the fool to "represent" the actions of the wise man as mere foolishness. Wisdom is what folly is like after the Menippean movement of representational estrangement has taken place. Hence, wisdom and folly are *aesthetic* and not *epistemological* notions (such as the notions of truth and falsity that we discussed a moment ago); and as we can only have good pictorial representations thanks to the presence of bad ones, or good historical representations in the presence of bad historical representations, so it is with what is politically wise and foolish.

Three conclusions follow from these Erasmian considerations. First, though knowledge may be an ingredient of or inspire wisdom, it is not essential to it. The domain of the true and of knowledge may, admittedly, overlap with aesthetics and with aesthetic representation, but they are governed by an essentially different logic. Second, if wisdom and folly presuppose the presence of each other, the attack on folly can, in the end, only result in an attack on wisdom as well. And, third, if wisdom and folly are to be situated in this logical space between human weakness and our view of weakness, folly is, no less than wisdom, an ineradicable part of human nature. We should therefore agree with Burke that the Enlightened attempt to eliminate folly from this world will be, in the end, an attack on human nature itself. The wise man will therefore be prepared to leave some freedom of movement to folly and be aware that it would be unwise, or even outright foolish, to strive for a world without folly. Or, as Pascal already put it: "Human beings are so necessarily foolish that it would require another feat of foolishness not to be foolish."[24] It is foolish not to be foolish.

And, indeed, three years before the Reign of Terror, Burke already correctly presaged what kind of horrors the folly of the relentless Enlightened attack on folly would lead to in actual political practice. Their attack on prejudice and folly was an attack on reality and human nature that had been inspired by the attempt to replace the regime of wisdom and folly by that of truth and falsity.

THE RIGHTS OF MAN, REAL AND IMAGINED

It will now also be clear what Burke found objectionable in the notion of human rights as defined by the French revolutionaries. He agreed with his opponents that these rights are inextricably connected with human *nature*. But human nature cannot be found in those shaky metaphysical principles on which the French revolutionaries liked to found their *droits de l'homme et du citoyen*, but only in how human nature articulated itself in the historical institutions human beings gave themselves in the course of time. Speaking about "the rights of man" *in abstracto*, apart from any real and historically existing sociopolitical order, is an attempt to toss anchor where there is no ground to hold the anchor: "The pretended *rights of man*, which have made this havoc, cannot be the rights of the people. For to be the people and to have these rights, are things incompatible. The one supposes the presence, the other the absence of a state of civil society."[25] The rights of man can only be *real* rights, expressed in positive law, and not metaphysical speculations. Even more so, not recognizing this may invite us to be content with these metaphysical speculations and to surrender real rights for metaphysical ones.[26] History must therefore replace metaphysical speculation, and this is why a substantial part of the *Reflections* presents us with an exposition of how, since the Magna Carta, since 1629, and especially, since the Declaration of Rights of 1689, all that Burke refers to as "our liberties as an *entailed inheritance*"[27] came into being.

One should avoid theorizing about rights and political freedom, since these things can only exist in their concreteness and inevitably something will be lost if rights and freedom are divorced from their actual historical contexts. Political theorists speculating about abstract human rights will, in the end, often discover that they have weakened rather than strengthened the cause of political freedom. In the discourse on freedom, people will be invited to introduce hypotheses, debatable claims, unproven assumptions, and doubtful inferences that can only provide additional ammunition to the enemies of freedom. We should, therefore, only speak about freedom and rights in the most concrete possible way: "The science of constructing a commonwealth, or renovating it, is, like every other experimental science, not to be taught *a priori*."[28]

Moreover, abstract reasoning will not contribute in any way to the solution of a concrete political evil—for "what is the use of discussing a man's abstract right to food or medicine? The question is upon the method or procuring and administering them."[29] And according to Burke, an even graver danger of abstract political discourse is that it tends to consider politics *sub specie* of the borderline case. For it is inevitably part and parcel of abstract political reasoning that the meaning and value of political principles can only be decided by considering their relationship in the most extreme political circumstances. It is only then that we can discover what hierarchy really obtains among political principles. Actual political debate, politics as a going concern, is ordinarily a complex and indecipherable muddle, presenting us with no reliable clue about what political principle overrides the application of others. It is only the state of emergency, as Carl Schmitt realized so well, that is the most reliable heuristic instrument in abstract political reasoning: "What always matters is the possibility of the extreme case taking place, the real war, and the decision whether this situation has or has not arrived."[30] Schmitt's political philosophy is an excellent example of the abject conclusions to which this kind of reasoning may give rise.

But, against Schmitt, we should agree with Burke that it is precisely the main purpose of the well-functioning political constitution to success-fully avoid such extreme cases at all times. It is exactly the reverse: we can only get to the heart of a political system by establishing the extent to which it succeeds in avoiding the emergence of extreme situations and the means it adopts to that end. The search for a principled politics is, ordinarily, in-spired by an aversion to the complexities of politics as a going concern. It is inspired by precipitation, ignorance, lack of respect for reality, or even by sheer intellectual laziness. Or, as Burke criticized this latent extremism of the revolutionary discourse of the so-called rights of man: "The pre-tended rights of these theorists are all extremes; and in proportion as they are metaphysically true, they are morally and politically false. The rights of men are in a sort of *middle*, incapable of definition, but not impossible to be discerned."[31]

Burke's rejection of the very idea of the *droits de l'homme et du citoyen* should therefore not be interpreted as a plea to surrender passively to the despotism of a tyrannical regime. Burke recognizes on several occasions the right to resist despotic government, though he emphasizes, in agreement with his distrust of abstract principles, that we should avoid theorizing about the question under what precise circumstances revolution against an existing regime would be legitimate. And we know that Burke's qualification of his rejection of idle speculations about the legitimacy of revolutions was far from being an empty proviso from his unequivocal support of the cause of the American revolutionaries against the British government.[32] Moreover, as heir and defender of the Glorious Revolution, and in his resistance against the attempt by George III to adjust England's constitution into a more au-tocratic direction, Burke proved to be a determined and courageous protag-onist of the rights of Parliament and of the citizen as these had been defined in the Declaration of Rights of 1689. But, once again, the point of his argu-ment is that one should fight not for abstractions but for *real* rights: "far am I from denying in theory, full as far is my heart from withholding *in practice* (if I were of power to give or to withhold) the real rights of men."[33]

We may discern here another ground of Burke's distrust of revolu-tions in general: in so far as revolutions draw their inspiration from specu-lations about abstract rights, they will result in lawlessness and despotism, whereas our *real* rights and our *real* freedom are best guaranteed by a pru-dent and careful adaptation of what exists. But, as Burke does not tire of saying, such adaptations are forever necessary because a state that lacks the means to change itself as is required by the circumstances, and that chooses to persist in an Egyptian immobility, will be condemned to political death—and rightly so. Therefore: *almost* always (i.e., not *always*) we should prefer reformation to revolution—and he expostulates with the French revolutionaries that there is no reason whatsoever to suppose that, in 1789, the French monarchy was really beyond reform and that revolution was therefore the only viable alternative.[34] Even when a political system has begun to show serious defects—and Burke never denies that this was truly the case with France at the time—even then, or better perhaps, *precisely* then, one should proceed from history and from what has grown historically and naturally. For it is history that may show us what has gone wrong and what historical antecedents may suggest an adequate medicine for our present political diseases. History should therefore never be hidden behind a Rawlsian "veil of ignorance." For what cabinet maker could repair a cabinet that he does not actually look at? Destruction can be the only result.

BURKE AND HISTORISM

Nevertheless, though Burke reminded the French revolutionaries again and again of the paramount political significance of history, he in fact kept amazingly close to the Enlightened conception of history. This may become clear if we consider a most telling aside in the *Reflections*. Meditating the disasters that have befallen humanity in the past,[35] Burke writes: "History consists, for the greater part, of the miseries brought upon the world by pride, avarice, ambition, revenge, lust, sedition, hypocrisy, ungoverned zeal, and all the train of disorderly appetites, which shake the public with the same troublous storms that toss the private state and render life unsweet."[36] And, as he continues, these vices are the *causes* of those storms: "Religion, morals, laws, prerogatives, privileges, rights of men [*sic*!], are the *pretexts* [Burke's emphasis]."[37] Hence, aspects of human nature (such as pride, ambition, and so on) are the real driving forces in human history; it is they that make history into what it has been, whereas all that the history books so painstakingly instruct us about is mere "pretext." We can now understand how Burke—in contrast to Rousseau and natural law philosophy in general—succeeded in giving so ample room to history, without being forced into abandoning the idiom and discourse of natural law philosophy. Indeed, it is the human being, and more specifically these less attractive human characteristics mentioned by Burke, that form history, and it is therefore history that will inform us about human nature. *Ex ungue cognosceris leonem.*

As has been emphasized by Meinecke, Burke was more eagerly and more attentively read in late-eighteenth- and early-nineteenth-century Germany than in his own, native England.[38] This is strange, in fact. For the German historical consciousness, as it would gradually develop into historism,[39] went far deeper and was far more pronounced than Burke's. Burke's conception of history, of its driving forces, does not yet transcend the Enlightenment view of history. There is even a striking similarity between Burke's thesis that historical forces are the mere pretexts that activate an unchangeable set of human passions (as described a moment ago) and David Hume's often quoted statement to that effect.[40] It is true that Burke was more sensitive to the life of political institutions than Hume, but he never saw them as formative of human nature. For Burke, as for Hume and the Enlightenment, history is like a play in which the decors are changed from time to time, but in which the dramatis personae always remain the same.[41]

For Burke, history was still primarily a matter of political expediency, rather than that strange world challenging all our cognitive powers that would so much fascinate the historists. The historist revolution was not in the last place an epistemological revolution, a revolution in our thinking about our cognitive access to the world. But Burke would never have understood the urgency of this revolution: for him history was the paradigmatically unproblematic, the *ne plus ultra* of what is simply *given* to us. History was to him like the air we breathe, or the water that we drink, and he would have experienced the historist's far more troubled and complex relationship to the past as an unnatural alienation from history. Even more so, precisely because of this, history could be such a secure and reliable foundation of our political constructions. It may well be true that Burke's conception of history was, in fact, a most fortunate *juste milieu* between the Enlightenment's indifference and the historist's devout prostration for history; it may well be that Burke's practical attitude toward history is most congenial to our own at the beginning of the twentieth-first century; it may well be that history should be our servant rather than an enigma forever escaping our grasp. Yet, it cannot be denied that the infatuation with Burke in the country of Möser and Herder is like Newton expecting intellectual revelations from Galileo.

The human passions that Burke still saw as the universal and unchanging agents in history were historicized by historism, and their causal significance was subordinated to that of the nation, or the *Zeitgeist*. The hierarchy between what Burke still saw as cause and as mere pretext was completely reversed by historism, so that nothing in human reality could any longer escape the control of history. This truly went beyond Burkean traditionalism and could no longer be understood in terms of it. Burke's conception of history, for all its emphasis on the gradual development of the nation's constitution, was still static; his traditionalism,[42] by excluding the very notion of something that might be fundamentally new, even further reinforces the predilection for the static that he had inherited from the Enlightenment and, especially, from Hume. But historism transcended traditionalism by historicizing traditions as well, and was capable of discerning (the possibility of) fundamental or even revolutionary change where Burke could only see continuity and tradition.[43] If the fight between Burke and the French revolutionaries was a debate about the possibility and desirability of a revolutionary rupture with the past, historism transcended this debate by allowing room for revolutionary change *without* dramatic ruptures with the past.

Historism had two ways to effect this utterly un-Burkean reconciliation. In the first place, historists often succeeded in seeing continuity where others used to see revolution. No nineteenth-century historist historian was more successful in doing this than Tocqueville, when, in his *L'Ancien Régime et la Révolution* (1856), he defended the amazing thesis that this revolution of 1789, which he disliked no less than Burke, was in fact nothing but the continuation of the *ancien régime*, albeit with different and far more effective means (i.e., administrative centralization). Neither did the German historists see in the French Revolution a rupture with the past; for them it had its roots deep in French history. For example, Ranke argued that the revolution was the delayed reaction to the failure of Louis XIV's foreign policy of the end of the seventeenth century.[44] This is also why historists felt no need to see in the revolution a refutation of their historism, whereas for Burke no such reconciliation between revolution and continuity was at all thinkable. By historicizing revolution—an intellectual device not yet available to Burke—historists succeeded in reconciling revolution with their own antirevolutionary political instincts. And a generation later, the leftist Hegelians even attempted to legitimate revolution historically.

In the second place historists reconciled revolution and continuity by discovering the truly revolutionary potential of gradual historical evolution. Indeed, this is how historists required the historian to see the past: he should always be aware that beneath the appearance of continuity and immutability, beneath everything presenting itself as being the merely "natural," revolutionary change is most likely to have hidden itself. In this way historism was not merely a new way of dealing with what had always been regarded as belonging to the realm of history. It effected, instead, a historicizing of what had always been experienced as belonging to "nature" as the appropriate object of investigation for the natural philosopher.[45]

ARISTOTELIAN AND MODERNIST
NATURAL LAW PHILOSOPHY

If, then, the historist's victory over the tradition of natural law philosophy was far more decisive than Burke's, if historism reduced natural law philosophy to the status of an obsolete irrelevance from which only two centuries later theorists like John Rawls, Ronald Dworkin, Robert Nozick, *e tutti quanti*, would (vainly) attempt to rescue it, we are well advised to ask how to account for this. Why did Burke stick to the idiom of natural law philosophy, in spite of his all too apparent distrust of its invitation to "metaphysical" speculation, whereas historism gave us access to a world that was both historically and politically without antecedents? If we wish to answer this question, a closer investigation of natural law philosophy will be necessary.

Now, the more than two-thousand-year-long history of natural law philosophy is one of the most complicated chapters in Western intellectual history. I could impossibly claim to do justice to it here.[46] It is most helpful in the context of the present discussion to distinguish, in the two and a half centuries preceding the birth of historism, between an older, traditional sort and a modernist sort of natural law philosophy.[47] The older tradition can properly be called Aristotelian, even though Aristotle never developed a natural law philosophy himself. This tradition is practical, empirically minded, shares Aristotle's disinclination to abstract and speculative reasoning, and has an unmistakable tendency toward conservatism. It is in agreement with the Aristotelian view of the human being as an intrinsically social being. More specifically, it is adverse to all political theory where the political subject is ontologically or epistemologically isolated from the world: here the given is social and political interaction, and not the interacting agents themselves. Thomas Aquinas most strongly contributed to this traditional, Aristotelian variant of natural law philosophy, which in this Thomistic codification dominated Western political thought down to the seventeenth century. Modernist natural law philosophy can be seen as the attempt to introduce rationalist and Cartesian methodology into political thought. It is aprioristic, abstract, deductive; can be ruthlessly metaphysical; and claims for itself a quasi-mathematical certainty. We find its first formulation in Grotius's *De iure belli ac pacis* (1625), in Hobbes's *Leviathan* (1651), whose last part, entitled "Of the kingdome of darknesse," is a merciless attack on Aristotelian political thought. Most natural law systems that were developed in the later seventeenth and eighteenth centuries belonged to it. In contrast to the Aristotelian tradition, it had, at least potentially, revolutionary implications, as the French monarchy would find out in due time.

Indeed, at first sight it might seem that little or nothing was left of the Aristotelian or Thomist tradition of natural law philosophy at the end of the eighteenth century. But here we should avoid hasty generalizations. Not only did the Aristotelian tradition manage to survive the modernist onslaught in the more out-of-the-way European universities. For example, though theorists like Samuel Pufendorf and Christian Thomasius were most successful in introducing the modernist tradition in Germany, the Aristotelian tradition never completely disappeared from German universities. Even such a supremely influential philosopher as Christian Wolff (1679–1754) remained quite close to Aristotelianism, especially in the German-language exposition of his political thought. Moreover, Aristotelianism possessed a striking capacity for survival by hiding itself in a guise that modernism did not always properly recognize as inimical to itself. In this way, the Aristotelian tradition may remind one of those rivers that sometimes go underground, only to come to the surface unexpectedly somewhere else.[48]

It is against this background that an explanation can be given of the differences between Burke's and the German historist's conception of history. Leo Strauss has been the first to remind us of Burke's Aristotelianism.[49] Indeed, as soon as we recall Burke's insistence that "experience" is our only reliable guide in politics,[50] and his repeated condemnation of "metaphysical" speculation, the Aristotelian inspiration of his political thought will be obvious to anyone. In fact, Burke's reaction to the French Revolution could well be seen as neither more nor less than the belated counterattack of the Thomist, Aristotelian tradition of natural law philosophy (which had been taught to Burke during his student years in Dublin) against the triumphant modernist tradition. But Burke is no less Aristotelian in his emphasis that politics is essentially a matter of "prudence."

"PRUDENCE" AND PRACTICAL PHILOSOPHY

This notion of "prudence" enables us to shed some light on what presumably caused Burke (and much of later Anglo-Saxon historical thought) to follow a path different from that of German historism. But before proceeding further a short remark will be necessary about the notion of prudence within the Aristotelian tradition. In our dealings with the nonnatural world of culture (roughly what we mean by the social, historical, and political world), Aristotle distinguished between "philosophical wisdom" and "practical wisdom." Sir David Ross, who edited of Aristotle's *Nicomachean Ethics*, defines the distinction as follows: "Philosophical wisdom is the formal cause of happiness; practical wisdom is what ensures the taking of proper means to the proper ends desired by moral virtue."[51] The idea is that philosophical wisdom (defined by Aristotle as "scientific knowledge, combined with intuitive reason") teaches us what ends we should pursue in order to achieve our perfection and happiness, whereas practical wisdom, or "prudence" (*phronèsis*) informs us how to attain these ends.

This relatively straightforward division is complicated, however, by Aristotle's recommendable realism and modesty, a caution that restrained him from being too specific about these "ends." In contrast to Plato, he was well aware that if we wish to avoid illiberal meddlesomeness and irrealist dreams, we had better not try to make universally valid claims about these ends. However, he always remained sufficiently close to Plato to believe that at least somewhere and somehow these universal ends are an indispensable part of the machine of practical philosophy.

Aristotle's wise solution to the problem was to shift the burden of his argument from philosophical wisdom to practical wisdom—though, of course, even for him the former is and will always remain logically prior to the other. This shift announces itself in the distinction made by Aristotle between practical wisdom (as instrumental for achieving noble ends) and mere "cleverness" or "smartness" (which may help us to realize ignoble ends),[52] as well as in his tendency to be more interested in this subaltern distinction than in a precise determination of what are the teachings of philosophical wisdom. Though, once again, the subaltern distinction is logically dependent on the one between philosophical and practical wisdom. Put differently, Aristotle was aware of the fact that the real problem in human action rarely originates from our ignorance of what are the relevant abstract and "Platonist" desiderata that it has to satisfy; the real problem always is how to apply these principles in practice. That is what really puts us in a quandary when confronted with moral problems. Indeed, universalist "Platonist" definitions of what is morally right or wrong are easy enough to give; as Goethe once put it, "A righteous person is, in spite of his darker impulses, well aware of what is right." The most difficult kind of problem in human action is that which typically confronts the politician; namely, the problem of how to apply a hierarchy of (Platonist) values to a political reality that takes impish pleasure in wreaking havoc within this hierarchy and in presenting itself to the politician in a guise that is completely at odds with hierarchical order.

In sum, Aristotle's wisdom was that inventing "Platonic" ideas about what is morally good is easy enough—a child could do that. But all real problems of human action are *application* problems. Ethics, it must be said, is a superfluous and stultifying science as soon as we leave the sphere of individual human action behind for idle abstraction[53]—and we had better turn, therefore, to "prudence," that is, the issue of the practical applications of that science. Nevertheless, if Aristotle's humane tact prevented him from formulating apodictic claims about the teachings of philosophical wisdom, this remained the keystone in the architecture of his ethical and political thought. Without it, the whole architecture falls apart.

Now, from the perspective of this account of Aristotelian ethics, one might agree with Strauss's argument that Burke eliminated philosophic wisdom completely from it and was thus left with practical wisdom, or "prudence," only.[54] Two arguments can be adduced in favor of this contention. First we must consider Burke's notion of "prescription." Since the sixteenth century, legal theorists debated the extent to which time could legitimate possession of rights or goods, and many of these theorists were indeed inclined to recognize prescription as legalizing possession. However, they rarely went as far as to accept prescription, even in the case of demonstrably unlawful initial acquisition. Yet Burke is prepared to make this ultimate step. As has been argued by Lucas, this means that in the relationship between the supreme dictates of philosophical wisdom and practical wisdom, the latter succeeded, in the Burkean doctrine of prescription, to completely vanquish the former. Practical wisdom of the *application* of a certain philosophical moral truth ("Do not appropriate another person's possessions") has now toppled over into the denial of that moral truth *itself*—and all that remained now was "prudence," the practical wisdom of the responsible statesman.[55]

Secondly, and even more importantly, we should consider Burke's view of the English constitution. It is true that he venerated the English constitution as the highest achievement of political wisdom. But, precisely because of this almost religious respect, we cannot fail to be struck by the peculiar impassivity and calm of Burke's account of the English constitution in his *Abridgement of English History* and in his *History of the Laws of England*. For contrary to our expectations, these essays on the history of the English constitution never suggest the existence of some aim, goal, or "idea" that has already been or still has to be realized in the course of time. First, such an aim or idea does not lie in the past. For example, when commenting on so important a document as Magna Carta, Burke writes: "It is here to be observed, that the constitutions of Magna Charta are by no means a renewal of the Laws of St. Edward, or the ancient Saxon laws, as our historians and law-writers generally, though very groundlessly, assert."[56]

Thirdly, nor is such an aim or idea part of the future or a promise of history. Though the Glorious Revolution was for Burke the highest stage in the development of the English constitution, he never implies that 1688 should be seen as the fulfillment of a promise that had always been present in British constitutional history. For when comparing the Glorious Revolution with 1789, Burke writes that "the people of England well know that the idea of inheritance furnishes a sure principle of conservation, and a sure principle of transmission, without at all excluding a principle of improvement. It leaves acquisition free; but it secures what it acquires."[57] This is, so to speak, Burkean prescription applied to the constitution. Just as infringements on the proper legal order, may, in due time, acquire legality, so constitutional history is a continuous adaptation to new problems and new developments that are always essentially unforeseeable and that gradually become absorbed as a legal part of the constitution.

As the old conservative wisdom goes, one must change in order to preserve. But these changes are necessitated by circumstances unrelated to the constitution itself (such as the appearance of an ambitious monarch in the person of James II); they are not guided by a continuous attempt to approximate as much as possible the "idea" or "ideal" of the English constitution. Of course, one may expect that the importance of the adaptations required by such unusual circumstances will or even should be in proportion to the seriousness of the challenges posed by them. Thus 1688 has been crucial in the history of the English constitution because the autocratic tendencies of James II posed such a serious threat to it, and therefore elicited so important an adaptation as the Declaration of Rights. But despite its obvious importance, the whole episode is contingent rather than necessary; for Burke there is no such thing as an English national character, or some equivalent, that made it inevitable sooner or later. Thus, in Burke's view of prescription and of the history of the constitution, we will look in vain for some sense of direction that organizes all these contingent adaptations into a logical and coherent whole and that is expressive of an "idea" or "mentality" of English political practice. Indeed, Burke does not hesitate to recommend to the French revolutionaries the remedy of 1688,[58] because this proved so extremely wholesome to the English nation in its hour of distress. Hence, there is nothing peculiarly or exclusively English about the Glorious Revolution: the political wisdom gained by the English is, in principle, open to any (European) nation[59] and can assist other nations in their political squabbles, if only one has the good sense to recognize the treasures of this wisdom. Thus, for all his veneration of the English constitution and of 1688, any hint of "Whiggism" à la Macaulay remains strangely absent from Burke's writings. There is no general principle, historical, metaphysical, or epistemological, or other, guiding the development of the English constitution, however gradual, natural, and beneficial this development may have been.

In sum, Burke's view of history could best be seen as an Aristotelianism from which the universalist dimension of philosophical wisdom (corresponding to that striking absence of universalist (Platonist) principles in Burke's political thought) has been completely eliminated. And all that remained was the practical wisdom, the "prudence," of the responsible statesman. And certainly much is to be said in favor of Burke's construction; it may well be that, *in politicis*, the dimension of philosophical wisdom should be recognized as the *arcanum imperii* whose existence we could not possibly deny but about which we should never speculate. For this *arcanum imperii* has the strange property of disappearing into thin air as soon as we start to theorize about it.

GERMAN ARISTOTELIANISM AND HISTORISM

Historism and its antecedents in eighteenth-century natural law philosophy present a different picture. The Aristotelian tradition was in Germany a far more stubborn and successful adversary of the modernist tradition than in England or, for that matter, in France. Its success was, at least
partly, due to the fact that in contrast to what happened in England and in
France, it managed to evade the conflict by timely concession or even by
grafting itself on the modernist tradition. It is illustrative that, all through
the eighteenth century, the titles of German political treatises tended include the phrase "practical philosophy" and that Aristotelian terminology,
definitions, and schematizations predominantly remained in use.

But the survival of Aristotelianism was due mostly to its success in
neutralizing the main disagreement between modernism and itself. This
main disagreement, so much will be clear from my exposition, originated
in the fact that Aristotelianism, by deemphasizing philosophic wisdom in
favor of practical wisdom (ultimately resulting in Burkean conceptions),
avoided formulating general and universalist rules for the good state and
the just society, whereas modernist natural law philosophy saw precisely
that as its exclusive purpose.

Now, what happened in eighteenth-century German natural law philosophy was the emergence of a fusion of the Aristotelian and the modernist
tradition.[60] This synthesis is most striking in Christian Wolff's *Vernünftige
Gedancken von des Menschen Thun und Lassen* (1720)[61]—and we should recall here that Wolff was the most influential German philosopher between
Leibniz and Kant.[62] We find in this treatise the typically Aristotelian division of practical philosophy into ethics, economics, and politics, whereas
the mode of argument is strictly modernist in its deductivism. Wolff's debt
to modernism also becomes clear from the pronounced etatism and the absolutist tendencies that his practical philosophy shared with the Leviathans
that were ordinarily called into being within the modernist tradition.[63] It
must be conceded, though, that Wolff's treatise was exceptional for its fusion of theoretical and practical philosophy and that his Latin writings are
less risque.[64]

But since it would be dangerous to base general conclusions on the
oeuvre of a single, albeit most influential author, I shall now deal with the
more fruitful question of what form this synthesis of Aristotelianism and

modernism more generally took in eighteenth-century German political thought and what occasioned this synthesis. From that perspective we should concentrate upon the so-called *Klugheitslehre* (or doctrine of *Weltweisheit*) and on cameralism (*Kameralistik*). In the seventeenth century, *Klugheit-slehre*, the doctrine of prudence, was identical with Aristotelian practical wisdom, that is, the discipline of the proper means to achieve certain ends. But even before the victory of modernism, a modification of Aristotelian-ism took place, in the sense that these means were ordinarily associated with a *Pflichtenlehre*, a doctrine of *duties*. This already tilted the balance be-tween philosophic and practical wisdom more strongly in favor of the for-mer than was ever the case in Aristotelianism generally: duties and the de-finition of their nature logically precede the problem of their fulfillment in actual practice.

Next, cameralism expanded this doctrine of duties from its original domain of individual behavior to that of the state's duties toward its sub-jects—needless to say, this was a most dramatic extension of the domain of duties. Above all, the state's duties were to guarantee public safety and public welfare. But this newly created *Staatsklugheitslehre*, or cameralism, as presented by Johann Theodor Jablonski, Johann Heinrich Justi, the great Frederick himself, and above all, by Gottfried Achenwall, was equally in-terested in mundane affairs like the building of roads and canals, building regulations, employment, schools and universities and their curricula, free (!) public health service, legal aid, and, more generally, all that we now call welfare services.[65]

In fact, cameralism can be seen as the logical counterpart and supple-ment to *raison d'état* thinking, as discussed in the previous chapter, for whereas *raison d'état* thinking took the state's interest as its guide, cameral-ism found this guide in the duties of the state toward the citizen. What the two approaches shared, however, was a pronounced awareness of what were the *specific* properties, interests, strengths, weaknesses, realistic aims, duties, and obligations of the individual state (and of its ruler). The link between cameralism and *raison d'état* was established almost automatically as soon as one added the more or less self-evident premise that it will ordinarily be in the state's (and the prince's)[66] interest to fulfill its duties toward the citi-zen—such as national safety and welfare. But apart from this material fu-sion of a doctrine of the state's duties and of *raison d'état* thinking, there was a no less important formal or methodological affinity between them. For in both cases, abstract and apriorist reasoning would be completely useless; only a knowledge of all the aspects of the *history* of the state, a knowledge as detailed and accurate as possible, could be the prince's (and his servant's) reliable guide.[67] Hence, by a most complex fusion of traditions, a situation gradually emerged within the intellectual jungle of eighteenth-century German natural law philosophy, in which the state's history presented the ruler with the relevant indications of how both interest and moral duty obliged him to act. And this would result in how historism conceived of the relationship between history and politics: history will inform the politician about the nature and true interests of the state—and is the only discipline capable of providing him with such information—and it will then be the politician's task to take this as his point of departure for present and future political action.[68]

In conclusion, it is history that will show the prince and statesman what are the proper "general goals" of their political enterprises. Or, to use the most appropriate terminology here, the historian has to discover the state's or the nation's Aristotelian entelechy and then it is the task of the prince and the statesman to realize this entelechy's *telos*. And indeed, with the help of the notion of the "historical idea,"[69] historists like Ranke and Humboldt succeeded in operationalizing this link between history and politics in a way that proved to be immensely valuable for the writing of history—and that would also appeal to many nineteenth-century German politicians. By means of the notion of the "historical idea," the Aristotelian natural law variant succeeded in grafting itself upon nineteenth-century historical and political thought—and, in a way, its grasp has never really slackened since then. Whereas for Burke history only teaches us the route along which we came to where we presently are, without implying what the future will or must look like, the political paragraph of German historism sought to teach us that history does not inform us merely about political *means* but also about the proper political *goals*. And it has been that very long road of political Aristotelianism that finally led historism, via the notion of the state's duties, via the *Staatsklugheitslehre*, and via the absorption of *raison d'état* thinking, onto this so very un-Burkean path.

The transition from the eighteenth to the nineteenth century is a watershed in the history of Western historical consciousness. As so often is the case with watersheds, on both sides we will find a countless number of streamlets, brooks, and rivulets running in all possible directions before uniting themselves in the few big streams that we all know from our maps—in this case the Christian understanding of the past as the history of salvation and, on our side of the watershed, history as formative of all cultural identity. And, similarly, as may be the case with watersheds, a coincidental and not at all impressive range of mountains or perhaps just a mere modest little hill may determine the watershed's course.

As I hope may have become clear from the foregoing, such a modest little hill has indeed played tricks in the history of Western political thought. For it has been so insignificant a fact as an ambiguity in Aristotelian ethics (and its almost inaudible echoes in Western eighteenth-century political thought) that has, to a large extent, determined how we relate to our past and how we conceive of the relationship between politics and history. This, then, is the lesson we may learn from the above comparison of Burke with German historism.

Whereas Burke's even most principled utterances "occur in statements *ad hominem* and are meant to serve immediately a specific practical purpose,"[70] and whereas for Burke history merely gave us the horizon for meaningful political action, German eighteenth-century natural law theorists discovered in history the origin of what Aristotle saw as philosophic wisdom. For Burke—as for most intellectuals in countries where the modernist tradition of natural law philosophy gained the upper hand—history is undeniably the scene where all our actions are enacted and in which their meaning is determined. However, to continue this metaphor, for German historism history is not so much the *stage* as the *text* of the play in which politicians have to display their talents.

The many differences between the political histories of the Western democracies and those of the German-speaking countries originate, to a considerable extent, in the ambivalences of Aristotelian practical philosophy. At the start of this chapter, we observed that in history small causes may sometimes have big consequences; the vagaries of political Aristotelianism and their impact on twentieth-century political practice can be considered a striking illustration of this "democratization" of causality.

3

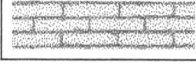

FREUD AS THE LAST NATURAL LAW THEORIST

In the eighty years that elapsed between 1789 and 1871, France was three times a kingdom, twice an empire, three times a republic, and had, besides, other episodic constitutional variants such as the Directory, the Consulate, and the presidential republic of Louis Napoleon. In the years after 1871, little suggested that an end had come to this depressing *va et vient* of constitutional tryouts, together with all the paraphernalia of revolts, massacres, coups d'etat, and revolutions. On the contrary, a comparison of the revolutions of 1830, 1848, and 1870 seems to show that the French were increasingly incapable of living together in peace and that their incapacity to do so resulted in ever more bloodshed. Even worse, an explanation of this continuous escalation of political conflict was all too easy to give. For if the social dimension was not yet prominent in the revolution of 1830, this dimension was obviously a large part of the revolution of 1848, while the revolt of the Commune in the spring of 1871 seemed the unambiguous announcement of a future total class war.

And indeed, if the cliché of living on a vulcano that may erupt at any moment ever became a reality, so it was during the two to three decades that followed 1870. The general expectation of the outbreak of an all-destructive class war culminated in the years around 1890. The celebrations of May 1 and the general strikes that the socialists had announced for that occasion were feared by the bourgeoisie as the beginning of the end. Charles de Mazade—and many with him—foresaw a bloody end to the Third Republic in 1889 on the occasion of the centenary celebration of the Revolution.[1] And a year later there was a general feeling that something horrible and of unprecedented proportions was at hand—and the government therefore prepared for the worst. "Paris was in a stage of siege," writes Mrs. Celia Barrows, "some 38,000 armed representatives of the army and the police were garrisoned within the city limits, the greatest number of troops since the Commune." Even though conscious of the unprecedented vigilance of the government, many conservative observers persisted in fearing a catastrophe. The May issue of *Charivari* described May Day as "an innovation which is not only *fin de siècle*, but could well be *fin du monde*."[2]

What the French bourgeoisie experienced in these years was the disquieting contrast between the apparent solidity and splendor of the French *fin de siècle* and a diffuse and unfathomable threat emanating from the deepest layers of society. The resplendent surface and the reassuring immediately observable realities of daily life thus seemed to be the caricatural reverse of a menacing and profoundly perturbing deeper social reality. The consequence was a peculiar inversion of what one might call the "social semantics" of the age: existing social peace and order were not read as an indication of the stability of the social order, but were interpreted, instead, as an indication of the depth and the scale of the total social revolution that could break out at any moment. The more stable society might seem to be at first sight, the stronger the repression had apparently been, and the more disastrous social revolution would be when, finally, the monstrous forces of revolution would succeed in overcoming those of repression. Hence, there was an experience of the existing social peace and order as the well-known silence before the storm. If the lower classes of society still seemed to respect and accept the existing political order, this was felt to be like a mere deceitful mask behind which a social revolution of unprecedented scale was silently being prepared.

A preeminently sensitive observer expressed it as follows:

I am under the full impact of Paris and, waxing very poetical, could compare it to a vast overdressed Sphinx who gobbles up every foreigner unable to solve her riddles. But I will save all this for verbal effusions. Suffice it to say that the city and its inhabitants strike me as uncanny; the people seem to me of a different species from ourselves; I feel they are all possessed of a thousand demons; instead of "Monsieur" and "Voilà l'Écho de Paris" I hear them yelling "A la lanterne" and "A bas" this man and that. . . . They are people given to psychic epidemics, historical mass convulsions and they haven't changed since Victor Hugo wrote *Notre Dame*.[3]

Thus Sigmund Freud in the autumn of 1885, in a letter to the sister of his future wife. French society, the French masses he experienced as the riddle of the Sphinx—a riddle formulated in terms of the conflict between what is on the surface and what lies hidden and concealed in the depth beneath this surface. And only the modern Oedipus who succeeds in solving the riddle may prevent us being swallowed whole by these Sphinx-like masses.

Exactly the same metaphor was used by Gustave Le Bon in his profoundly influential *La Psychologie des foules* (The psychology of crowds; 1895). The task that Le Bon gave to himself and to his contemporaries was defined as follows: "Crowds are much like the sphinx of ancient fables; no one should succeed in solving the riddles that are posed by their psychology or resign to being devoured by them."[4] This is why, in Le Bon's eyes, mass psychology was the most important social science for the Western world at the end of the nineteenth century. For only when the mass psychologist succeeds in solving the riddle propounded by the "Sphinx crowd" may we hope to prevent the total destruction by those masses all that Western civilization has created in the course of two millennia. "The advent of the masses will probably be one of the last stages of Western civilization"[5]—according to Le Bon, it is only mass psychology that may help us prevent this desperate scenario from becoming historical reality.

Now, one should realize that the mass psychologist who took on this sublime task of rescuing Western civilization from the onslaught of the masses was in a strangely ambiguous position. The crucial datum here is that this ambitious task could only make sense to the extent that the coming of the masses was an indubitable and definitely established fact. Hence, the mass psychologist had to be the announcer of as well as the fighter against mass society. The position was obviously uncomfortable because the fight against the masses could only be successful if the advent of the masses were somehow *not* inevitable—and thus the cure most inconveniently contradicted the diagnosis.

The paradox can be given a more concrete content. All the mass psychologists of the end of the nineteenth century—Alfred Espinas, Gabriel Tarde, Scipio Sighele, and Le Bon, to mention the best known of them— were convinced that democracy and mass society were intimately related, and this may explain their antidemocratic propensities. For in the first place the egalitarianism that they ascribed to democracy had its obvious counterpart in the fact that all distinctions between individuals tend to disappear when these individuals coagulate into a crowd. Next, it is the explicit purpose of democracy to reconcile the will of the individual with that of the community. And this is exactly what fascinated the mass psychologists about the new psychological phenomenon of the masses: they also observed in the masses a complete willingness of the individual to surrender his own personality to the crowd without feeling curtailed in his freedom of movement or individuality. In other words, the masses seemed to be a kind of orgiastic cult of democracy in which all the evils of democracy clearly demonstrated themselves in their most pathological extremes. And for the same reason, mass psychology could be seen as the social psychology of democracy—and was therefore entirely dependent on a social reality that it so unconditionally and so enthusiastically abhorred. Once again, we may observe here the curious paradox that the mass psychologists had to start by presenting themselves as the standard-bearers of democracy in order to justify their claim, at a later phase, that only they might succeed in saving Western civilization from democracy's horrors. If democracy and the crowd constituted a merely temporal, avoidable, and transitional phase in the history of the West, then exactly the same would necessarily be true of the writings of these mass psychologists. In this way, the mass psychologists were the best solicitors of democracy that they (with the exception of Tarde, by the way) so much urged their readers to fear.

This inevitable "infection" of mass psychology by democracy is already apparent from the question that is absolutely central to all mass psychology. In the crowd we may observe a (temporary) disappearance of the usual barriers between the individual and society, and thus the crucial question must be: thanks to what psychological mechanism does the crowd succeed in bridging this gap? Self-evidently, this is a *psychologistical* formulation of the *political* problem with which all democracy typically has to deal. It is this problem that preoccupied all the mass psychologists and that they tried to answer each in their own way (though liking to copy what others colleagues had already said on the subject). The question is already addressed in Espinas's *Des Sociétés animales* (1877), which is ordinarily seen as the first mass-psychological study. In a somewhat awkward formulation, Espinas first argued here that the group possesses a certain autonomy with regard to the individual:

We shall say that a society is, on the one hand, a living organism, but, on the other, an organism distinguishing itself from others in that it is mainly constituted by its consciousness. A society is a living consciousness, or an organism of ideas. In this way we may sidestep the criticism that is correctly addressed at several sociologists when they explain a superior mode of being by an inferior one.[6]

But this (methodological) collectivism or holism is kept in balance by his observation elsewhere: "The individuality of the whole is in proportion with the individuality of its constituent parts; and the better the identity of the parts is articulated, the more their action is independent, the more the unity of the whole and the force of its action will be guaranteed."[7] Apparently Espinas is looking here for a reconciliation of what we presently call methodological holism and methodological individualism (and, in the attempt, he transformed the *political* problem of democracy into what is, basically, a *philosophical* problem).[8] And, anyway, it remains unclear whether in Espinas's writings this balance is really more than a concealed *coincidentia oppositorum*. Perhaps we can best do justice to Espinas's exposition by granting him the honor of having been the first to put this problem on the agenda of mass psychology, without, however, finding a solution to it that is satisfactory from either a philosophical or socioscientific point of view.

Later mass psychologists dealt with the issue more fruitfully. In the first place, they were more successful in avoiding the trap of diluting an essentially scientific problem in the watery abstractions of philosophical debate. And, second, this invited them to identify a domain of human psychology where the dissolution of the individual into the crowd could actually take place. Thus, Tarde offered a description of what he described as the "laws of imitation," explaining how the human individual might, under certain circumstances, come to exchange individuality for the properties of a collectivist self. Something similar was offered by Le Bon. In his view, if a flush of victory, by suggestibility or by some kind of "mental infection," invites individuals to merge into a crowd, the usual opposition between the individual and the collectivity will disappear.[9] And this loss of the individual self into the collectivity is not at all a brutalization of the individual by the group or crowd; we see here rather a voluntary self-amputation by the individual of those personality aspects that stand in the way of loss into collectivity. The adaptation of the individual to the collective crowd arises spontaneously from the individual and is emphatically not the result of some external constraint or of the tyranny of the crowd's leader.

It was this that both intrigued and appalled Le Bon and the other mass psychologists about the new phenomenon of the masses. And the awareness of this fundamental and characteristic feature of the masses would, in the end, result in the proud first sentences of Freud's "Group Psychology and the Analysis of the Ego," where the opposition between the individual and the collectivity, between a psychology of the individual and one of the masses, is explicitly rejected:

The contrast between individual psychology and social or group psychology, which at a first glance may seem to be full of significance, loses a great deal of its sharpness when it is examined more closely. . . . In the individual's mental life someone else is invariably involved, as a model, as an object, as a helper, as an opponent; and so from the very first individual psychology, in this extended but entirely justifiable sense of the words, is at the same time social psychology as well.[10]

Freud wanted to emphasize in this way that the opposition, described a moment ago, between methodological holism and individualism loses its meaning and raison d'etre from the perspective of mass psychology: for the point of the quoted statement is that this opposition between the individual and the collective (which is, self-evidently, presented as a reality by those who believe in the meaningfulness of the opposition) is simply not present in human behavior. So, according to Freud, this whole debate about individualism versus collectivism—in both its philosophical and psychological variants—proceeds from a profoundly mistaken conception of the realities of human psychology.

But let us return to Le Bon. We may, then, observe how, unintentionally, his writings on mass psychology provided democracy with a psychological basis instead of being the attack on democracy that Le Bon expected them to be. Illustrative of these unintended and unwanted tendencies in his mass psychology are the contradictions in which Le Bon entangles himself in *La Psychologie des foules*, which he concludes with a kind of speculative philosophy of history, including a sketch of the rise and fall of civilizations. He presents his readers there with a cyclical view of the history of civilizations: that we will find "at the dawn of these civilizations a scattering of human beings, of different origins and united by the fortuity of migrations, invasions, and conquests."[11] Out of this disparate sociological material, a civilization is then formed under the influence and guidance of some religious or political ideal that inspires and unites these individuals in a common effort. The initial sociological "dust" of isolated individuals is thus transformed into the perfect unity of a successful civilization. And this is what Le Bon, following Taine, refers to as a "race," that is to say, as a homogeneous group of individuals that is capable of the highest perfections of human civilization. If, however, we approach our own age, defigured so much by masses and by democracy, we will observe that "with the final loss of its old ideals a race will, in the end, also lose its soul. It is nothing but a 'dust' of isolated individuals and becomes again what it initially was: a crowd."[12]

This truly is an amazing exposition. For elsewhere in his book Le Bon finds the explanation of the origin of a crowd in the animation of an amorphous chaos of individuals by some collective religious or political ideal that is imposed on that chaos by a powerful and charismatic "leader" (*meneur*). But in Le Bon's philosophy of history, as presented above, it is precisely *civilization* that we are required to see as a "race" inspired by some shared ideal, while it is said to be characteristic of the masses not to possess such a shared ideal and to disintegrate into mere sociological "dust." Hence, the pre-nineteenth-century and predemocratic order idealized by Le Bon is credited here with all the features that Le Bon exclusively ascribes to the masses in the major part of his study. And, next, Le Bon's philosophy of history grants to the democratic individual precisely the same autonomy and independence that his mass psychology had taken away from it. All value judgments of mass society and of what, according to Le Bon, is opposed to it are now confused and get into each other's way.

The explanation is, obviously, that in Le Bon's mind "civilization," crowd, and democracy do not find themselves in such a clear and well defined opposition to each other as he liked to believe. And this implies, again, that Le Bon's mass psychology cannot offer a believable solution or *alternative* to the "age of the masses": mass psychology itself does not find itself on a platform outside or beyond mass society; it presupposes mass society and makes no sense in its absence. Mass psychology is, in a crucial sense, a theory about itself; it is self-referential in this way because it essentially is a characterization or explanation of the conditions of its own possibility. And the riddle posed by the Sphinx-crowd therefore is, in fact, the riddle of mass psychology's own origination together with democracy—a riddle that certainly is not insoluble but that cannot be solved by mass psychology itself. The origin of a discipline cannot be explained by that discipline itself (the writing of history might be the sole exception to this rule): for example, the coming into being of physics is not itself a physical phenomenon.

BOURGEOISIE AND MASS PSYCHOLOGY

To continue this line of thought, if we ask for the conditions of the possibility of reliable knowledge within a certain discipline, we may expect to be given some kind of conceptual framework defining the discipline in question. If, encouraged by this success, we move on to the question of what the conditions of the possibility of knowledge are, not only in this, but in science in general, we may expect to be presented with some variant of Kantian transcendentalism—or with an epistemological account of the relationship between language and the world, to mention one of those variants of transcendentalism that have become so popular in our own time, in which we all adore the god of language. If, next, having become still more audacious by our successes until now, we decide to ask the even more ambitious question of what the conditions of the conditions of the possibility of knowledge are, it is only history that may satisfy our curiosity. For it is only history that is capable of giving a satisfactory answer to the question of why humanity, in some phase of its evolution, decided to put scientific and philosophical issues on its agenda. But even then we may wish to move onward and ask about the conditions of the possibility of history. But if we ask *that* question, the only reasonable answer to it will be a *historical* answer all over again. So history is where, in the end, it all stops, and the historical question is, thus, the last and most fundamental question that we may ask about the origins of science, philosophy, and culture in general. Philosophy, art, science—they are all embedded in history.

Bearing in mind all this, we will be all the more ready to turn to history when we wish to account for the coming into being of mass psychology—the question that we asked ourselves at the end of the previous paragraph. But it will not immediately be clear how to operationalize the question in a meaningful and helpful way. For what precisely are we asking when we ask for the historical origins of a discipline? An obvious and uncontroversial answer would be that humanity (or Western civilization) was somehow in need of the discourse and the results of the discipline in question. If, then, we want to answer *this* question with regard to mass psychology, we had best turn to Bernard Groethuysen's *Origines de l'esprit bourgeois en France* (1927), one of the great, but unfortunately almost forgotten, history books of the first half of the last century.

With powerful but accurate strokes, Groethuysen paints in this book the conflict between the traditional Christian *Weltanschauung* and what the bourgeoisie put in its place in the course of the eighteenth and nineteenth centuries. Groethuysen's main idea is that there was no room for any compromise in this conflict since the bourgeois and typical bourgeois concerns had no real overlap with the Christian *Weltanschauung*. The poor and the powerful had their trusted and fixed role in the order that was presupposed in the Gospel. But the advent of the bourgeoisie presented Christianity with something that had not and could not possibly have been foreseen in the Gospel: "the god of the Christians, when creating this world and preparing for the advent of the church, seems not to have foreseen that one day the bourgeois would claim its place and might wish to play an important role in it."[13] The sins and the duties of the prince, of the aristocracy, and of the poor were all defined in the Gospel, and precisely because they derived their meaning and social function from an embrace of the Christian order, they could never be a serious threat to this order, but were, instead, a continuous and ever repeated confirmation of it. By contrast, the sins and the triumphs of the bourgeois did not have their well-attested antecedents in the Gospel; and it therefore made no sense for the Church to remind the bourgeois of the vanities and the miseries of this world, as it had always successfully been able to do for the aristocracy and the poor. The regime that governed the bourgeois's life and from which all his happiness and his fears stemmed, that regime was neither known to nor recognized by the Bible.[14] The resistance, or rather, the incapacity of the Church to keep pace with the development of bourgeois capitalism, and to fit it in some way or other into the matrix of the Christian faith, was both the sign and the exact measure of this ever-growing alienation between the Church and the bourgeoisie.[15] In one word, the bourgeois basically has always been a *corpus alienum* within the Christian conception of the world and humanity.

Hence, from the perspective of the Christian West, one could justifiably say that the bourgeoisie has created itself: in contrast to the aristocrat and the poor, the bourgeois could truly say about himself that he owed the confirmation and the recognition of himself only to *himself*. On the scene of world history the bourgeoisie therefore unites in itself both the doubtful grandeur and the despicableness of the parvenu—and with all its self-doubt the bourgeoisie is aware of this down to the present day (assuming with Fukuyama that the entire world has become "bourgeois"). For this painful uncertainty has always been the hallmark of the bourgeois, all the more painfully so because—once again, unlike the aristocrat or the poor—the bourgeois really succeeded in changing all that he touched and had thus set into motion: "He has taken everything in hands," writes Groethuysen, "he has removed everything from its place and subjected it to a new order."[16] So, what is so extraordinary about the role of the bourgeoisie in world history is that it created this role itself—even more, it rewrote the whole scenario of world history after its own image. This preeminently uncertain social class, the bourgeoisie, took upon itself a responsibility that no previous social class would ever have dreamed of. In this way, the bourgeois is at once prince, priest, aristocrat, poor—and, indeed, everything falling outside or going beyond this traditional social hierarchy.

"God has in no way contributed to the greatness of the bourgeoisie," says Groethuysen about the origin of the bourgeoisie. And about its taking over the control of "the business of this world," he rightly observes the following: "As long as he remained in his humble sphere the bourgeois was part of God's order, like all the others possessing a fixed role in society, but he ceased to be part of that order as soon as he stood up. Since then he enacted his own providence, he put himself in God's place."[17] Indeed, the bourgeoisie had taken for itself the place of God and of Providence. Thus, in contrast to the representatives of the traditional social orders of Christian Europe, the bourgeoisie no longer had a foundation *outside* itself; it could no longer experience itself as being safely embedded in an order wider and more comprehensive than itself. The bourgeoisie could only find out about its grandeur and its miseries, about its unsurpassed creativity and its no less unsurpassed lust for destruction, by investigating the depths of its own soul and of its own heart—and this is why psychology is a typical bourgeois science. And what religion used to discover in the word of God, the bourgeois psychologist now had to find in the dark forces hidden in the depth of the soul of the bourgeoisie. Consequently, the old Christian fear of sinning against the order imposed by God was now transformed into a fear of those deeper and disquieting layers of one's own self. The aristocrat and the poor still coincided with themselves thanks to the very coherent role that the Gospel had accorded to each of them; the bourgeois, by contrast, was divided in and against himself—an inner division of the self that expressed itself most clearly in its uncertainties of what might be hidden underneath its so (desperately) rational(ist) self-presentation on the scene of world history. The dreams of reason produce Goyaesque monsters. In sum, the parable, or *figura* in Auerbach's sense, of the bourgeoisie can be found no longer in the Gospel, but in the darker ranges of the psyche of the bourgeois that continually threaten to overtake his personality—and far more often do so than the bourgeois likes to admit. Hence, the bourgeoisie's propensity to hypocrisy or repression and neurosis. And the Book of the Soul thus became the bourgeoisie's Bible.

The evolution sketched here is nowhere more clearly expressed than in Stevenson's well-known novella *The Strange Case of Dr. Jekyll and Mr. Hyde.* And it certainly is no coincidence that this novella, dating from 1886, is contemporaneous with the meditations of the mass psychologists about the advent of a new "age of the masses" in which even educated and intelligent people willingly transformed themselves into the brainless and primitive components of a human crowd. The novella expresses the realization that the bourgeois is capable not only of the greatest, but also of the most horrendous crimes, and it therefore voices the bourgeois's fear of *himself,* of the awful realities that he may be expected to find in the depths of his soul. Indeed, the traditional fear of God and of sinning against God's commandments was now transformed into a fear of oneself and of one's own aggression.

Certainly Stevenson was more likely to appreciate this transformation of religious into psychological fears and to give an adequate literary expression to it. We must recall, in this context, that Stevenson came from a strictly puritanical Scottish family and that all his life he continued to wrestle with a Christian obsession with sin. In this way, we can agree with G. K. Chesterton's apt observation that "Stevenson was a Christian theologian without knowing it."[18] But this is the less interesting part of the whole truth. For what is so interesting about Stevenson is that his morality had a profound affinity with the uncertain no-man's-land between the Christian and the bourgeois world order that we tried to define a moment ago, with the help of Groethuysen. More to the point, therefore, is Chesterton's observation elsewhere that Stevenson exchanged "the prison of Puritanism" for the "prison of Pessimism" and that he replaced the Calvinist's somberness with Schopenhauer's secularized, bourgeois variant of that somberness—just as, for that matter, many cultural pessimists at the end of the nineteenth century became enthralled by Schopenhauer's bleak picture of the *condition humaine,* in which the absence of unhappiness is the best that we can hope for.[19]

Indeed we may discover several reminiscences of the Christian notion of sin in Stevenson's novella: thus Hyde preferably wrote his blasphemies in the margins of the religious treatises that Jekyll had always valued so much, and he destroyed the portrait of Jekyll's father—the evident psychological equivalent of God's authority.[20] But the most interesting aspect of Stevenson's construction is to be found in two other aspects of his novella. The first element is Jekyll's insight into the *double* nature of man and of himself: "It was on the moral side and in my own person, that I learned to recognize the thorough and primitive duality of man. I saw that, of the two natures that contended in the field of consciousness, even if I could rightly be said to be either, it was only because I was radically both."[21] Jekyll realized that his personality comprised both Jekyll and Hyde, and that in the depth of his personality the very paradigm of bourgeois respectability lived shoulder to shoulder with a hideous and dangerous monster. Even more so, as becomes clear at the end of the novella, the monster proved to be the stronger and the more prominent partner of the two. The second element is this. Science—this "prothesis" that, according to Freud, elevated man to the status of a quasi God—the *science* of chemistry enabled him to achieve this most unnatural segregation of both his natures. It was therefore science—another typical bourgeois device that did not fit into the *Weltanschauung* of the aristocrat and of the poor—that enabled Jekyll to disrupt "the God-willed order" of the integral personality and to effect the fateful segregation of his self—for which suicide proved, in the end, to be the only resolution.

And this brings me to the point of the novella. The result of this disruption of God's order was that the individual no longer found himself placed *integrally* before his judge (i.e., God), as had been the case in Christianity: for this traditional opposition between the integral personality and God was now transformed into an opposition *within the individual himself.* The individual broke apart in a God-like and criminal part, and all that used to happen between God and the individual Christian now happened in the transaction between these two components of the bourgeois personality. Hence, Jekyll no longer feared God; rather, he feared Hyde—and thus *himself.* It should be noted in this context that Stevenson is at pains to suggest that Hyde, with all his monstrous behavior, must not be seen as a challenge to the Christian order and its commandments but first and last as a challenge to Jekyll's moral integrity. And it is neither God nor the Devil who takes possession of Jekyll at the end of the novella, but Hyde, that is, his own *alter ego*. As personified by Jekyll, the Christian God is changed into this uncertain God of the bourgeois personality, divided against and afraid of himself: no longer is God the supreme judge of the indivisible individuality of the aristocrat or of the poor, but now one part of the bourgeois personality has become the judge of another part of the bourgeois self and of its impulses and transactions. Religion is thus exchanged for psychology. And in this way Stevenson's novella most lucidly expresses the bourgeois's fear of the order that he has created *ex nihilo*, and it similarly explains how this fear would manifest itself in the writings of the (mass) psychologists.

From this perspective, it need no longer surprise us that the transformation that Jekyll undergoes when he temporarily becomes Hyde is closely similar to what, according to the mass psychologists, happens to individuals when they lose themselves in the crowd. For what always struck the mass psychologists about this was the elimination of self-awareness, of that part of the self that holds itself responsible for what it does. And precisely this was achieved by Jekyll's strange potion:

Men had before hired bravos to transact their crimes, while their own person sat under shelter. I was the first that ever did so for his pleasure. I was the first that could plod in the public eye with a load of personal respectability, and, in a moment, like a schoolboy, strip off these lendings and spring headlong into the sea of liberty.[22]

Just as the individual subsumed in the crowd is so miraculously successful in divesting himself of all that distinguishes him from his fellow human beings, so that, during a short moment of collectivist inebriation, he can enjoy total social freedom, so Jekyll succeeded in momentarily laying aside all the attributes determining his place in society when he deliberately transformed himself into Hyde. In both cases the effect is, as Stevenson puts it twice in exactly the same words, "a solution of the bonds of obligations"[23] and the coming into being of a creature that is only capable of aggression and destruction. And thus of a creature that inspires every "decent" bourgeois with a feeling of intense aversion, disgust, and fear (probably because he knows this creature all to well from his *own* deeper self).

It requires no clarification that Hyde is Jekyll's *unconscious*. Hyde gave to Jekyll the opportunity to freely indulge in all his desires; desires that he would never have tolerated in himself as a decent bourgeois, and insofar as he had suspected their existence at all, would have relegated to the unconscious, animal part of his personality. And here, too, Stevenson's novella is a parable of mass psychology and of the fears of self that the bourgeoisie projected on the masses. For when Espinas speaks about the animal character of the group, or crowd, when Tarde speculates about the laws of imitation that invite the individual to lose himself in the crowd, when Le Bon theorizes about the "collective soul" dominating the crowd, the intuition is, at all times, that because of a temporal paralysis of intellectual capacities the individual is reduced to some (collective) unconscious. The individual in the crowd is not aware of himself; he acts on the basis of impulses originating in the unconscious for the simple reason that he has divested himself of his individuality and therefore no longer possesses a self that he could possibly be aware of. Ideas lent from Schopenhauer or from Hartmann were used to demonstrate the destructive and primitive character of the collective unconscious.[24]

Stevenson's Hyde clearly is a product of this school. It is therefore his unconscious that the bourgeois feared most; it is his "other," what is outside and alien to his rational self, never in the grasp of his rational consciousness and yet decisive of what his history will be. When seen in this way, the unconscious is the bourgeois perversion of the Christian God and of Christian Providence. But no matter how far the bourgeois might like to move away from his unconscious, it is and will always inexorably remain a part of himself. This is also why for the aristocrat and the poor of the Christian era, to whom this urge to effect such a segregation in their psyche was wholly alien and incomprehensible, the notion of the unconscious could not possibly have made any sense. If psychology is a typical bourgeois science, then the unconscious is, again, the prototypical bourgeois product of that bourgeois science.

The contrast between Jekyll and Don Giovanni, the prototypical aristocrat of Mozart and Da Ponte, may be illuminating here. Just like Jekyll, Don Giovanni was in the possession of the respectability that was part of his social role status—and like Jekyll he sincerely enjoyed this social respectability and even exploited it in his dealings with Zerlina, for example. And once again, just like Jekyll, there is also a darker side to his personality. But Don Giovanni does not permit this tension to tear his personality into two separate parts, even when the Commendatore (and the sublime music that Mozart wrote for this part of the opera) made it abundantly clear to him that hell will be his fate forever if he persists in his refusal to do so. And precisely this is where the aristocrat Don Giovanni crucially differs from Jekyll the bourgeois. The explanation is that within the kind of view that Don Giovanni had of himself, the situation could not arise that one part of himself found itself in outright opposition to another part: Don Giovanni saw himself from the outside, as it were, and then one typically sees a unity only (though this unity itself may well be a mixture of what is good and what is bad). For Don Giovanni, with his "decentered self-assessment," there is no reason at all to believe that moral depravity and social respectability could not be aspects of one and the same integral personality. And what is united by this decentered self-awareness is dearer to him than the salvation of his soul. The bourgeois, on the contrary, divides his self into a number of conventional elements, into elements that he may or may not share with his fellow human beings and that may then become the subject of psychological investigation. The aristocrat unites a number of conventional elements (being a man of the world, being an erotomaniac) into something that is essentially new and would therefore escape psychological analysis. The psyche of the aristocrat is synthetic, that of the bourgeois is analytic, and it is therefore most suitable that the psychoanalytical therapy of the bourgeois individual is called "psychoanalysis." The Freudian self as a box of Pandora with all kinds of unsuspected and generally unpleasant gifts would never have occurred to the aristocrat and to people whose minds and mental outlook had been formed by aristocratic society.

Freud, here also more radical and more cynical than any of his predecessors, abandoned the idea that the lower, animal strata of the human psyche are responsible for the individual's propensity to become part of a crowd. Freud situated this propensity at the opposite pole of the psyche, in what he initially referred to as the *Ich-Ideal*, and later as the *Über-ich* or the "superego." For the later Freud, in contrast to Le Bon or Stevenson, it was not our animal and most primitive instincts that might, under certain circumstances, succeed in achieving this fusion of the individual and the crowd. According to him, this fusion could only take place after some religious or political ideal has been instilled in the individual(s) by an artful demagogue. The not implausible intuition here is that mere animal and primitive instincts could never effect the extreme degree of social cohesion that we find in the crowd. For Freud the social cohesion so typical of the crowd is therefore, in contrast to what Le Bon and others believed, not a denial of civilization, but the most impressive proof of the things that civilization may achieve.

However, in this way all the negative associations that we all have with the notion of the crowd are also attributed to the notion of civilization. Albeit for quite different reasons, Freud would therefore agree with the critique of civilization as had been formulated, for example, by Rousseau. And, as we shall see in a moment, there is much more that he would share with Rousseau's pattern of argument. In a way, Freud's critique of civilization is even more radical and uncompromising than Rousseau's. Rousseau's famous exhortation *retournons à la nature* was intended to be an invitation to construct a civilization that would respect human nature. But for Freud such a reconciliation of civilization and human nature is *sui generis* impossible, since civilization has no other task than to restrain and to frustrate human nature.

FREUD ON THE NATURE AND ORIGIN OF CIVILIZATION

The nature and origin of civilization are intimately related for Freud. On the face of it, this is what historism also had always argued for: according to historism, we should turn to a thing's history in order to find out about its nature and identity. But we could make no graver mistake than to link Freud's analysis of civilization to that of historism. For when the historists so closely, perhaps even logically, related nature and history,[25] Freud is much closer here to natural law theory.

Natural law theorists such as Hobbes, Locke, or Rousseau had always tried to derive a conception of civil society from speculations about the nature of the presocial and prehistoric human individual. After having produced a definition of human nature, natural law theorists ordinarily proceeded by postulating a contract that was supposed to have been agreed on by all these presocial individuals in order to overcome the inconveniences of the state of nature. Natural law theorists widely differed with regard to the details of this hypothetical scenario, but this is nevertheless the plot that one will discover in the writings of most of them. And exactly the same pattern of argument is repeated in Freud's theory of human society—this is why my thesis in this chapter is that Freud could well be seen as the last of the great natural law theorists.

Just as natural law theorists reduced all of human history to one all-decisive event—the creation of civil society by the unanimous acceptance of the social contract—so Freud reduces all of human history to one extremely dramatic event in a prehistoric past. And just as the natural law theorists saw the original contract as the matrix for all later historical phenomena, such as states, law, civilization, social organization, and so on, so Freud derived all of individual and collective human behavior from that profoundly dramatic and traumatic event in mankind's prehistory. Both natural law theorists and Freud argue that all that we know as "history" is nothing but a mere repetition, a continual atavistic reexperience, either on the scale of the individual or on that of the collectivity, of the all-decisive event, however defined, with which all history began. And with which, in fact, it also ended, in a certain sense. For since that primeval event nothing has or could have happened in all of human history that might significantly have changed the social reality that came into being with it. "History" as it is so eagerly studied by historians is a mere "inconclusive clutter," in the words of Philip Rieff,[26] if compared to that single and all-decisive moment when civil society was created.

Freud's psychological variant of natural law theory is most clearly outlined in his *Totem and Taboo*, the book in which he proposed his hypothesis of the murder of the father by the primitive horde. The idea is that the primitive father monopolized all the sexual contacts with the females, thus forcing the younger males to sexual abstinence or to exogamy. Out of frustration about this state of affairs, the younger males finally murdered the primeval father—and after the murder they ate his corpse in the belief that they could thus appropriate his strength. That they did this is certainly no mere bizarre and accidental detail; for Freud, this cannibalistic act contains the origin of the ritual totem meal and, therewith, much if not all of later human society. For during that meal the sacrosanct totem animal is collectively consumed in a remembrance of the murder of the primeval father, and thanks to this remembrance the foundation of society can be passed on to later generations. Furthermore, Freud likes to point out (as we might have expected from such a fierce enemy of revealed religion) that we may find all these cannibalistic elements carefully preserved in the Holy Communion of the Christian religion. For, on this most solemn occasion, the faithful are supposed to eat and drink the body and the blood of Christ in order to express the unity of the Christian community. A most eloquent and succinct summary of all the elements of the murder of the father is formulated by Freud himself in the following passage:

One day the brothers who had been driven out came together, killed and devoured their father and so made an end of the patriarchal horde. United, they had the courage to do and succeeded in doing what would have been impossible for them individually. (Some cultural advance, perhaps, command over some new weapon, had given them a sense of superior strength.) Cannibal savages as they were, it goes without saying that they devoured their victim as well as killing him. The violent primal father had doubtless been the feared and envied model of each one of the company of brothers: and in the act of devouring him they accomplished their identification with him, and each one of them acquired a portion of his strength. The totem meal, which is perhaps mankind's earliest festival, would thus be a repetition and a commemoration of this memorable and criminal deed, which was the beginning of so many things—of social organization, of moral restrictions and of religion.

In order that these latter consequences may seem plausible, leaving their premises on one side, we need only suppose that the tumultuous mob of brothers were filled with the same contradictory feelings which we can see at work in the ambivalent father-complexes of our children and of our neurotic patients. They hated their father, who presented such a formidable obstacle to their craving for power and their sexual desires; but they loved and admired him too. After they had got rid of him, had satisfied their hatred and had put into effect their wish to identify themselves with him, the affection which had all this time been pushed under was bound to make itself felt. It did so in the form of remorse. A sense of guilt made its appearance, which in this instance coincided with the remorse felt by the whole group. The dead father became stronger than the living one had been—for events took the course we so often see them follow in human affairs to this day. What had up to them been prevented by his actual existence was thenceforward prohibited by the sons themselves, in accordance with the psychological procedure so familiar to us in psycho-analyses under the name of "deferred obedience." They revoked their deed by forbidding the killing of the totem, the substitute for their father; and they renounced its fruits by resigning their claim to the women who had now been set free. They thus created out of their filial sense of guilt the two fundamental taboos of totemism, which for that very reason inevitably corresponded to the two repressed wishes of the Oedipus complex. Whoever contravened those taboos became guilty of the only two crimes with which primitive society concerned itself.[27]

This event—and like most of the natural law theorists, Freud is quite candid about this being a *hypothetical* event—concentrates all that transformed the presocial father-horde into the "brother-horde" that our society has remained down to the present day. And, once again, as in the contract theories of the seventeenth and eighteenth centuries, all the essential features of the social or civil order can be derived from the nature of this event, thanks to which human society was founded.

It need not surprise us, however, that the psychologist Freud was especially interested in a number of sociopsychological properties of all human society about which natural law theorists cared little. For example, his account of the murder of the father makes it easy to see why incest is taboo in all human societies. This taboo expresses the memory of the sexual abstinence that the father had imposed on the younger males and that these younger males continued to respect thanks to this peculiar mechanism of the *nachträgliche Gehorsamkeit* (deferred obedience). No less interesting (especially from the point of view of the tradition of contract theory) is that society does not have its origin in the attractive prospects offered by future cooperation as defined by a contract agreed upon by all the members-to-be of civil society, but in the oppression of a permanent awareness of shared guilt. The members of the "brother society" that civil society essentially is down to the present day can only recognize each other in this memory of the murder of the father for which they are all responsible. So, right from the beginning there lies a curse on human society, and it emphatically is not born from some promising and liberating collective action. Not the welcome fruits to be expected from collective action, but an unspeakable tragedy and the traumatic memory of it, mark the beginning of history and of human society.

Furthermore, a remarkable aspect of Freud's account of the origin of human society is that, unlike traditional contract theory, it presents a solution for the dilemma of methodological individualism versus collectivism that we discussed above. These contract theories were necessarily and invariably individualist. This certainly has its recommendable implications from a political point of view; surely we should oppose political philosophies presenting the individual as a mere emanation of the collectivity. But the price that these theories had to pay—as nineteenth-century historism pointed out ad nauseam—was a dangerous blindness to what the individual owed to society. This blindness could be dangerous, in that it tended to ignore to what extent the collectivity, and what transcends the individual, can paradoxically serve the cause of the individual's freedom.[28] For this dimension of the collectivity has its elective affinities with history, which functions as a kind of reservoir or repository of previous collective action.

And, as the historists went on to argue, radical breaks with history, such as had been attempted during the French Revolution, even if these attempts had been inspired by the best of individualist political theories, will in practice often result in a destruction of individual human liberty.

Within Freud's account of the origin of civil society, the dilemma of methodological individualism versus methodological collectivism simply evaporates, so to speak. For we should observe that within this account there is neither a temporal nor a logical hierarchy between society and the individual: both come into being *at one and the same time* in Freud's peculiar brand of natural law theory. The individual only becomes an *individual* thanks to his participation in the *collective* guilt of the murder of the father—that is, at the very same moment that *society* comes into being. The individual and the collectivity are, so to speak, collateral; neither of the two has priority over the other. Freud succeeds so much more in removing the dilemma that traditional natural law philosophy is unable to solve because he emphasizes the complete psychological metamorphosis that the individual undergoes in the transition from the father-horde to civil society. He truly becomes a completely different kind of human being—and in this new human being, what we associate with the individual is indissolubly linked with what we associate with the collectivity. Hence, after the foundation of civil society, the distinction between the individual and the collectivity is a most tenuous and helpless abstraction that will produce misunderstanding rather than clarification. Similarly, if we follow Freud rather than traditional natural law theory, or the (Marxist) collectivists who preferred the other horn of the dilemma, it will be easier to avoid the kind of political disasters arising from a denial of a synthesis (Freudian or otherwise) of individualism and collectivism in human nature itself.

Next, in the traumatic memory of the murder of the father lies not only the origin of conscience but also of the domain of human communication. The idea is that conscience creates in the individual a *forum internum*, a domain of potential experience of the self that is an indispensable condition of the possibility of all human communication. It is such a condition since without this domain of potential inner experience there would simply be nothing that communication could possibly be *about*—mere data provided by external reality would be insufficient. Only after external reality has, so to speak, *passed through* this *forum internum*, will meaningful communication about reality be possible. The crucial datum here is that this *forum internum* will be decisive with regard to what we say, not only about ourselves, but about external reality *as well*. This is what distinguishes meaningful communication from mere animal exclamations of pain, fear, or happiness. The statements that we, as human individuals, make about external reality can only meaningfully be made because our *forum internum* both enables and requires us to formulate them. For even if we seem to speak exclusively about objects outside ourselves without explicitly adding anything about ourselves, we should think of all our statements as accompanied by a short introduction, such as "I think," "I believe," "I think it is of importance to observe, that . . . ": in all such cases the "I" refers to the *forum internum* that, from a psychological point of view, was created with the murder of the father. Hence, without this *forum internum* created by conscience, mankind would never have made the transition from mere mechanical exclamation (the level to which animal communication is restricted) to the truly social level of meaningful interhuman communication.

We should observe, furthermore, that this *shared* sense of guilt also provides mankind with a shared *topic* of communication: obviously, the discourse of the brother-horde will tend to focus on how this sense of guilt is experienced by the individual members of the social order and how it should be dealt with. In this way, history as a past that is shared by all and the discourse of moral behavior came to be introduced into human communication and to play such a prominent role in it. This sense of guilt has thus also been the basis for all speculation about and knowledge of the nature of the moral and social order in which human individuals live. As Freud points out, the etymology of the German word for conscience (*Gewissen*; related to *Wissen*, or "knowing") makes this clear already: "For what is conscience? On the evidence of language it is related to that of which one is 'most certainly conscious or aware.'"[29]

Furthermore, Freud emphasizes that civilization and society came into being under the aegis of a peculiar but no less important ambivalence in the feelings that the younger males had for the father. On the one hand, they had loved and admired the father, but on the other they had hated him. The human psyche does not care about our rationalist intuition that hate and love should mutually exclude each other. On the contrary, Freud even has the courage to claim that those we love most are necessarily those who provoke in us the strongest feelings of hatred. And, as Freud goes on to argue, this has left its indelible traces in how human individuals relate to each other in society. Freud has in mind here what Kant had referred to as the *ungesellige Geselligkeit* of human society, that, in his relationship with other human beings, the human individual will discern in his fellow human being an "other" that he "he cannot suffer or live without." Freud himself preferred in this context the fable of the shivering porcupines that had been proposed by Kant's epigone Schopenhauer. On a cold night these porcupines huddled together in order to benefit from each other's warmth, but when they hurt each other with their quills they were forced to look for the narrow optimum of proximity and distance. And so it is in our dealings with our fellow human beings: the duke de Saint-Simon's so accurate and compact description in his memoir of the Président de Harlay—"never at his ease, nor anybody else with him"—is true of all of us to a greater or lesser extent.

Lastly, the prehistoric murder of the father could usefully be compared to the Big Bang that astronomers see as the origin of the universe. Just as the Big Bang formed all the matter in the universe and crystallized all the laws that still obtain in physical reality, so this social Big Bang of the murder of the father produced human society and all the psychological and sociological laws determining its functioning down to the present day. And, to continue this astronomical metaphor, astronomers have measured a so-called background radiation that they interpret as a kind of echo, still observable today, of the Big Bang of fifteen billion years ago. A somewhat similar echo of the social Big Bang is still audible according to Freud in the depths of our own souls. For Freud, the Oedipus complex is structurally identical to this murder of the father with which human history began.

In order to see this we have to go back to the earliest phase in our mental development, namely, the phase in which the child that we were still lived in a quasi-solipsistic union with the world, where the separation between self and not-self has not yet been achieved. This act of separation resulted in what was arguably our life's greatest loss: in the most literal sense of the word, we lost the whole world, in opposition to and in fear of which we now have to live as puny individuals. Small wonder that we all wish to undo in some way this terrible and traumatic event in our psychic history and to attain once again the state of solipsistic bliss. This is, so to speak, the logical and psychological underlife of our libido, the impulse that we feel, sometimes weaker, and sometimes stronger, but that always aims at a reunification of ourselves with reality, or parts of it.

Since, for the child, reality consists mainly of mother and father, the child has two options for achieving this reunification with reality. In the first place the child can opt for an appropriation of the world (Freud uses here the term *Objektwahl*); in the second, the child can aim for an identification (*Identifikation*) with the object of reunification. Hence, the libidinous desire to reestablish the solipsistic original situation can take the form of either a "having" or "being" reality. For the male child, the father invites the mechanism of identification (i.e., of "being") and the mother that of *Objektwahl* (i.e., of "having"). Hence the child's subconscious desire to murder his father in order to sexually possess his mother—and the plausibility of Freud's at first sight so absurd and bizarre claims about the child's psychic life. Obviously, if seen in this light, we may discern in the Oedipal matrix a repetition of the original drama of the murder of the father in order to achieve sexual freedom. Thus prehistory has determined our psychic life down to the present day. History has had nothing of any real significance to add to this; it both began and ended with the murder of the father.

THE PESSIMISM OF FREUD'S NATURAL LAW THEORY

Earlier we noted that there is in Le Bon's book on mass psychology a contradiction: the psychological mechanism responsible for the creation of the masses is also presented as the mechanism to which civilizations owe their existence. Apparently, Le Bon's psychological approach to civilization made him confuse what is good and what is bad from a sociological or historical perspective: civilization became indistinguishable from such a deplorable phenomenon as the modern crowd. And we have seen that something similar is true of Freud's theory of the masses, though for different reasons. Freud believes that the superego is the ally of civilization in the human psyche but also the indispensable accomplice of the masses in the human psyche. No superego, no masses—but then no civilization either. So, once again, psychology has the curious effect of provoking indifference with regard to civilization and what might threaten it.

But at a later phase of his life Freud went beyond even this. In his later writings, psychology not only invites indifference or indecision with regard to civilization, but even an outright opposition between our deepest psychological needs and civilization. This is the case, for example, in his *Civilization and Its Discontents*—as the book's title make abundantly clear—which presents us with a way of thinking that is essentially different from that of

Le Bon's mass psychology and the one presented in Freud's earlier piece, "Group Psychology and the Analysis of the Ego." A surprising *renversement des alliances* has now taken place. Le Bon and the younger Freud, in spite of the uncertainties mentioned a moment ago, clearly were in sympathy with culture and civilization at the expense of the psychological mechanisms, however defined, that might threaten them. But this attitude, to which we all will feel naturally inclined, is abandoned by the later Freud when he takes up the cudgels for instinct rather than for civilization.[30] As the case is presented in *Civilization and Its Discontents*, we feel unhappy and disappointed about civilization—and have every reason for doing so—since civilization continuously and often needlessly frustrates our instinctive desires.

As long as the libido, with its directedness toward unification, still played the main role in Freud's analysis, an outright conflict between instinct and civilization could be avoided. Even more so, within this conception civilization may even, in its own way, contribute to the unification for which the libido always aims. But all this changed profoundly when Freud, especially after the crucial *Beyond the Pleasure Principle*, began to construct an opposition between the libido on the one hand and the instincts of death and aggression on the other.[31] Self-evidently, this death and aggression instinct is, by its very nature, a threat to and an implacable enemy of civilization and a well-ordered civil society, but of even more importance is what one might call, paraphrasing Hegel, "the cunning of civilization." I have in mind here Freud's claim that civilization, in its effort to protect itself against the potential onslaught of the death and aggression instinct, succeeds in redirecting this instinct against the self. Initially the instinct is directed against what is outside the self, but it has been civilization's supreme triumph (and, arguably, the condition of its very existence) to transform the instinct into a powerfully ally by making it attack the self. Thus we are confronted with the strange spectacle of an alliance of what is highest and what is lowest in the human psyche, of what has produced the most sublime achievements of human civilization and of what is darkest and most dangerous in the human mind. And the victim of this most unlikely alliance is the self, which is only capable of these achievements to the extent that it allows itself to be bullied and maltreated by its own instinct of aggression.

An obvious example of this new mechanism is offered by sexuality. First, Freud now associates sexuality with the death and aggression instinct rather than with the libido and its nostalgic yearning for a solipsistic reunification with the world. Sex is aggression. And, precisely because of this, civilization wishes to enforce sexual behavior within the narrow limits still acceptable to it, so that it need no longer fear an attack from sexuality and all that sexuality symbolizes. Civilization achieves its aim by making the instinct of aggression into a kind of psychological whip that disciplines individuals in their social behavior. The torture that sexually unacceptable behavior might be to others is now transformed into the self-torture of sexual abstinence. Small wonder that civilization produces in us a permanent state of frustration and discontentedness, sometimes resulting in neurosis. And this is also why Freud is not unwilling to take sides with the death instinct rather than with civilization. So much becomes clear from Freud's tendency to put sexual abstinence in an unfavorable light: it is a sign of weakness rather than of strength when the individual so easily allows himself to internalize the harsh, merciless, and, ultimately, self-serving prescriptions of civilization.

And it certainly is one of the most depressing implications of Freud's arguments here that such apparently praiseworthy things as *Triebverzicht* and self-discipline proceed from weakness rather than from strength. Before Freud came along, the individual succeeding in restraining his socially undesirable (sexual) behavior could still console himself with the certainty that his behavior was proof of his high moral standards and his sense of responsibility; since Freud, the individual who so easily denies himself the satisfaction of his desires has acquired the contemptible features of the *Überguter* (naive sucker).[32] Thus Freud adds to the self-torture demanded by civilization the humiliation of self-contempt. Freud's contempt of the *Überguter* clearly resonates in his hard verdict on the individual living "decently": "Only the weaklings have submitted to such an extensive encroachment upon their sexual freedom."[33] As Nietzsche had done before Freud, morality is presented here as the hypocrisy of the weak.[34]

Thus the conflict between the individual and civilization is a direct result of the nature of both, and inevitably results in an infringement upon the individual's freedom. Indeed:

The liberty of the individual is no gift of civilization. It was greatest before there was any civilization, though then, it is true, it had for the most part no value, since the individual was scarcely in a position to defend it. The development of civilization imposes restrictions on it, and justice demands that no one shall escape those restrictions.[35]

The creation of a well-ordered society can only be successful to the extent that civilization does not care about the individual's happiness and psychological well-being. And the neuroses that are provoked in the individual's psyche by ruthless self-restraint are the sign and proof of the victory of civilization over the individual's desire for the satisfaction of his desires. Hence, for the later Freud neurosis and civilization are not alternatives to each other, in the sense that our psychic energy is invested either in neurosis or in civilization, but are placed on exactly the same level. We will be civilized to the extent that we are neurotic. And the sad picture now is that it has been neurosis to which we owe the greatest achievements of art, philosophy, and, perhaps, science.[36]

Consequently, because of the inevitability of this conflict between the individual and civilization, Freud expects little from programs for social reform.[37] The human capacity for freedom and happiness depends on the individual's psychic constitution; the way that society is organized only marginally and negligibly affects it. One can be happy in the worst of societies and unhappy in the best.[38] Each social reform, even if inspired by the most sublime (revolutionary) ideals, will only result in the creation of new social *Ich-idealen* and thus be little more than the substitution of one psychological dictatorship for another. Freud was therefore not surprised by the *Kurzlebigkeit und klägliche Erfolglosigkeit* ("lamentable lack of any long-term success") of revolutionary experiments such as the French or the Russian revolutions. Neither need we be surprised by humanity's habit of trying out the revolutionary experiment again and again, despite all their previous failures: the desire to exchange an older social order for a new one is as old as the rebellion of the younger males against the father of the primeval horde, and as persistent as the perennial Oedipal rebellion of the male child against his father.[39]

Hegel gives us the following characterization of the difference between man and animal:

What man is in reality, he must also be in ideality. Since he possesses ideal knowledge of reality, he ceases to be merely a natural being at the mercy of immediate intuitions and impulses which he must satisfy and perpetuate. This knowledge leads him to control his impulses; he places the ideal, the realm of thought, between the demands of the impulse and their satisfaction. In the animal, the two coincide; it cannot sever their connection by its own efforts—only pain or fear can do so. In man, the impulse is present before it is satisfied and independently of its satisfaction; in controlling or giving rein to his impulses, man acts in accordance with ends and determines himself in the light of a general principle.[40]

The striking similarity between Hegel's argument here and Freud's thesis about why civilization compels us to *Triebverzicht* will need no further elucidation. Nevertheless, Hegel and Freud did quite different things with this same insight. Whereas for Hegel *Triebverzicht* is the condition of the triumphal march of Reason through History, for Freud it results merely in an endless *Wiederkehr des Verdrängten* ("return of the repressed")[41] from which, *sui generis*, no progress in history could possibly be expected.

So our question must be why Hegel and Freud drew such so widely different conclusions from the same datum. Within the present context, the most interesting explanation is that whereas Hegel focused on the use, or rather the "abuse," by Reason and History of the instincts and passions of man, Freud identifies with the individual and with the havoc wrought by History and Civilization on the human psyche. In contrast to Hegel, history for Freud is a mere background; and the many different ways in which civilization manifested itself in the course of history are of little or no interest to him.

One important qualification must be made, though. In a certain sense history is no less important for Freud than for Hegel. However, "meaningful history" is reduced by Freud to just one single event: the prehistoric murder of the father of the primitive horde. For Freud the meaning of history should be situated neither in the genesis of the present nor in an evolution of both the present and the past from an earliest beginning, but exclusively in that earliest beginning *itself*. Needless to say, in Hegel's philosophy of history we observe exactly the reverse. As Rieff expressed it in a most appropriate metaphor: "for the very reason that Hegel thought Africa no proper subject for the historian, Freud would consider it most proper."[42] What happened in human history after this earliest beginning—after "Africa," so to speak—is for Freud nothing but an endless repetition of a repressed prehistorical event. Analogy, parallelism, the prototypical, displacement, and repetition are the favorite categories of psychoanalysis—and all these categories are invariably inimical to history and to historical development.[43] A distrust of the historist conception of the past (i.e., of the belief that nothing, neither society, civilization, nor the nature of the human individual and his psychology, should be considered exempt from historical change) is therefore part and parcel of the psychological or psychoanalytical paradigm. In other words, the animosity between history and psychology is the inevitable result of the very nature of these two disciplines.

Rieff's metaphor of "Africa" is thought-provoking for one more reason. Africa symbolizes here our prehistoric past, the event that we can see as the "social Big Bang" with which all social organization, culture, religion, language, philosophy, art, and science began. And, as we have seen, this is exactly the same kind of argument that we find in natural law theories down to its most recent offshoot, namely, Rawls's "original position." In both cases, the coming into being of human society is explained by means of a hypothetical event that is supposed to have taken place in a prehistoric past. As a political or social theorist, Freud can therefore be seen as the last great natural law theorist. But unlike contemporary liberal theorists who added relatively little of enduring value to the natural law tradition, Freud brought an amount of psychological sophistication to natural law theory that rendered it interesting again. I am mainly thinking here of Freud's claim of the inevitable and tragic opposition between society (or, to use Freud's own term, civilization) and the individual, a dimension for which contemporary contract theorists have remained wholly insensitive.

Traditional natural law philosophy never spotted the Freudian problem and therefore failed to investigate its political dimensions. The only arguable exception to this rule might be Rousseau, who was undoubtedly the most psychological among the natural law theorists of the seventeenth and eighteenth centuries. And it need not surprise us, therefore, that both Freud and Rousseau saw history, or civilization, as an attack on human nature. Though both Freud and Rousseau were not at all times insensitive to the temptation of utopianism, their main outlook was pessimistic with regard to the possibility of a substantial improvement in the human condition. And this is what we must expect from all political theory that takes its point of departure in a description of human psychology. Psychology cannot but invite cultural pessimism—for our own time one may think of the writings by David Riesman or by the late Christopher Lash. Surely this pessimism with regard to what we may expect from history and political reform is far less pronounced in natural law theory in general than is the case with Freud—once again, with the possible exception of Rousseau's political philosophy. But the more natural law theory becomes dependent on psychological insight, the more pessimistic it will inevitably become.

And we may conclude that the political theorist had better keep clear of natural law theory. For it may suggest ways of improving our political fate—but then it will be based on a poor psychology; or it may be psychologically sound—but then all our hopes and efforts to achieve political improvement will be unmasked as naive illusions.

PART II

DEMOCRACY AND HISTORY

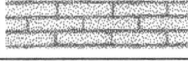

ON THE ORIGIN, NATURE, AND FUTURE
OF REPRESENTATIVE DEMOCRACY

History teaches us that every political system can or even should be regarded as the response to a particular type of political challenge. Thus, feudalism was the answer to the problem of collective safety occasioned by the collapse of the Carolingian empire and the invasions of the Norsemen; consciously or unconsciously people were aware at the time that the severely enfeebled political center could not sufficiently ensure public safety, and that this task now had best be delegated to the individual baron, count, or church dignitary. And seventeenth- and eighteenth-century royal absolutism, to mention another example, was the response to the European religious civil war that had begun in the sixteenth century and that threatened to result in collective political suicide. The absolute monarch was now given the power either to settle the conflict to the advantage of either of the two religions, or to keep both parties separated from a position of neutrality. In our own time, Carl Schmitt has brilliantly shown why and in what way this settlement of the religious conflict was the overture to much if not most of later Western political history, with its continuous alternation of depoliticization and repoliticizations. A political problem arises, is recognized as such, and politicization results. At a later stage, the problem is adequately solved, is no longer recognized as being an urgent one, or simply disappears spontaneously. Depoliticization takes over, only to be followed by repoliticization in the wake of the emergence of some new and urgent political problem. But, as Schmitt goes on to say, our age will witness the death of politics, for politics will no longer be possible after economics and technology have taken possession of all human relationships.[1]

It follows from this historist conception of political systems that every political system must be expected to possess an affinity with a particular type of political problem—that is to say, the sort of problem to which it was supposed to be a response. And if we wish to understand the nature, the possibilities, and the impossibilities of a political system, we will have to examine the sort of political or social problem which that political system was originally expected to deal with. For this will continue to determine the functioning, the reflexes, and, more generally, what we might call the "political psychology" of that system.

I do not claim to be original for this way of looking at political systems and their nature. The approach, implicitly and perhaps even explicitly already present in nineteenth-century historism, was defended some thirty years ago by Quentin Skinner in an influential essay,[2] and it has since become one of the basic tenets of the so-called Cambridge school of political theory. Strangely enough, however, this so natural and generally accepted approach has never been applied to representative democracy. At least as far as I know, no political theorist has ever investigated the nature of representative democracy by asking what exactly was the nature of the political problem that representative democracy was expected to solve— and to what extent the nature of our contemporary democracies is determined by that specific kind of problem. The explanation is, perhaps, that we are immediately inclined to see feudalism or absolute monarchy as the naive and somewhat peculiar experiments of an earlier and politically less mature age than ours. They were, as we think, sorts of political phlogiston theories that lost their right to exist as soon as democracy was (re)discovered in the course of the eighteenth and nineteenth century. And just as people such as Newton, Lavoisier, and Maxwell put the sciences on the right path during that same period, just as they developed insights that are still accepted and that proved to be the best point of departure for all further scientific research, so we also conceive of democracy as if it were some kind of everlasting political truth and we tend to believe that democracy is the final solution to each conceivable political problem that might confront humanity. This is, of course, both naive and mistaken. For if people had attempted to solve the problems of public safety in the ninth and tenth centuries, or those occasioned by the religious civil war of the seventeenth century, by means of representative democracy, this would only have (tremendously) lengthened, not shortened, the list of their disasters.

Hence, democracy does not escape the fate of all those other political systems that have been constructed since the dawn of mankind. No less than all these other political systems—forgotten, ridiculed, or even abhorred—it also is a product of a unique and specific set of historical circumstances and should be assessed accordingly. And it follows that we must begin by asking ourselves to what kind of political problem democracy was the appropriate answer if we wish to grasp the nature of that best known, but least understood of all political systems. In undertaking such an assessment, we must first of all avoid the temptation of equating democracy with universal suffrage. Even Athenian democracy, still now glorified by so many adherents of direct democracy, excluded large parts of the population without thereby ceasing to be a democracy. And though it certainly is a matter of the greatest importance who is or is not entitled to vote in a representative democracy, this is not an issue involving the nature of that political system. Naturally, this is not an attempt to disparage the historical significance of the struggle for universal suffrage. My point merely is that this struggle was not identical to the struggle for representative democracy as such.

THE ROMANTIC ROOTS OF REPRESENTATIVE DEMOCRACY

The origins of representative democracy lie in a remoter past than the struggle for universal suffrage. They can be found in the beginning of the previous century, when parliamentary democracy was first tried out in several countries of continental Europe, when the first more or less durable constitutions were adopted, and when the traditions of parliamentary government gradually developed and became accepted by most participants in the game of politics. The politicians of continental Europe at the time of the Bourbon Restoration and Romantic Europe after the fall of Napoleon feared civil war no less than their predecessors had done two centuries before during the wars of religion. As in that earlier period, one part of the population found itself in a mortal opposition to another. If in the religious wars the opposing groups had been the Protestants and the Catholics, now two secular religions or ideologies divided the population. On the one hand, many believed that the revolution had been ended prematurely in 1794 and that the social and political revolution should be taken up again as soon as a suitable occasion arose. On the other hand, many nobles and members of the higher bourgeoisie recalled with a feeling of nostalgia the prerevolutionary social order and were prepared to do all that they believed necessary to prevent further revolutionary experiments or, perhaps, even to return to the world of the *ancien régime*. (And between these two extremes there were, of course, all kinds of more moderate variants, which, moreover, differed from one Western European country to another according to circumstances prevailing there.)

But as this rudimentary sketch of post-Napoleonic continental Europe makes clear, the conflict in nineteenth-century Europe was essentially different from that of the religious civil wars of the seventeenth. The nature of the earlier religious conflict was such that it almost created the state as an institution independent of society. If there had been no state at the time, it would have had to be invented in order to arbitrate between the fighting parties from a position that was fundamentally independent of these parties themselves. And this demand for an independent arbitrator was so strong that even though the state most often took sides with one of the conflicting religious parties, this never really compromised its aloofness from society. In retrospective, this is perhaps one of the most amazing features of how the European state emerged from the wars of religion; the state might just as well have been pulled into the religious conflict and shared in the demise of the warring parties in their remorseless internecine fight. Interestingly enough, this did not happen (though France in the decade prior to Henry IV's accession to the throne came dangerously close to the above dismal scenario). Even in Germany, which the religious conflict tore apart, within each of the principalities originating from the arrangement of 1648 the state was no less victorious than elsewhere in Europe. So, generally speaking, when the state identified itself with the cause of one of the religious parties, the religious party favored by the state was elevated to the sublime position of the state itself; and the state was not degraded to the level of the religious party it endorsed. In sum, the nature of the conflict was such that the state could only benefit from it as an independent political entity; this explains why absolute monarchy was the almost inevitable outcome of the conflict, and why the distinction between a civil society and a state that had now successfully emancipated itself from civil society gradually became regarded as a matter of course. And it certainly is one of the paradoxes of Western political history that absolute monarchy and the distinction between state and civil society share so much in terms of origin and political logic that we might arguably never have had the latter without also having had the former. If only because of this, we should be a little kinder about absolute monarchy than we often tend to be.

In any case, the situation after 1815 was a completely different one. The state could now no longer place itself as a neutral arbiter above the conflicting parties. For the state had now itself become the main issue in the conflict. The revolutionaries, the liberals, the conservatives, the Bonapartists, and the rest were now fighting about who would be in control of the state. And this, self-evidently, was a problem that could no longer be settled by the state itself. Thus there arose a political problem whose extreme urgency no one could sensibly doubt and that could not possibly be made to fit the existing political machinery. Even worse, this problem had all the characteristics of being unsolvable. For one possibility was to allow the discord existing within society to be expressed at the level of the state as well; but such a divided state would precipitate, rather than prevent, the as yet latent social civil war. And that scenario would result in the same sort of quandary as existed at the beginning of the religious wars two centuries earlier; once again, a divided and powerless state would have been submerged in a chaos of social conflicts and all the ensuing disasters. Even worse, the state now could no longer play, as it had done two centuries before, its role of *deus ex machina* in order to get society out of its political morass. The alternative possibility was to allow the state to be controlled by one of the fighting parties, but what would then guarantee the other parties that their interests would still be sufficiently addressed? All the considerable powers that the state had acquired during its absolutist adolescence could now be used by the party in control of the state against its rival(s). And civil war seemed the inevitable result of this alternative strategy as well. In short, the Restoration's political problem had all the features of having to square a political circle.

Parliamentary, representative democracy was the highly ingenious political system devised during the Restoration in order to take the sting out of this conflict and to prevent Europe from plunging into another endless series of revolutions and ideological wars. At its heart was the so-called *juste-milieu* policy that we ordinarily associate exclusively with François Guizot but that in fact sums up the political mentality of most of post-

Napoleonic Western Europe. This complicated notion contains several components, but in this context the most significant is the following. To begin with, people at the time realized that it would be impractical, in view of the existing irreconcilable political disagreements, to strive for consensus. The gap between the different ideologies was correctly perceived to be too deep to allow consensus. And, more importantly, they were profoundly aware of the fact that the political challenge of the time was not to create consensus out of political disagreement, but how to square the political circle that I mentioned a moment ago. Hence, the best they could realistically strive for was not *consensus*, but *compromise*. And (as will be explained in Chapter 6) compromise is governed by a kind of political logic other than consensus: for compromise, unlike consensus, retains the possibility of co-operation even when people hold different views and are also determined to maintain these. So, people now resigned themselves to the fact that others could think completely differently on even the most essential and urgent political questions, on the condition that a compromise with these others would prove to be feasible. The invaluable gain of the acceptance of compromise was that they could now live more or less safely under one and the same political roof with political opponents who only a few years previously would gladly have imprisoned or guillotined them. In sum, thanks to this readiness to compromise, civil war could be avoided; and clearly, representative democracy was the political system that was ideally suited for achieving such compromise. Lastly, the many revolutions of nineteenth-century continental Europe further contributed to the willingness of all responsible statesmen to discover in compromise and representative democracy the only feasible solution for Europe's profound political divisions and the only means to avoid a permanent social civil war.

To us, the heirs of the *juste-milieu* policy, all of this will sound like a platitude. One should keep in mind, however, that the idea—and the willingness—to compromise about political principles (like those of the *ancien régime* and the revolution) for which people had been ready to sacrifice their lives only a couple of years before, was at that time experienced as being little less revolutionary than the great revolution of 1789 itself. After all, it meant the embrace of a "principled unprincipledness" by a generation that only shortly before would not have hesitated to stake its own life for the principles in question. Such a supremely intelligent and acute observer of the political realities of his own time as was Alexis de Tocqueville never succeeded in accepting this, in his eyes, contemptible perversion of politics. And this has nothing to do with Tocqueville's conservatism, for exactly the same attitude can be found in a "left-winger" such as Alphonse de Lamartine. Tocqueville and Lamartine's contempt for *juste-milieu* politics and the July monarchy—a contempt that found its most perfect personification in Julien Sorel, the main character of Stendhal's *Le Rouge et le noir*—amply demonstrates how difficult it must have been for our ancestors of two centuries ago to get used to a political practice in which the highest and most sublime political principles were now negotiated as if one were haggling about the price of a house or of a sack of potatoes.

For two reasons, it has been history that provided the model for the potential successes and advantages to be expected from *juste-milieu* politics. In the first place, the *juste-milieu* politicians realized that the ideologies that they attempted to reconcile by means of compromise were the products of Europe's revolutionary and prerevolutionary past: a profound awareness of these historical realities was therefore a first requirement for the success of their enterprise. The present and the future of the nation could only be constructed on historical foundations, and so each politician had to be a historian. But there was also a "methodological" affinity between *juste-milieu* politics and the writing of history. The willingness to compromise requires a capacity to transcend (existing) political strife, to see oneself from the outside as it were, and the willingness to muster a certain degree of impartiality. Similarly, as (historist) historians were all arguing at the beginning of the nineteenth century, historians can only succeed in doing justice to the past if they are impartial and to the extent that they do not identify themselves with the political parties whose conflicts they are describing. In this way, one might say that politicians became historists in this period and that historians adopted a kind of *juste-milieu* politics with regard to their subject matter. And it need not surprise us, therefore, that the *juste-milieu* politicians (such as Pierre-Paul Royer-Collard, Charles de Rémusat, Amable-Guillaume-Prosper Brugière de Barante, Adolphe Thiers, Guizot, or Benjamin Constant, if we restrict our gaze to France) were often excellent historians in their own right, nor that historians, in their turn, felt little reluctance to pronounce on contemporary political issues. And this certainly gave a depth and penetration to political debate so sadly absent from our own contemporary politics, which is so estranged from any long-term vision and drowned in bureaucratic technicalities.

Two conclusions can be drawn from this insight into the romanticism of representative democracy. First, we ordinarily consider democracy to be a product of the Enlightenment—and certainly for good reason. The notion of the equality of all citizens, so essential to democracy generally, definitely stems from the metaphysics of Enlightened natural law philosophy. Natural law metaphysics was in the habit of freely speaking of "the" citizen, or "the" human individual in general, thereby availing itself of a figure of speech not allowing of any empirical distinction between one citizen or human individual and another. This metaphysical discourse therefore had the (probably unintended) result of powerfully contributing to the doctrine of the political equality of all citizens. Whatever hesitations one may have with regard to metaphysics, at least in this time metaphysics presented itself as the "democratic" discipline par excellence. Furthermore, Enlightenment natural law philosophy taught that the state originated from a well-considered decision by the citizens wishing to put an end to the inconveniences of the state of nature. And however absolutist natural law philosophy could sometimes be, the inevitable implication was that the state exists for the benefit of the citizen and not the other way round. Next, it also followed from this construction that the state would automatically lose its legitimacy if it placed its citizens in a situation worse than that in which they had been in the state of nature. And this could be reformulated in the state's obligation to respect certain civil rights under all circumstances. Now, undoubtedly, these were all excellent political principles, and for this reason we undoubtedly are heavily indebted to Enlightenment political theory. Last but not least, as shall be expounded below at some length, eighteenth-century political theory and political practice introduced a conception of political representation without which democracy could never function. Arguably this has been the Enlightenment's most substantial contribution to the cause of democratic government as we presently know it.

But what the Enlightenment did not teach us, and what we therefore owe to political romanticism, to the Restoration and to *juste-milieu* politics, is the possibility of achieving a minimum degree of peaceful coexistence in a society in which opinions are deeply divided on political principles, and even to use these divisions to the advantage of all parties. It was political romanticism that taught us the blessings of this attitude of a "principled unprincipledness" that is so essential to representative democracy generally and that enabled the nations of continental Western Europe to escape the conflict between the revolution and the *ancien régime*. Several decades later, when the even more threatening conflict between capital and labor announced itself, it was, once again, this *juste-milieu* mentality (though, of course, no longer described in this way) that enabled the nations of the European continent to survive this conflict largely unscathed. Nothing is a more convincing proof of the unprecedented capacity of representative democracy to resolve conflicts than how it managed to absorb the tremendous shock of this, the most serious social conflict in European societies since the wars of religion.

Moreover, this was a lesson the Enlightenment was neither able nor willing to teach us, because it was incompatible with the desire for clarity, transparency, and consistency so important to the Enlightenment. As Carl Schmitt already observed in *Politische Romantik* (1919), the Enlightenment's mentality was completely at odds with this "principled unprincipledness" of parliamentary democracy. Only romanticism—with its respect for multiplicity, for all the paradoxes, oppositions, and contradictions inherent in sociopolitical reality—created the intellectual climate in which parliamentary democracy could thrive. We have been most unjust toward political romanticism by forgetting what it contributed to representative democracy and to the emergence of the political mentality necessary for its proper functioning. For political romanticism is much more than mere nationalist pathos or the excesses of (utopian) socialism: it *also* gave us the practice of representative democracy.

ANGLO-SAXON AND CONTINENTAL DEMOCRACIES

I said a moment ago that two conclusions can be drawn from the recognition of the romanticism of representative democracy. The second conclusion that I have in mind is my answer to a question that many readers must have had in mind for quite some time already. In the foregoing, I posited—without considering any alternative views—that parliamentary or representative democracy came into being in the romantic climate of post-Napoleonic continental Europe. But is this not completely at odds with one of our few uncontested and universally accepted certainties about the origins of representative democracy? For did we not all learn in school that the English parliament is "the mother of all parliaments" and that in the course of the eighteenth century a system had emerged in England that could well be seen as the model for all parliamentary democracies to come? And did these *juste-milieu* theorists and politicians themselves not always point across the Channel in order to demonstrate both the workings and the successes of representative democracy? Moreover, it might well be argued that the most successful democracy in world history—the United States—was constructed by its "founding fathers" on an exclusively Enlightened foundation. Just as I would neither dare nor wish to disparage what we owe to Enlightened natural law philosophy, so it would be quixotic to deny the immense plausibility of this objection. However, precisely because the objection is such an obvious and natural one, we tend to forget what we owe to political romanticism—and why the standard view is in need of some correction and completion.

In order to deal with this issue, I will take as my point of departure Michel Albert's much discussed *Les Deux Capitalismes* (translated as *Capitalism Against Capitalism*)[3] of several years ago. The basic idea of this essay is that debate on politics and in political theory should situate itself within a spectrum determined by the most extreme political positions in existence. For example, when Soviet communism still existed, political debate ought to have focused on why we should prefer Western democratic systems to Soviet-style communism. And so it did. Differences within Soviet communism as well as within Western democracies were thus reduced to a lesser relevance. This changed with the collapse of communism. The whole world has now become democratic—at least theoretically. And this means that political debate should now focus on the question of what is the most successful and desirable variant of (Western) representative democracy.

The two relevant variants are identified by Albert as the Anglo-Saxon democracies (of England and the United States) on the one hand, and the "Rhine democracies" (the democracies of the Western European continent and of Japan) on the other. This also explains the title of his essay: two forms of capitalistic parliamentary democracies are opposed. And between these two kinds of democracies there are, according to Albert, previously neglected but now all-the-more-relevant differences. Albert describes the main difference between these two democracies as follows:

The neo-American model is based on individual success and short-term financial gain; the Rhine model, of German pedigree but with strong Japanese connections, emphasizes collective success, consensus and long-term concerns. In the last decade or so, it is this Rhine model—unheralded, unsung and lacking even nominal identity papers—that has shown itself to be the more efficient of the two, as well as the more equitable.[4]

If, then, we recall our methodological rule that each political system should be seen as the response to a specific kind of challenge, we cannot doubt that these two kinds of democracy must be different in important respect(s), and that Albert must have been right when presenting them as the two main alternatives for our political future. For a consideration of both the Glorious Revolution of 1688, which so strongly contributed to the emergence of the English parliamentary system, and the decade or so following 1776, in which the American constitution was created, shows us that both these cases posed political challenges of a wholly different kind than those facing continental Europe after the fall of Napoleon. Both the English in 1688–89 and the Americans from 1776 onward were looking for a solution to the problem of the relation between the king, sovereign, or the president and a representative body—Parliament or Congress—and of what system of checks and balances could best regulate their interaction. Ambitious kings, such as James II and George III, or a too powerful president were the dangers against which constitutional safeguards were sought. The continental European problem of a nation divided against itself did not play a role of much significance in England and was a problem of only minor importance in the eyes of the founders of the American constitution. In both these cases, people did not fight *against* each other about the question of who was to control the state, but fought *together* to keep the power of the sovereign or president within acceptable limits. And whatever was taken away from the king or president in this conflict came into the common possession of the representative body that had waged this battle against king or president. In Anglo-Saxon countries, the recollection of the political power united in the person of the (absolute) monarch still survives in the two-party system, where usually one political party can have an absolute majority in parliament. In this way the party in power can, within the logic of Anglo-Saxon democracy, be seen as the successor of the absolute monarch, whereas such an assertion would make no sense at all in connection with continental democracies. It might be argued that Anglo-Saxon democracy has thus been more successful than its continental counterpart in combining the virtues of absolute monarchy with those of representative democracy.

Perhaps we ordinarily fail to recognize that the former still is closer to absolute monarchy than the latter because the Tocqueville of *L'Ancien Régime et la Révolution* was so extremely convincing in demonstrating this continuity between the absolutism of the *ancien régime*, the revolution, and democracy. In contrast to continental democracies, in Anglo-Saxon democracy the absolute monarch is still present insofar as the possession of political power and of having an absolute majority in the representative body ordinarily go together there. If an Anglo-Saxon democracy had a number of smaller parties, as continental democracies do (none of them possessing a majority), this would be, according to the logic of that system, as if there were a king wanting several things at the same time but unable to decide between them. This is why compromise and "principled unprincipledness" play so much more of a prominent role in continental democracies than in Anglo-Saxon democracies. And this is also where most differences in style and functioning between the two types of democracy have their origin and explanation. Admittedly, these are mere outlines; but they may, nevertheless, clarify to what extent Anglo-Saxon and continental democracies differ from each other with regard to their respective nature, origins, reflexes, relative successes, and weaknesses.

It therefore is no coincidence that up to this very day the most evident difference between Anglo-Saxon and European continental democracies is that the former have a two-party system, whereas the latter have always had coalition governments. The countries of the European continent, having all experienced in one way or another the upheavals following the French Revolution and the regime of Napoleon, all ended up after 1815 with politically strongly polarized populations, and therefore had to face a kind of major political problem that had no precedent in European history. Hence, the coalition governments of the Continent, striving for a balance between different political ideologies, are a lasting reminder of the Napoleonic regime of nearly two hundred years ago. Without the revolution and Napoleon, the struggle against royal prerogative would probably have prevailed on the Continent as well, which would, in all likelihood, also have resulted in variants of the Anglo-Saxon two-party system, including that system's method of party formation and political style. Unfortunately, most history books on the post-Napoleonic period present Restoration politics as a mere repetition of what England and the United States had already gone through several generations before. And, certainly, this is part of the truth. Nevertheless, this historical shortcut may blind us to what was really new and different about the political situation after 1815, if compared to that of 1688 and of 1776, and in what ways this difference affected the nature of later continental democracies.

Naturally, this raises the question of which of the two democracies is to be preferred (and here we may well disagree with Albert's declaration of love for continental democracies). Categorical answers are hard to give, since each kind of democracy will also generate its own kind of problem, which it will have to deal with in the future in its own way. From this perspective, the two kinds of democracy are truly incommensurable. However, having taken this qualification into account, the following can perhaps be said. The political problems with which the Restoration struggled were undoubtedly more complex and involuted than those facing the Anglo-Saxon countries in 1688 and 1776. And the predictable consequence of this datum is that the continental democratic machine will also be more complex than its Anglo-Saxon counterpart. One could reasonably draw the conclusion from this observation that, as usual with complicated machines, continental democracies will function both better and worse than their less complex Anglo-Saxon counterparts.

Anglo-Saxon democracy may be expected to continue to function fairly well under even the most adverse circumstances, but never perfectly. The more subtle and fragile instrument of continental democracy will, under favorable circumstances, function more satisfactorily than the Anglo-Saxon model, achieving better, more efficient and economic results for its citizens than its Anglo-Saxon counterpart. However, if a continental democracy gets stuck for whatever reason, repair will prove to be very difficult, and a total catastrophe, like that of the Weimar Republic, is then no longer inconceivable. It is of the utmost importance, therefore, never to neglect the necessary maintenance of continental democracies. To mention just one appropriate example to which I shall return below, it may well be that Anglo-Saxon democracies will be able to survive the impending death of the political party relatively unscathed, whereas it might take away the lifeblood of continental democracy. Since it has always remained closer to absolute monarchy than has continental democracy, Anglo-Saxon democracy is better equipped to survive the death of the political party than its continental counterpart. Whereas the disappearance of the political party will affect only part of the Anglo-Saxon political machinery, it would irrevocably throw out of balance the whole of a continental democracy. Ideological differences as expressed by political parties are the political fuel of a continental democracy, and its constitutional logic becomes a meaningless fraud without it. One need only look at the contemporary United States to see how very different this is for an Anglo-Saxon democracy: U.S. democracy functions no worse apparently than continental European democracies, though the two main American political parties are ideologically the mere shadows of their European counterparts. The U.S. parties have become mere organizations for winning elections. For achieving this aim, fixed and well-defined (ideological) convictions about the nation's future tend to be a serious handicap, since these may have the counterproductive effect of alienating those potential voters who do not happen to share this ideology. So in the United States, as different from most Western European countries, ideology is a liability rather than an asset.

OLD AND NEW TYPES OF POLITICAL PROBLEMS

Since parliamentary (continental) democracy, thanks to *juste-milieu* politics, succeeded in finding creative solutions to such potentially dangerous conflicts as those between the *ancien régime* and the revolution or between capital and labor, we have every reason to be deeply grateful for how it guided us through one of Europe's most difficult periods.

The question arises, however, of whether the challenges facing our contemporary social and political order are still the same kind as those for which parliamentary democracy was invented. Clearly, the question is a crucial one from the perspective of the present exposition. For I have been arguing that political systems should be seen as answers to specific types of political problems. In this way, history will most valuably contribute to our understanding of the kind of political machines that mankind has invented over the centuries, and of the kinds of problems these machines can and cannot be expected to fix. Hence, if the nature of political problems changes in the course of time, it is by no means certain that a political system antedating this new type of problem will be able to recognize it as a political problem at all, let alone deal with it in a satisfactory way. And it can indeed be argued that our most urgent political problems today are categorically different from those of the not too distant past. For one of the most conspicuous characteristics of our current political situation undoubtedly is that it is no longer primarily a question of one part of the population being pitted against another; rather, we have problems that affect all of us equally and in a more or less similar way.

It is, admittedly, not easy to think at the beginning of the new century of what kind of serious political problem we have to face, either now or in the foreseeable future. Almost fifteen years of sustained economic growth may have eroded our belief that such serious political problems are possible; for cannot almost each imaginable political problem be solved by financial means? And do we not have every reason to be more optimistic about the availability of such means than in almost the whole history of representative democracy? And do we not witness everywhere "the death of politics"? And is there not an almost universal consensus that politics has played its role and that civil society itself will be more effective in dealing with whatever social problems we might have? Such optimism, however, might well prove to be short-sighted. For as long as the thesis of "the new economy" has not been proven conclusively, economic recessions are still a possibility and—with them—potential consequences such as "jobless growth" (we then all run the risk of being fired) and the collapse of the welfare state under the heavy burden that might be imposed on it. But even if economic prosperity could last, serious social and political problems would still manifest themselves, such as crime, a defective infrastructure, the decline of education, an aging population whose health care and pension claims will involve an ever increasing demand on public finance, the deepening gap between the rich and the poor, and the juridification of all human relationships, and, perhaps paradigmatic of them all, problems of the environment.

These new political problems have several things in common that differ from the kind of problems that democracy was originally made to solve. In the first place, we are all no less the authors of these problems than their victims. Think, for example, of the problem of traffic jams that ideally exemplifies our new kind of political problem: when we are stuck in a traffic jam, we both contribute to it and are paralyzed by it. In the second place, these political problems typically have their origin in the unintended consequences of our decisions. We invented cars and constructed motorways in order to promote mobility, and the result is that we get stuck in a congestion; we desire excellent social services and higher wages and thus bring about unemployment; and so on. And all these problems do not divide society against itself—in the way that traditional political problems did—but they have become a part of the lives of all of us. Rather than polarizing society or the electorate as a whole, they polarize the individual cit-izen—insofar as they polarize at all. Conflict *between* citizens is exchanged for a conflict *within* the mind of the individual citizen.

Indeed, we may daily understand from our newspapers that our representative democracies are insufficiently equipped with the means to handle this new type of political problem adequately. So much may be inferred from their tendency to see these problems as merely technical problems of how to achieve a goal that is never questioned as such, instead of as problems requiring truly political decisions about the desirability of these goals them-selves. And the paradox is, consequently, that our current political problems have become curiously "democratic," in the sense that we are all confronted with them in a more or less similar way, whereas at the same time traditional democracy does not know how to cope with exactly this sort of "demo-cratic" problem. Perhaps democracy is better at solving the kind of problem that we inherited from our aristocratic past (i.e., conflicts arising from social inequality), while it is relatively helpless when it has to cope with the kind of democratic problem that it tends to generate itself. And, alas, this would be only too understandable, since representative democracy was not created in order to deal with this type of political problem. And one might well ask oneself whether political systems will ordinarily feel most at ease with the type of political problem that was created by a previous system while re-maining relatively blind to those that are created by itself.

Lastly, it may be argued that Anglo-Saxon democracies will probably have less difficulty than their Western European continental counterparts in digesting this new type of political problem. For let us recall here from what challenges the two democracies emerged. The challenge of Anglo-Saxon democracy was the problem of royal or presidential prerogative; that of continental democracy was the problem of a state whose paradoxical task was to *both express and reconcile* political polarization. It will be clear that the new kind of political problem identified above has a greater formal re-semblance to the original challenge of Anglo-Saxon democracy than to that of its continental counterpart. For in both cases the problem confronts the whole citizenry in a more or less similar way; the struggle about royal or presidential prerogative was a struggle about the "constitutional environ-ment," to put it metaphorically. And it is illustrative that this struggle pro-voked far less political polarization in England in (or after) 1688 and in the period from 1776 to 1787 in the United States than existed in Western European societies after 1815. But though the political machinery of an Anglo-Saxon democracy may be better equipped for dealing with this kind of political problem, it may be less inclined than continental democracies to see a political problem here at all. Whereas continental democracies will have a visceral sensitivity to how these "democratic" problems stimulate conflict in the mind of the individual voters, and to respond to this in one perhaps rather helpless way or another, no such sensitivity is to be expected in Anglo-Saxon democracies because of their relative indifference to this whole issue of the reconciliation of (political) conflict. In sum, Anglo-Saxon democracies are handicapped with regard to this new kind of political problem since they will simply not see political problems here at all, and continental democracies are handicapped because this kind of problem does not fit well into their political machinery. And in both cases an adaptation of democracy to this new kind of political problem seems to be a matter of some urgency.

In sum, the main challenge for our contemporary democracies—both Anglo-Saxon and continental—is to reform themselves in such a way that they may recognize and digest the new kind of political problem that has emerged in the last few decades of this century. And democracy will certainly be in danger if they fail to do so.

POLITICAL REPRESENTATION

But this is not the only danger threatening our contemporary democracies. The other danger, which is the main topic in the remainder of this chapter, arises from the logic of (political) representation itself. As we shall see, there is an inevitable limit to what representation can do and where representative democracy will necessarily fail. In order to identify this danger, we had best start with the following observation. We describe our political system as "representative democracy." Now, "democracy," in the sense of government by the people, was founded in classical Athens. But classical democracy was direct democracy, and direct democracy left no room for (political) representation (this is precisely what so many people, such as Hannah Arendt, always found so extremely attractive in the Greek polis). (Political) representation, on the other hand, is a medieval notion. One may think here of the assemblies of the three estates that were sometimes summoned by the king, and in which the nobility, the clergy, and the third estate were represented. And this certainly was not an early medieval tryout of any form of democracy. Hence, democracy has no intrinsic link with representation, and representation has no intrinsic link with democracy. The miracle of contemporary parliamentary representative democracy is that it nevertheless succeeded in combining these two completely different concepts in an extremely fruitful and creative way. Consequently, representative democracy as we know it is the result of this most unlikely marriage of Athens and the Middle Ages. And this observation invites the then obvious question of how these two notions of democracy and of representation had best be related. For since there is no necessary connection between the two of them, we shall have to develop an answer to that question independently of what democracy was in Athens and of what representation was in the Middle Ages. In order to develop such an answer, I shall start with a few remarks about the notion of representation. We shall see, next, how this may clarify our conception of representative democracy.

Representation is a notion borrowed from the world of aesthetics: the work of art, a painting or sculpture, will often be a representation of part of reality. Two theories about the nature of aesthetic representation need to be taken into account within the present context: the resemblance theory and the substitution theory of representation.[5] According to the former theory, a representation should resemble what it represents. There are three problems with this theory, so attractive at first sight. In the first place, as is demonstrated by the history of the visual arts, no generally accepted or acceptable criteria of resemblance can be given. For each artistic style in the history of art could be seen as the definition of a new set of such criteria. And what could be the use of the notion of resemblance in the absence of such criteria? Next, as was pointed out already by Nelson Goodman, the resemblance theory gets entangled in absurdities. For if we have in front of us (1) Blenheim Castle, (2) a painting of that castle and (3) a painting of the duke of Marlborough, the resemblance theory would urge us to see (2) as a representation of (3) rather than of (1). For paintings resemble each other more closely than what they represent: one piece of canvas with dots of paint on it resembles such another piece of canvas rather than some huge building in the Oxfordshire countryside. In the third place, since words and sentences cannot in any noncircuitous way be said to resemble what they are about, the resemblance theory is helpless with regard to language as a medium for representing reality. And this would have the counterintuitive consequence that we could not speak of, for example, historical representations of past reality.

According to the substitution theory of representation—for the first time defended by Edmund Burke and, more recently, by Ernst Gombrich and Arthur Danto—the etymology of the word "representation" is our best clue for understanding the nature of representation. Representation is a making present (again) of what is absent. Or, more formally, *A* is a representation of *B* when it can take *B*'s place; hence, when it can function as *B*'s *substitute* or as *B*'s *replacement* in its absence. Words and texts present no problems for this theory: for we may well say that we have the writing of history in order to compensate for the absence of the past itself. Neither do we need to worry about criteria of resemblance, since this theory does not require a representation to resemble what it represents. Nevertheless, it may well be that in specific cases (for example, in the visual arts) a certain amount of resemblance (however defined) may make us see something as a satisfactory substitute for something else. So the resemblance theory could, perhaps, best be seen as a special case of the more general substitution theory.

All this can be transposed without any difficulty to political representation. In the first place, the resemblance theory of political representation is one that we will all intuitively accept. According to this theory, the opinions of the electorate's representatives should be exactly the same as those of the electorate itself. This view of political representation was admirably defined by the anti-Federalists during the debate about the American constitution:

The very term representative, implies that the person or body chosen for this purpose, should *resemble* those who appoint them—a representation of the people of America, if it be a true one, must be *like* the people. . . . They are the sign—the people are the thing signified. . . . It must then have been intended that those who are placed instead of the people, should possess their sentiments and feelings, and be governed by their interests, or in other words, should bear the strongest *resemblance* of those in whose room they are substituted.[6]

The Federalists, in their turn, were struck by the egalitarian undertones in this conception of political representation. And they therefore wished to convince their anti-Federalist opponents that the abandonment of the identity of the represented and his representative did not in the least imply a return to aristocratic conceptions:

Who are to be the electors of the federal representatives? Not the rich, more than the poor; not the learned more than the ignorant; not the haughty heirs of distinguished names, more than the humble sons of obscure and unpropitious fortune. . . . Who are to be the objects of popular choice? Every citizen whose merit may recommend him to the esteem and confidence of his country. No qualification of wealth, of birth, or religious faith, of civil profession is permitted to fetter the judgement or disappoint the inclination of the people.[7]

Not the identity of the represented and their representative is what we should demand of representation, but how we can succeed in finding those people who are most suitable to function as the people's representatives and who will be least inclined to abuse their powers. Or, as James Madison put it: "The aim of every political constitution is, or ought to be, first to obtain for rulers men who possess most wisdom to discern, and most virtue to pursue, the common good of society; and in the next place, to take the most effectual precautions for keeping them virtuous whilst they continue to hold their public trust."[8] And Madison even explicitly inferred from this that the person represented and the representative will not only most often differ from each other (insofar as we may expect the latter to possess a greater political wisdom than the person represented), but that they even *ought* to differ on this scale of political wisdom. For one of the main aims of political representation is precisely to select the best and the wisest candidates for this so important and responsible office of being the people's representatives.

Strangely enough, the anti-Federalists had no reply to this argument. The obvious response would have been to say that the kind of identity at stake in political representation is an identity of opinions and not of persons and that therefore nothing would be wrong with sending the most worthy and best educated people to Congress as long as they would express exactly the same political opinions there as those whom they represent without ever deviating from these opinions in any conceivable way. Perhaps the anti-Federalists did not think of this obvious answer since they did not yet separate opinions from the persons having them. And such a disjunction certainly is a rather modern notion. Within the premodernist conception of politics, the social roles and opinions of individual are still indissolubly related, and the idea of a cake of political opinions, out of which everybody can cut the piece that he or she likes best, belongs to a later and fundamentally different political consciousness.

But some twenty years before this discussion of the American Federalists and their anti-Federalist opponents, the resemblance view of political representation had already effectively been demolished by Rousseau.[9] As a proponent of direct democracy, Rousseau rejected all forms of representation. There are, as Rousseau pointed out, two possibilities: either this requirement of exact resemblance has been satisfied or it has not. In the first case representation is a useless redundancy. For if the requirement has been, or will be met, we must be able to establish as much. And if we can do that, we know already what the electorate wants—and this obviously makes representation superfluous. But if the requirement has not been met, representation should be rejected on the basis of the resemblance theory of representation itself. The resemblance theory therefore either presents political representation as an irrelevance or it is in contradiction with itself.

So let us now turn to the substitution theory of political representation. Like its aesthetic counterpart, it was formulated for the first time by Edmund Burke. Burke wrote in 1774 a letter to his voters in Bristol in which he explained, first, what is wrong with the resemblance theory and, next, what view of political representation we should hold:

Certainly, Gentlemen, it ought to be the happiness and glory of a representative to live in the strictest union, the closest correspondence, and most unreserved communion with his constituents. Their wishes ought to have great weight with him; their opinions high respect; their business his unremitted attention. It is his duty to sacrifice his repose, his pleasure, his satisfactions, to theirs,—and above all, ever, and in all cases, to prefer their interest to his own.

Even the staunchest defender of the resemblance theory will have rejoiced in this eloquent statement by Burke. But then comes the decisive turn:

But his unbiased opinion, his mature judgment, his enlightened conscience, he ought not to sacrifice to you, to any man, or to any set of living men. These he does not derive from your pleasure,—nor from the law and the Constitution. They are a trust from Providence, for the abuse of which he is deeply answerable. Your representative owes you, not his industry only, but his judgment; and he betrays, instead of serving you, if he sacrifices it to your opinion. . . . To deliver an opinion is the right of all men; that of constituents is a weighty and respectable opinion, which a representative always ought to rejoice to hear and which he always ought most seriously to consider. But *authoritative* instructions, *mandates* issued, which the member is bound blindly and implicitly to obey, to vote, and to argue for, though contrary to the clearest conviction of his judgment and conscience,—these

are things utterly unknown to the laws of this land, and which arise from a fundamental mistake of the whole order and tenor of our Constitution.

And then follow the famous words:

Parliament is not a *congress* of ambassadors from different and hostile interests,
which interests each must maintain, as an agent and advocate, against other agents
and advocates; but Parliament is a *deliberative* assembly of *one* nation, with *one* interest, that of the whole—where not local purposes, not local prejudices, ought to
guide, but the general good, resulting from the general reason of the whole. You
choose a member, indeed; but when you have chosen him, he is not a member of
Bristol, but he is a member of *Parliament.*[10]

The tie of identity between the represented and his representative postu-
lated by the resemblance theory has thus decisively been cut through by
Burke. Just as the work of art has an (aesthetic) autonomy with regard to
what it represents, so has the representative a certain independence or autonomy with regard to the voters who sent him to Parliament or Congress.
After having been elected, not the opinions of his voters, but his own opinions, what he himself believes to be reasonable or acceptable in the views
of his political opponents, the compromises for which he himself is prepared, and so on, these should now be the people's representative's compass in his political actions. Of course the representative will continuously
bear in mind the views of his voters, since he knows that after a period of
four years he will be face to face with his voters again and that he then
must be able to explain to his parliamentary performance in a satisfactory
way to his voters. In sum, the political opinions of his voters will be an *ingredient* in the representative's decision making, but his decisions ought
not to have been *determined* by the voter's opinions. So, in practice, there
will often be a *gap* or *difference* between the voter's opinions and those of
his representative in Parliament or Congress.

IMPLICATIONS

We observed a moment ago that there is this (aesthetic) gap or difference separating the representation from what it represents and that the
same observation holds for political representation. A few comments on
this gap or difference are in place here. We should realize that this gap or
difference is not necessarily an indication of *conflict, distortion,* or *incorrect-
ness.* Admittedly, we may be justified in ascertaining distortion or incor-

rectness under certain circumstances. For example, when Cromwell had his portrait painted, the painter asked him whether the wart on his face would have to be left out or not. As a true Puritan, Cromwell was free from personal vanity (or at least that is how he liked to present himself)—and thus Cromwell went down in history accompanied forever by his wart. But, obviously, if Cromwell would have had the less Puritanical character of, let us say, a Louis XIV, distortion would in all likelihood have been the result. So there exists such a thing as misrepresentation. But ordinarily things are different. Portraits will differ dramatically from the persons portrayed, yet this fact alone will not make us say that the portrait is a distortion of reality, or a misrepresentation. For the crucial datum here is that we know and expect portraits or representations to be different from what they represent. That simply is what art is all about.

And so it is with political representation. The adherent of the resemblance theory of political representation is like the person who does not understand art and aesthetic representation and therefore believes that each difference between the electorate and its representatives is an indication of distortion and political misrepresentation. But if one accepts the Burkean substitution view of (political) representation, one will recognize that it is part and parcel of political representation that there will be an (aesthetic) gap or a difference between the electorate and its representatives. Interestingly, it will be less easy in political representation to distinguish between simple misrepresentation (as in the case of Cromwell's wart) and the kind of difference between the representation and what it represents that belongs to the nature of all representation. This probably is what the voter will have to ponder after four years, trying to decide how well he or she has been represented by the elected representative or political party. Being able to properly distinguish between these two things probably is a measure of a nation's political sophistication. A politically naive electorate will see all difference between itself and its representatives as an impermissible distortion; a politically lazy and indifferent electorate will not see distortion even if its representatives have recklessly reneged on all their political promises (politics has then become something like modern or abstract art, so to speak)—whereas a politically mature electorate will know how to find the *juste-milieu* between these two extremes and how to distinguish between mere aesthetic difference on the one hand and such a serious thing as (political) misrepresentation on the other.

This has an interesting implication. When we speak about representation, we assume that the represented is more or less unproblematically given to us. We exactly know what a person, a landscape, or a still life looks like (or so it may seem)—and next we may see how the painter has represented these things in paintings. But if the sophisticated voter will be searching for this *juste-milieu* between misrepresentation and the kind of aesthetic difference necessarily inherent in all representation, the implication is that the represented (the voter) is not such an unchangeable and objective datum. We recognize that voters may change their political opinions because of what their representative or preferred political party does over the four years in office. Some kind of interaction between the representative and the voter seems to have developed—an interaction transforming the represented, that is, the voter, from a hard and objective given into a kind of fuzzy continuum. But if we think a little harder, we shall see that it is no different with pictorial representation and that the phenomenon therefore is part of representation as such.

If we compare Titian's famous portrait of Charles V with the one painted by Bernard van Orley, we would probably all prefer the former. And this is not because Titian came closer to the ideal of photographic precision than van Orley but because Titian somehow succeeded in penetrating deeper into the psychology of the aging emperor than did the Flemish painter. Both Titian and Van Orley painted what they saw—but they saw *different* things. Titian saw a man who had carried the fate of the whole Christian world on his shoulders and had been deeply aware of the immense responsibilities involved in this and of the tragedy of his failure; van Orley saw a man whose princely duties had not yet become part of his personality. What they saw, they painted. This may make clear why, contrary to what we are inclined to believe, the represented is not independent of its representation. There is not a Charles V who was exactly the same to Titian as he had been to van Orley—or to anybody else in the emperor's entourage—and who functions as a represented that is somehow objectively given to us. Representations partly determine the nature of what they represent. Historical representation perhaps illustrates the phenomenon in question even better. There is no French Revolution that is exactly the same to a Michelet, a Tocqueville, a Labrousse, or a Lefebvre; they all represent it in different ways in their texts. We have no French Revolution apart from all these texts (of course I am not upholding here the silly idealist or postmodernist thesis that texts actually create the past). The French

Revolution as a represented is defined by its representations and has neither face nor contours without these representations. Speaking generally,
historical reality—as a represented—only has its face and contours thanks
to the representations historians have offered of it.[11]

The recognition of this fact about representation in general may make
clear why political representation is such a supremely important phenomenon in politics. We need political representation, not so much in order to
compensate for the practical impossibility of assembling the whole nation
in one national agora so that the whole nation can participate in political
decision making. Political representation is much more than that. For without political representation we are without a conception of what political
reality—the represented—is like; without it, political reality has neither face
nor contours. Without representation there is no represented—*and without
political representation there is no nation as a truly political entity.* Hence, to
put it provocatively, even if it were possible to get the whole nation together, or to achieve the same effect by some variant of direct democracy
such as electronic voting, even then we should prefer representation. Political reality only comes into being after the nation has unfolded itself in a
represented and in a representation representing the represented. Without
representation, no democratic politics.

FOUR CONSEQUENCES

Several consequences follow from the foregoing. In the first place, we
should be wary of the referendum and of (variants of) of direct democracy.
Direct democracy can be an improvement on representative democracy
only if we are dealing with political problems that cannot meaningfully be
discussed in political or public debate. In such cases, representation will
make things more rather than less complicated. Examples of this are small-
scale problems such as the quality of life in a neighborhood, the facelift of a
decrepit area in a town, the reorganization of the center of a city, shortcomings in the public transport system, or what should be the precise trajectory of a road or a railway. In cases like these it will often be best simply
to listen to the people involved and to follow their preferences. People will
have pronounced opinions on issues like these that they are not likely to
abandon even if they have been intensively discussed, and then it is best just
to do what people want.

Political scientists recently discovered that local bureaucracies tend to be unexpectedly responsive to this kind of issue and to react in a creative way to how problems are perceived by the people involved. So this kind of relatively local and isolated problem had best be left to the interplay of direct democracy and bureaucracy—*bien étonnés de se trouver ensemble*. And on a larger, or even national scale one might think of issues like abortion or euthanasia, in the unfortunate situation, at all times to be avoided, that such issues have become thoroughly politicized and polarized by tactless political handling. Here, also, discussion is not likely to make people change their minds; discussion will probably even tend to entrench them ever deeper into what they already saw as the only morally satisfying option. And in cases in which the postponement of a decision about such issues has, for whatever unfortunate reason, become impossible, the referendum may often prove to be the best way out. Normally, however, such issues had best be kept out of politics and left to the evolution of public debate, since their politicization can only damage politics, hamper the openness of public debate about them, and result in decisions that a later generation will generally have good reasons to deplore.

Finally, representation is the procedure we will rely upon if we wish to put things into their wider context. Historical representation best exemplifies this general truth: when historians represent the past, they want to show readers how the individual aspects of the past under investigation all hang together, how they are "contextually" related. And it follows that we should make use of representative democracy if the political problem in question is such that it can only adequately be dealt with after all its relationships to other political problems have been carefully explored and discussed. And, conversely, it also follows that direct democracy may be the most sensible way to deal with political problems that can more or less be isolated from a wider context.

The second consequence can be seen in terms of the artist's creativity, which has its natural and exclusive locus in the gap or difference between art and reality—this is where creative genius may express and demonstrate itself. And so it is in politics. The politician's talent to solve problems, his talent to reconcile seemingly irreconcilable political positions in a manner acceptable to all concerned, depends on his ability and success in reformulating problems and disagreements in such a way that reconciliation becomes possible. Or, to put it differently, the politician must possess the essentially *aes-*

thetic talent of being able to represent political reality in new and original ways. And we can expect little of the politician who does not have this talent and who can only give us "photos" of political reality.

The third consequence is that many authors have recently argued that one of the major problems confronting our contemporary democracies is the gap between citizen and representative. Both seem to live now in completely different worlds and no longer to be much interested in what the other is doing. The result is a growing political indifference of voters and a political practice that no longer seems to be responsive to their wishes. Of course there is much truth in this sad picture of *Politikverdrossenheit*, to use the untranslatable, but most appropriate German term for the phenomenon in question. The virtual death of ideology and of the political party, the bureaucratization of government that has reduced the people's representatives, parliament, and often even politicians to the lowly status of a mere constitutional ornament (think of the hilarious but profoundly unsettling TV series *Yes, Minister!* of a few years ago), the dissolution of political issues into the unfathomable depths of abstract and technical argument, have certainly transformed politics into an arcane bureaucratic science with which no citizen can any longer be expected to identify. In the next section I shall return to the issue of how government bureaucracy has affected representative democracy and of how it succeeded in transforming representative democracy into something essentially different.

But two things should be borne in mind in this context. In the first place, we observed a moment ago that this aesthetic gap between voter and representative is not necessarily a bad thing: the existence of this gap is even indispensable to the proper functioning of representative democracy. In the second, against this background one might well venture the paradoxical thesis that this gap has now become too small rather than too large: for is not bureaucracy what we get when politics attempts to come as close to the citizen as possible? Bureaucracy is the politics of closeness (and therefore favored so much by totalitarian regimes). I remind the reader here of this strange alliance of direct democracy and bureaucracy that we observed a moment ago. Politics, political issues, and political debate all require a certain amount of distance between government and the citizen. Think of a painting: we can only adequately interpret what we see on a painting if the painting is at some distance from us. If we keep it right under our noses all contours get blurred into meaningless brush strokes. In politics it is no dif-

ferent: political "meaning" can only come into being after we have exchanged bureaucratic "closeness" for aesthetic "distance." So instead of trying to get as close to citizens as possible, explaining to them in what way
government bureaucracy will affect their *individual* lives, politicians had
better tell them what political plans they have (if any, that is) with the *whole*
of the nation. Paradoxically, this is what voters can discern far better than
the microdecisions with regard to their personal existence. But it seems that
in most contemporary Western democracies the future of the "whole of the
nation" is no longer considered to be the most appropriate background for
the identification and the prioritization of the items that should be on our
political agenda. No effort is made any more to transcend the fragmentation
of political reality and of the problems posed by it.

The fourth and last consequence referred to in the title of this section
is that this distance, gap, or difference between voter and representative also
makes clear what is the nature and origin of legitimate political power in
representative democracy. If we move from the citizen on the one end of
the aesthetic gap to the representative (or the state) on the other, then we
move from the domain of those who are subject to legislation by the state
to the place where this legislation is realized and to where its observance can
be enforced. To put it metaphorically, when a population unfolds itself into
a group of people that is represented and another group of people representing the former one, legitimate political power wells up, so to speak, in
the hollow between the two groups. Hence, the origin of all legitimate political power must be situated in the aesthetic gap between voter and representative (the state). This would justify, to begin with, the probably amazing and certainly unorthodox conclusion that *in a representative democracy
all legitimate political power is essentially aesthetic.* It follows, next, that in a
representative democracy legitimate political power is possessed by neither
voter, representative, nor state. At most, one could say that the voter entrusted for a period of four years the *use* of legitimate political power to the
administration of a certain political makeup. But political power as such,
apart from its mere use, is not owned by anybody in a representative democracy. Consequently, we should abandon the doctrine of popular sovereignty just like that of the divine right of kings: in representative democracy
nobody, no segment of society and no institution, can properly be said to
"own" the state and the political powers embodied by it. Sovereign power
exists but is in nobody's possession in a representative democracy.

FROM REPRESENTATIVE TO PLEBISCITARY DEMOCRACY

We have every reason to praise representative democracy as the most successful and subtle political instrument ever invented by mankind. Its capacity of identifying the most urgent political problems, of solving them creatively, and of guaranteeing a fruitful cooperation of state and civil society is unequaled by any other political system. Nevertheless, it also possesses an inherent weakness that has insufficiently been noticed by political theorists, for which, moreover, it will be difficult to find an adequate remedy within the logic of representative democracy. To put it succinctly, representation gives us all that is so immensely valuable in representative democracy, but it is also its Achilles' heel. For if representative democracy is so remarkably good at solving our social and political problems by means of political representation, there is one category of problems that necessarily will remain outside its reach: namely, the ones originating in or occasioned by the democratic state itself. This limitation is like a painting's, which can represent everything except itself. Thus the democratic state's marvelously powerful arsenal for solving political problems by means of political representation becomes inaccessible as soon as the state gets entangled in problems of its own. In agreement with the logic of representative democracy, the state's efficiency at solving problems is lost as soon as it has to deal with problems of its own instead of those existing in the civil society that is represented by it. This is why the democratic state itself is the most inefficient, clumsy, and stupid institute in our "sophisticated" Western societies and why it is so extremely difficult to fit the conflicts that have arisen in the state itself on the political agenda of a representative democracy. This also explains why there are no effective brakes on the growth of the state's size. The state resembles the well-known Barber of Seville, who styled everybody's hair so very neatly, with the inevitable exception of his own, and who, as a result, always presented himself so sloppily and slovenly to his surprised fellow citizens.

It will be instructive to consider briefly an objection that might be made against the foregoing. It might be argued that my thesis of this weakness of representative democracy obfuscates a distinction that is absolutely crucial precisely in this connection. I have been speaking above rather loosely and carelessly about "the democratic state," but it might be objected that precisely in the context of the present discussion it is more necessary than ever to carefully distinguish between the legislative and the executive power as the two components of the that state. For as soon as this distinction is made and respected, it may be pointed out (1) that this alleged weakness of the democratic state is, if anything, a weakness to be attributed to the executive power only, and (2) that the legislative power (which has been elected by the people) is meant to control the executive power and to remedy its shortcomings. It would follow from this that the foregoing argument about the essential weakness of representative democracy is based upon a failure to properly distinguish between the democratic state (as a whole) and the executive power (as part of that whole). But this objection is actually less effective than it may seem at first. It should be observed that there is a telling imbalance between how the legislative functions when the state deals with problems in civil society and how it functions when it has to deal with problems concerning itself. In the former case, the legislative functions as the representative of those who are subject of the state's actions (i.e., the people). This is in complete agreement with the logic of (political) representation: the electorate elects its representatives so that, in public decision making, these representatives function as the substitute or replacement of the electorate itself. And then they may try to solve the conflicts that had arisen among the people represented by them. Obviously, no problems there. But things are fundamentally different when it comes to dealing with the state's problems and, more specifically, those of the executive. For the legislative represents the electorate, *not* the state or the executive, so that, in discussions of the state's problems, the legislative relates to them in a way that is different from how it relates to the problems of civil society. Because of the logic of (political) representation, the role of the legislative is, here, essentially that of an outsider to the problem in question.

And to the objection that the political leaders of government bureaucracies "represent" these bureaucracies in their interaction with the legislative, our reply must be that that they do not *represent* those bureaucracies in these interactions, but *are identical* with them from the perspective of the logic of our constitutional, representative democracies. Constitutionally, these bureaucracies are mere extensions of themselves, enabling them to do what they could never do alone. So the problems, internal conflicts, failures, and shortcomings of these bureaucracies are, from a logical point of view, really their *own* problems and internal conflicts, so that dealing with them necessarily places us outside the scope of representative government and what representative government allows us to do. These are essentially management, and not political, problems. And we can think of a different argument leading to the same conclusion. We observed a moment ago that in a representative democracy nobody can properly be said to be in the *possession* of legitimate political power, though there are people and institutions to whom the *use* or *exercise* of this power has been entrusted for a certain period. Self-evidently, government bureaucracies are the institutional instruments that one has to rely upon for this use. So what can legitimately be discussed within the logic of representative government is the *use* that political leaders have or will make of these bureaucracies (for example, in their attempts to solve the social and political problems of civil society), but not these bureaucracies *themselves.* These bureaucracies are a kind of heritage, so to speak, that are handed over more or less as is from administration to administration. It follows, then, that upholding the distinction between the legislative and the executive power will enhance rather than weaken my argument about representative democracy's inevitable incapacity to adequately deal with problems of, or occasioned by, the democratic state itself.

As long as the state still was relatively small and ministers could still be expected to be in control of their (departmental) bureaucracies and of the civil servants working in them, this weakness of representative democracy only rarely manifested and never really got out of hand. And this is probably why—at least as far as I know—political theorists have never cared much about the problem. Most of the really fruitful and creative political thinking about democracy dates from the time when government bureaucracies had not yet become a political problem themselves. But now that almost half of the GNP of a nation passes, in one way or another, through the hands of these bureaucracies, we can no longer afford to remain indifferent to this most dangerous lacuna in the political practice of representative democracy and be content with the many (useful) things that political scientists since Weber have had to say about this. Moreover, the extent to which government bureaucracies now determine the political agenda of Western democracies has given extra urgency to the issue. Government bureaucracies identify the most urgent political problems; they initiate the decision-making procedures with regard to them, carry decision making beyond the point of no return, and finally realize its implementation. Moreover, they are depressingly effective at all these things and are given the chance to evade discussion (which, paradoxically, makes the problem so much worse). In comparison to the actual powers wielded by government bureaucracy, the role of the legislative has gradually dwindled to that of a naive, ill-informed, and therefore increasingly irrelevant onlooker; parliaments nowadays often do little more than acclaim what has been devised already by government bureaucracies. Within the original Weberian conception of bureaucracy, government bureaucracies faithfully worked out the decisions that had been made by politicians. Now the situation is the reverse: bureaucracies make the real decisions and the politicians' task is to sell these to their rank and file and to the public. Their political significance is thus restricted to the public debate of a few spectacular items that happen to fit well into the (narrow) matrices of what the media can report to the public. But long-term policies that tend to be technical, complicated, and dull, but also decisive for the nation's future, have thus gradually (been) moved outside the grasp of the legislative power and of that of the people's representatives.

Put differently, Montesquieu's doctrine of the balance of powers obfuscates rather than contributes to an understanding of the realities of actual decision making in our contemporary democracies. The legislative power's privileges have gradually been eroded and absorbed by the executive; as soon as we realize this we must recognize that we had better speak of the democratic state as a whole (as I did above), rather than continuing to distinguish, with Montesquieu and official constitutional law, between the legislative and the executive powers.

Or, to put the dots on the constitutional *i*, citizens no longer vote for a legislative of a certain political composition as they used to do in representative democracy; elections have gradually acquired the character of a plebiscite on the state's most recent behavior. In a plebiscite the citizens are asked to pronounce on the state's past actions and on its plans for future action, regardless of the ideological origins of these actions. In the plebiscite, the state is a mere black box to the citizen; the state is seen only from the outside, as it were, and not as an entity whose actions may be subject to the citizens' influence, via their representatives, for example. All interaction between the citizen and the state has ceased to exist in a plebiscitary democracy, with the sole exception of the citizen's right to pronounce once every four years an unqualified but decisive "yes" or "no" on the state's most recent behavior. Thus our contemporary democracies, both Anglo-Saxon and continental, could all be said to have become plebiscitary democracies to a greater or a lesser degree. Though it must be added that this movement toward plebiscitary democracy on the national level is to a certain extent counteracted by a movement toward variants of direct democracy on the local level. In this way a polarization can be observed in our contemporary democracies: they tend to become less democratic on the national scale but more sensitive to pressure by the people on the local level. And this polarization is not without its dangers, since it undermines the unity of democratic government; unless a great deal of care and attention is paid to the issue, a political system may be pulled apart eventually if it continues to move into opposite directions on the national and the local levels.

Obviously, this gradual transformation of our Western democracies into plebiscitary democracies is in many ways an infringement on what representative government used to be. The common denominator of these infringements, I would suggest, is that plebiscitary democracy is a far cruder instrument for controlling government than representative democracy was, for it is operative really only once every four years and it exercises control at a far greater distance from actual government than is the case in representative democracy. In the latter, the people's representatives may freely interfere with government decision making when all options are still open and in all stages of the decision-making process. Plebiscitary democracy, on the contrary, is the democracy of the *fait accompli* and it can only legitimate (or reject) what has already come into being. Moreover, the signals emitted by the electorate in a plebiscitary democracy are far more open to interpretation than in representative democracy, where the people's intentions are continuously detailed and refined in the ongoing interaction between its representatives and the government. In fact, in a plebiscitary democracy, the people's electoral pronouncement is little more than an expression of public happiness or unhappiness—or anything between these two extremes—and it can always be interpreted accordingly. This robs the people's pronouncement of much of its political significance, for each electoral result can now be constructed as, for instance, a reaction to what the economic climate happened to be like at the time when elections take place, instead of being the electorate's well-considered verdict on the doings of the administration. Elections have then been reduced to the status of official inquiries into the citizen's feelings of happiness and well-being; and though such inquiries often yield fascinating material, we ordinarily interpret their results sociologically rather than politically. And this undoubtedly is the proper way to see these inquiries—for, *pace* Jefferson, happiness is not a political category. Something has clearly gone wrong if elections are robbed of the political character that they ought to have.

In sum, what takes place (or, rather, has taken place) in this transition from representative to plebiscitary democracy is a shift in the center of gravity of the interaction between the state and the citizen. In representative democracy this center of gravity was transferred by the people's representatives right into the heart of the administration; now that the political party, the people's representative, and the legislative all tend to disappear from the political scene, this center of gravity is shifting from the state to the citizen. Surely, it may well be that we have acquiesced in this shift because of the generally responsible and responsive behavior displayed by most Western democracies since World War II. On the whole, we tend to trust our democratic governments and, fortunately, have sufficiently good reasons for doing so. Moreover, the advocates of the referendum and of variants of direct democracy may even gladly applaud this shift in the contact between the citizen and the state, though I expect that their enthusiasm will be considerably dampened as soon as they discover the disheartening paradox of all democratic government: the closer this center of gravity is to the citizen, the less political influence he will have. The price to be paid for this apparent "triumph of direct democracy" by means of plebiscitary democracy will be an irretrievable loss of control of the government by the citizen. For it is far more advantageous to have someone representing you at the center of political decision making (though the decisions that have been reached there will be binding for you), than to be miles away from this center yourself and without such a representative (even though you retain the nominal right to say "yes" or "no" after the decisions in question were made).

As may be clear from this brief and certainly not exhaustive list of what we stand to lose by the transition from representative to plebiscitary democracy, we presently have every reason to welcome a contemporary Montesquieu who would identify all the dangers to be expected from this gradual and insidious corruption of our representative democracies, and who may tell us how we had best try to avoid them. It is all the more to be regretted, then, that contemporary political philosophy has so completely lost itself in useless abstractions and focuses so exclusively on the citizen. For if political philosophy is to be of any use in our present predicament, it had best give us a theory of the democratic state that at least accounts for developments such as the one described above. What we really need at the present moment are not still more abstruse theories about the rights and duties of the citizen, about political rights or the "good life,"[12] but an up-to-date theory of the contemporary democratic state. And, surely, this is not such an unreasonable and unprecedented demand, since for most of its history political philosophy has been precisely an effort to develop such theories of the state. Is this not where we have always discerned the genius of philosophers like Hobbes, Locke, or Montesquieu?

WHENCE THE REMEDY FOR OUR PRESENT POLITICAL ILLS?

Since I have neither the capacity nor the ambition to be such a new Montesquieu myself, my question in the remainder of this chapter will be not how to adapt our constitutional matrix so that it fits best the realities of plebiscitary democracy as described a moment ago, but rather the (perhaps somewhat reactionary) question of how to counteract the attraction of plebiscitary democracy so that we may return to the matrices of representative democracy. Where can we expect a remedy for what I shall consider as the illnesses of (representative) democracy rather than as inescapable political facts that we shall have to accept for better or for worse?

Three agents in the political domain will require attention in this context: the state, the voter, and the political party. Least is to be expected from the state. For as we saw a moment ago, mechanisms operative in the state and deriving their movement and impetus from the development of the modern state have been the main cause of the degeneration of representative into plebiscitary democracy. Perhaps this evolution was, in the end, bound to happen. Organisms always isolate themselves from their surroundings as well as they can, and see in their success at doing so an important part of their identity and independence. It has been argued, in this vein, that the skin, demarcating ourselves from the outer world, is our most important organ.[13] Much the same will be true for organizations—the shared etymological roots of the words *organism* and *organization* are most instructive here. Hence, we can expect that each institution will try to demarcate itself as much as possible from what is outside itself and enclose itself within its own skin, so to speak; if so, representative democracy, by keeping open the wound of the body of the state through which the demos could more or less freely enter, must always have been a cause of potential trauma to the state. This consideration contributes still further to the above thesis about the transition from representative to plebiscitary democracy. For from the state's perspective, the main effect—or rather, benefit—of this transition has been that the people's influence now seems far less threatening. In representative democracy the citizenry exercises its influence in the heart of government through its representatives and thus forces the state to speak and listen to a language that is not its own. Put differently, being open to something alien to itself has always been one of the most peculiar features of the state in a representative democracy. For the citizen, of course, this was the main benefit of this system of government, but from the state's perspective this has always been rather a source of irritation and of frustration. From the state's viewpoint, this arrangement was tantamount to an organism's being forced to welcome infection by certain viruses. I apologize for this most unbecoming metaphor, but I deliberately use it to reinforce the sense of why it has always been in the state's own interest, as an institution with a logic of its own, to stimulate the switch from representative democracy to plebiscitary democracy. There truly is something intrinsically unnatural about the state in a representative democracy, which will always motivate it to avoid or to render inoperative as much as possible the mechanism of political representation. If the state has to react to and to submit to the demands of the electorate and of civil society at all, it will *sui generis* prefer to do so as a closed whole rather than as an institution that can be penetrated from the outside. This is also why the democratic state prefers direct contact between its own bureaucracies and the citizen to a contact that is channeled by representation: the former leaves the state's skin intact, so to speak. This is why, with regard to our contemporary political predicament, little or nothing can be expected from the state.

As for the citizen, let us return to what was said earlier in this chapter about the new kind of political problem facing us after the death of ideology. Our political problems no longer have the character of setting one part of the electorate against another, as was paradigmatically the case in the struggle between labor and capital. Political conflict has typically become a conflict within the individual voter's mind. It has become a conflict that has two axes: the voter's short-term versus his long-term interests, and the realization of social and political interests versus their potential unintended consequences. The citizen may now desire higher wages and more social security, but the unintended consequence may well be that this will contribute to his being unemployed at some later stage; he wants medical aid to prolong his life, but will then have to go through all the degradations of old age; he wishes to use the world's resources for his own purposes, but will discover that this will result in an irreparable destruction of the environment; he wants to enjoy the conveniences of twentieth-century technology, but also finds himself confronted with all the inconveniences (like the traffic jam) created by modern technology; and so one may go on indefinitely. The search for the *juste-milieu* between these alternatives no longer puts the citizen's own interests in opposition to other people's interests or to public interest, the way it did reassuringly in the age of ideological politics. For now the conflict is between mutually exclusive self-interests; the old and comfortable dilemma of having to choose between self-interest and public interest (or anything in between) has ceased to be the Archimedean point for the citizen's political orientation.

On the one hand, we have every reason to rejoice in the end of ideological politics; on the other, one could maintain that the current situation is hard to reconcile with both human nature and the nature of politics in a democracy. As for human nature, we tend to define our political identity by distinguishing between our own interest and that of the community (which does not in the least exclude a considerable amount of overlap between the two—think of the police or of national defense). From this perspective, the new kind of political problem tends to rob us of our political identity—and this will certainly make us feel that our own fate no longer is at stake in politics and that we therefore had better leave it to the naive dupes who have not yet recognized the complete irrelevance of politics— or, worse, who seek some personal gain from it.

Next, if we define democracy (very generally) as the political system that takes into consideration all the interests of (groups of) individuals in a reasonable and responsible manner, it also follows that this new kind of political problem will dislocate (representative) democracy's political machinery. For it is hard to see what work will be left for democratic politics in the absence of political conflict. If all our individual (long-term) interests lose their specific contours and are dissolved into one comprehensive public interest, the only question still left to us will be how the cause of public interest can best be served. Then we will want to put an end to the practice of politics and leave it all to government bureaucracies and their experts. And this would, once again, compel us to embrace plebiscitary democracy. For the only (pseudo)political question left to us then would be that of the state's efficiency and its capacity to realize the public good at the smallest cost. It would then be enough to have two nonideological, so-called catchall parties, so that the electorate can express in a general way its dissatisfaction with the state's behavior over the last few years by voting against the party that had been in power until then. More and clearer signs coming from the electorate would not be necessary in plebiscitary democracy. The presence of these two parties will be sufficient to prevent gross abuses of the state's (considerable) powers and to safeguard civil society from unwanted interference by the state. The doings of all other potential inhabitants of the public domain could then only complicate this simple picture and jeopardize what we may hope to gain from (plebiscitary) democracy.

In sum, in our present political predicament plebiscitary democracy seems to be the inevitable and, perhaps, even best outcome from the perspective of both state and citizen. Since most of the dramatis personae of representative democracy—the political party, the ideological opinion makers either inside or outside the political party, the party's representatives in the legislative body, the legislative power itself, the executive power—are all on their way out, so that only the citizen and the state (within which the legislative and the executive coagulated) are now left on the political stage, we probably had better start to like plebiscitary democracy, however much we may regret the disappearance of representative democracy. For if the political domain is divided between these two remaining political agents, plebiscitary democracy is inevitable—as is amply demonstrated by the United States, where plebiscitary democracy has been victorious on the federal level for many decades already.

Nevertheless, if one finds it hard to acquiesce in the (impending) victory of plebiscitary over representative democracy, one may feel tempted to ask oneself the admittedly quixotic question of how to lengthen the life of the latter. Self-evidently, this will amount to asking which of the now moribund political agents that I enumerated a moment ago we had best try to bring back to life. Since the political party has always been the link between the individual citizen and the state in representative democracy, and since the political party always provided representative democracy with its lifeblood, the political party will be our most obvious candidate. For if the political party cannot halt the dying off of all intermediaries between the citizen and the state on the national level, no other agent can do it either.

First of all, it should be noted that the state and the citizen can much less easily and safely be reformed than can the political party. Any attempt to reform, change, or influence the state or the citizen has a great many more risks than experiments with the political party. Reform of the state involves a change in the instrument we possess for the sake of social change, and clearly no source is richer in the production of unintended consequences than attempts to change the instrument for change itself. Reform of the state is only a realistic option in those very rare cases in which a revolution is inevitable—and history has indeed taught us that this ordinarily is a leap into the dark whose consequences are invariably much worse than the political inconvenience(s) for which the revolution was supposed to have been the remedy. Besides, history also teaches us that nations paradoxically often seem to prefer their ruin to constitutional change (the French lust for constitutional change since 1789 being, of course, the obvious exception to this rule). So, even if one were willing to consider constitutional change, the chances that proposals to that end will effectively be realized are next to nil. All of this is *a fortiori* true for the attempts to reform the citizen. The fortunately rare attempts to do so were undertaken by totalitarian dictatorships proclaiming a new humanity and a new society. This has invariably resulted in the greatest horrors in the history of humankind (and it also follows that we should be wary of the undoubtedly well-intentioned efforts of the communitarians to educate the citizen: political philosophy had best accept, for better or for worse, the citizen as is).

Attempts to change the political party, however, are not only eminently practicable but even an absolute must for the survival of (representative) democracy. And if we have reason to be dissatisfied or even worried about our contemporary political predicament, part of the explanation undoubtedly is that we have cared too little about the well-being of the political party. The political party, if noticed at all, has most often been seen as a mere intermediary between the citizen and the state, instead of a political agent in its own right. Illustrative is the fact that both its birth and its (impending) death have remained unsung in the writings of political philosophers.

We should recall, first of all, that the political party bridges the aesthetic gap between the state and the citizen, between representation and the represented. The political party encompasses the entire trajectory between the citizen and the state, and its main political task is to do precisely this.

Thus the supreme political "secret" of democracy, that is, the aesthetic gap between the citizen and the state discussed earlier, is right at the heart of the political party. Three conclusions follow from this. First, whenever we feel dissatisfaction with the state's functioning, whenever repairs of representative democracy seem to be required, we are addressing a kind of problem that can best be diagnosed and analyzed in terms of the (dys)functioning of the political party. The focal point of the state's and the citizen's activities is to be found within themselves: that of the state is to be identified with public decision making and that of the citizen with activities in the private sphere. However, the political party is far more part of *both* these two spheres than the state or the citizen (who both try to shut themselves up as much as possible within their own sphere) could ever be. The political party overlaps the spheres of both the state and the citizen, it functions as a *trait d'union* between the two—which is, in fact, its raison d'être. Hence, if representative democracy functions inadequately in the sense that something seems to have gone awry in the relationship between the citizen and the state, then the political party is the perfect medium both for analyzing the nature of this deficiency and for determining how this relationship could best be improved. In sum, the macrocosm of (representative) democracy's vicissitudes can be derived from the microcosm of the fate of the political party.

And this brings me to my second conclusion. It was pointed out above that the political party can safely be manipulated, whereas the manipulation of the state and the citizen, if possible at all, is always fraught with the gravest dangers. In the field of the political party, politics still has a human dimension; it is still enacted on a human scale, so to speak; it is still possible to have a reasonable overview of causes and consequences; one can still make well-considered plans on the realistic assumption that these plans will not diverge from the outcome too much. At first sight, this clearer cause-effect relation may seem surprising, since it is precisely the political party where this *arcanum imperii* of the aesthetic gap between the state and the citizen is most prominently present. And this may make us believe that if we wish to understand political reality and to act on it on the basis of sound understanding, we had best avoid the political party and its dark and unfathomable secrets and turn to the state and the citizen instead. But this would be putting the cart before the horse: we may know all that one could possibly know about both the state and the citizen and still be in the dark about how the two relate in a (representative) democracy. Similarly, even if you know all about a landscape and a painting of this landscape, you will not, on the basis of this knowledge, be able to define the exact nature of the representational relationship between the two—only in terms of representation can one clarify what happens when we move from one to the other. However, precisely because the political party spans both ends of the aesthetic gap around which all politics gravitates in a representative democracy, the politically relevant features of both state and citizen can best be investigated from the perspective of the political party. On the level of the political party, we can freely observe any potential problem of and in the relationship between the state and the citizen *in statu nascendi*, so to speak. For the same reason, the political party is also the most appropriate area of research for finding out how problems in the relationship between state and citizen might best be solved. Any adverse consequences of experiments with political parties are far less disastrous than experiments with other elements of the political domain. On the contrary, all political parties can learn from the experiments that have been tried out by any of them and, in this way, even unsuccessful experiments may be beneficial to democracy as a whole. In short, the political party is, as a result of its position in the political field, not only a pure culture of all problems that might besiege (representative) democracy, but also our best, if not our only, compass for how to deal with them.

Thirdly, and most importantly, because of its location in the political domain the political party is both the embodiment and the custodian of the aesthetic dimension inherent in representative democracy. Take the political party away from representative democracy and the aesthetic relationship between the citizen or civil society and the state will be exchanged for a merely causal relationship between the two. The creative potentialities of the interaction between the two (to be discussed in Chapter 7) will be lost, the citizen will no longer be represented in the proper sense by the state, and representative democracy will have been exchanged for its bastardized variant, plebiscitary democracy. Thus there is an indissoluble link between the fate of representative democracy and that of the political party. Without the latter we can not have the former, and without healthy political parties there is no way to avoid plebiscitary democracy in the future.

If we have reason to assume that representative democracy is about to enter another and perhaps less fortunate phase in its history, and if we wish to preserve this exceptionally successful political system for the future and to adapt it as best we can to new social and political challenges, then the political party provides the key to the future. It is advisable to consider substantial alterations to the state only in very exceptional cases; only disaster can result from attempts, whether inspired by ethics or by any other well-intentioned program for social and political reform, to influence or to improve the citizen politically. Adaptations of the political party to the changing challenges of our time are least risky, and the political party is also, due to the hold that it has on the state, the most effective instrument to realize elsewhere those changes in the system of representative democracy, either long-term or short-term, that might be required. The political party is, consequently, the place where we may still succeed in *cutting the world at its joints.* Our success or failure to revive the political party will be decisive for the future of representative democracy. Such a renaissance of the political party can best and perhaps only be achieved on the condition of a reideologization of party programs. However, little is to be expected in this effort at reideologization from the liberal or sociodemocratic ideologies that we have inherited from our past. Rather, the political party's point of departure should be the citizen's self-division after and because of the death of ideology, and the resulting conflict between short- and long-term interests and in how these conflicts can be expressed and articulated in terms of conceptions of the nation's future. Only in this way can the political party take up again a clear and widely recognized position in the dilemmas with which the citizen feels confronted, thus resolving the citizen's present political paralysis. Only in this way will the political party succeed in rediscovering the road to the heart of the citizen. And only this may therefore save democracy and prevent its degeneration into the political impotence and disgrace of plebiscitary democracy.

If the state is, as we have seen, our greatest and most urgent political problem at the beginning of the next millennium, then the political party is our most appropriate instrument to solve this problem. Democracy will stand or fall with the political party. This is the most important lesson that aesthetic political philosophy may teach us.

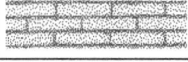

POLITICAL STYLE: SCHUMANN AND SCHILLER

In any given case political style might be unimportant or dangerous, but obviously it can't be both.

—Robert Hariman, *Political Style*

One can distinguish between two paradigms in political thought. The first focuses on the individual agents active in the political domain. One may think here of the actions of politicians, of voters and their representatives, of bureaucrats, and so on, and, next, of the interests, wishes, ideologies, and institutional rationality from which their actions originated. Within this view political reality is seen from the perspective of the political agents themselves. Obviously, most of historical writing and most of political theory can be situated within this paradigm; and I would add to this company writers like Hegel or Marx. It is true that Hegel's concept of Reason or History and Marx's class struggle and notions of capital and labor enriched political reality with new kinds of political agents—and this is where we may discern their genius. But once we are ready to work with this new kind of hypostatized political agent, the instances of it will function in much the same way in political reality as its more traditional inhabitants—kings, ministers, trade unionists, and so on. And the same can even be said about what the variables in the theories devised by social scientists refer to. One might even argue that the effort of the social sciences precisely is to identify causal agents in sociopolitical reality with the greatest possible precision in terms of such variables—a consideration inviting us to grant to the social sciences pride of place within this paradigm.

It may well seem, and for good reason, that this paradigm exhausts pretty much all of existing history, politics, and political and social theory.

Nevertheless, a number of political theorists do not fit this paradigm. Think of Tocqueville, in whose writings we will find the same kind of hypostatized political agents as in the writings of Hegel or Marx. But where Hegel and Marx closely follow in their writings the doings of Reason or of the class struggle and require us, next, to see the past and the present (and even the future) from the perspective of these supraindividual political agents, Tocqueville invites us situate ourselves in the still "empty space" *between* the supraindividual agents discerned by him (such as aristocracy, democracy, liberty, equality). What will strike us most in Tocqueville— and where he so conspicuously differs from a Hegel or Marx—is that he does *not* identify himself with anybody or anything whatsoever in his writings. Here political reality is truly seen from the perspective of the moon, so to speak. And this eerie effect is achieved by his focus on the *interaction* between his political agents rather than on these agents themselves.

Much the same is true of Machiavelli. We are shocked by Machiavelli's immoral advices to the prince since we feel invited by his writings to identify with him. And I shall be the first to concede that this was part of Machiavelli's intention when he wrote his so ill famed portrait of the princes. From this perspective, Machiavelli surely is an exponent of the first paradigm. Yet Machiavelli's most amazing insights derived from his refusal to identify with either the prince or the people, and from his decision to situate himself instead in the field where the interaction between the prince and the people takes place. This is why Machiavelli—and the same is true of Tocqueville—can be seen as a proponent of an *aesthetic* political philosophy.

In sum, apart from the well-known first paradigm of political philosophy, we should discern a second paradigm focusing not on political agents and their respective perspectives but on their interaction. And at all times theorists working within this paradigm avoid the temptation to elevate this interaction into a new kind of political superagent.

Both paradigms can be contrasted in terms of the distinction between content and form or style. One may think here of the following. A painter may depict *different* things in reality though making use of *one and the same* style. For example, even the layman will be able to see that a portrait by Fragonard was painted in the same style as one of his genre paintings—both paintings may have the same *style*, regardless of however much they may differ with regard to their *content* or *subject*. Now, transposing this contrast between content and style to political thought, the content of thought and action is the object of study within the first paradigm. Someone working within the second paradigm, on the other hand, will occupy the "empty space," still devoid of any political content, between the political agents, and focus on the way or manner in which political contents interact with each other in this space. Hence, this question of form or style is the natural question to ask after a shift of perspective from political agents to "empty space" between political agents. In short, within the second paradigm one will preferably focus not on *content*, but on the *style(s)* of interaction.

But this is only part of the truth. The distinction between content and style is certainly useful and inevitable. However, there is a continuity between the two of them, as has so often been pointed out already.[1] For instance, it undoubtedly belongs to Watteau's style that in his paintings we often see an elegant group of people seeking each other's company in a park surrounded by dense woods. Content (what was depicted in Watteau's paintings) and style (how Watteau experiences and represents the world) here merge into each other. And surely, one could not possibly determine whether the nostalgic and unreal atmosphere of Watteau's paintings belongs to the content or to the style of his work.

The fact that style and content cannot always be clearly separated can be interpreted in two ways. The most obvious reaction would be to say that this impossibility results from a lack of clarity in the two notions themselves. This is what could be labeled the "connotative" view. But one could also maintain a "denotative" interpretation, saying that things or aspects of *political reality itself*, as denoted or referred to by the notions of "content" and "style," tend to interfere and interact with each other. The first interpretation is a statement about the *words* "content" and "style," whereas the second is a statement about those parts of *reality* itself that we may refer to when using these words. The second, denotative interpretation is the right one. For conceptually the distinction between content and form can be maintained with all the clarity desired. On the other hand, we can truly make the *empirical* observation that style and content sometimes merge into each other when we apply these two notions to certain aspects of reality—like in Watteau's paintings mentioned just now. To put it more generally, one of the peculiarities of the reality we are living in is that apparently style sometimes generates content, and vice versa.

With this, the plot of my argument in this chapter has been indicated. I want to investigate here how within the second paradigm of politi-

cal thought we may account for the coming into being of a new, or extra reality, political *style*. Of course, this is a political reality, or content, to which
the first paradigm will inevitably remain blind. Thus, this chapter will not
deal merely with political style as such, but above all with the question of
how political style may contribute to political content and with how political style can create a new (and rarely noted aspect of) political reality.

THE 'INNERE STIMME' IN MUSIC AND POLITICS

Robert Schumann's *Humoreske* (1838) is one of the most remarkable
passages in the history of music. The historian of music Charles Rosen, in
his brilliant *The Romantic Generation*, wrote the following about it: "There
are three staves: the uppermost for the right hand: the lowest for the left, the
middle, which contains the melody, is not to be played." Hence, the pianist
plays with right and left hands the accompaniment of a melody that is
clearly and unambiguously suggested by the score and that the listener will
also hear, while, at the same time, the score explicitly forbids the pianist to
play this melody. The melody here is, as Schumann indicates himself in the
score, an *innere Stimme*, an inner voice, which listeners, without being aware
of it, will furnish themselves. Put differently, the melody, also for Schumann
the heart of the composition, will be *listened to* by the listener, without actually being *heard* by him. Hence, what one listens to, according to Rosen,

is the echo of an unperformed melody, the accompaniment of a song. The middle
part is marked *innere Stimme*, and it is both interior and inward, a double sense
calculated by the composer: a voice between soprano and bass, it is also an inner
voice that is never exteriorized. It has its being within the mind and its existence
only through its echo.[2]

Certainly precedents can be found in polyphony for this paradox of
inaudible music; indeed, for the more subtle composers in polyphony this
was a musical trope as obvious as it was popular. Who does not recall this
really "shattering rest," louder then the loudest kettledrum beat, in the
midst of the *Sind Blitze, sind Donner in Wolken verschwunden?* of Bach's *St.
Matthew Passion*? The classical tradition, on the other hand, with its emphasis on transparency and the unambiguous, forbade this paradox and
therefore its theory of music left no room for it. It was only romanticism
that operationalized and eagerly exploited all the possibilities of making silence audible and of transforming into music what was not yet music.

Now, we may ask ourselves, is this *innere Stimme* a *reality* or a mere *illusion*, if we, as we have seen, did *listen* to it but could not possibly actually have *heard* it? Probably the answer to this question will depend on what one's musical affinities happen to be. Whoever is used to classical music will undoubtedly prefer to see Schumann's invention as an illusion, as mere musical rhetoric: we were deliberately and artfully deceived, for we believed to have heard what we could not possibly have heard. Schumann achieved this invention by means of a reality effect, an *effet de réel* in the terminology of Roland Barthes,[3] offending a healthy and recommendable sense of what reality is. And this certainly is how one could look at the matter.

But the romanticist will not be at a loss when confronted with this argument, pointing out that this melody that was listened to but could not be heard can be identified with just as much precision as what we actually did hear. There is an amount of quasi-mathematical precision in music ensuring that the *innere Stimme* is completely and unambiguously fixed by what we *could* or *did* hear. And, the romanticist continues explaining, if we customarily associate reality with what can objectively be established, whereas fiction indeed permits us to leave this objective reality, then we should situate Schumann's *innere Stimme* in the domain of reality rather than in that of fiction and illusion. And that would also justify the amazing inference that what is *not* there can nevertheless be part of *reality*.

But what has all this to do with politics? The main point of my argument will be that if we want to give content to the notion of "political reality," and to define what we should see as such, the paradox of Schumann's melody that can be listened to without being heard will prove to be a most valuable and fruitful analogy. For, in a way much reminiscent of Schumann's *innere Stimme*, two answers can be given to the question about the nature of political reality. On the one hand we have, to use the musical terminology adopted above, those "classical" political theorists and political scientists according to whom there is a measurable political reality that should be the basis and starting point of all reflection on politics. To press the analogy with music a little further, within the classical conception of politics, nothing can be *listened to* in politics that had not been actually *heard* before. Political "input" on the one hand and political "output" on the other, what "really" happened in the domain of politics on the one hand and our perception of it on the other—at all times these two are most directly and intimately interconnected. There can and should be no "gap" or "discrepancy" between this "input" of objective political reality and the "output" of how we subjectively experience this reality. For if such a gap or discrepancy were to present itself, we would seem to perceive something in the political world that is not "really" there; we would then have become the will-less plaything of illusions and of political myths. The fact that we naturally and immediately resort to this kind of pejorative qualifications in this context clearly suggests already how objectionable we would tend to think such discrepancies to be. We are therefore naturally inclined to agree with the "classical" political theorist's view that such a discrepancy would lack a *fundamentum in re* and must therefore be considered an expression of irrationality, of primitive instincts, if not worse.

On the other hand, there are the political "romantics," who reject the input/output model of their "classicist" opponents. They will not deny that in many cases, perhaps even most cases, the model will be adequate and helpful—just as in music we will ordinarily have *listened* to what we have actually *heard*—but they also want to leave room for cases in which in political reality something new is produced that transcends the input/output model. When such a new political reality comes into being, we seem to be listening to a political *innere Stimme* for which the classical input/output model is unable to account. And, as will become clear in this chapter, this disagreement between the "classical" and the "romantic" political theorist is not of mere academic importance; the sound functioning of our Western democracies requires that we are able and prepared to listen to that political *innere Stimme* in the complex symphony of democratic politics.

Perhaps we might observe here another argument in favor of the elective affinities between democracy and the market that have already been emphasized by so many writers. The value of a company or of a national currency will not be found by figuring out the values of the company's buildings, machines, assets, bank accounts, and so forth, nor by determining a country's natural riches, its trade balance, and national savings. All these things may seem to be very "real" and determinate and therefore the obvious and solid basis for establishing value; nevertheless it will be the unpredictable and often unexplainable vagaries of the stock exchange that give us the best definition of the economic realities of a company or a nation. Hence, both in democracy and in economics it is in the *innere Stimme* of political and economic interaction that "reality" reveals itself. And there is no surer way to disaster than the decision not to listen to this *innere Stimme*— as will invariably be the case when we decide to ignore what reality is like.

WHAT IS POLITICAL "REALITY"

If we wish to determine our own position in this debate between "classical" and "romantic" political theorists, it will above all be necessary to propose a concretization of the notions of political input and political output. A most suggestive example of such a concretization is presented by Murray Edelman, when he writes that the citizens in a democracy are always urged "to look upon government as a mechanism that is responsive to their wants and upon these in turn as rational reflections of their interest and moral upbringing and therefore as stable and continuing."[4] Put differently, on the one hand there is the input of the political interests and desires of the citizen, and, on the other, the output of political decision making. And the classical model of the nature of (democratic) political reality requires us to conceive of the output of political decision making in terms of the input of those interests and desires of the citizen—which does not in the least preclude, however, that in actual democratic practice this relationship between input and output may be very complex and untransparent.

This plausibility of the classical conception of the machinery of democracy is still further reinforced by what Combs and Nimmo recently referred to as "the myth of the Good Citizen." That is to say, by the widespread presupposition that democracy is supported by peaceful citizens who by taste or by interest sincerely desire the well-being of their country."[5] This myth of the Good Citizen seems to endow the classical political model with a solid and reliable foundation in the reasonable interests and desires of the citizen and presents democratic politics as a more or less complicated calculating machine that figures out the correct resultant of all these individual interests and desires—without adding anything of itself, if things go as they should. In short, there is a popular ideology of democratic politics—this myth of the Good Citizen—that seems to grant an immense plausibility to the classical conception of democratic politics.

When the romantic political theorists wish to attack the input/output model, two arguments are at their disposal. Or, rather, as will become clear in a moment, it is only the second argument which is really decisive. But since the first argument offers a few interesting perspectives, it deserves our attention within the present context as well.

Within the first argument, the input/output model is rejected since it is said to be impossible in politics to identify clearly and unambiguously what functions as input for the output of public political action. Input and output simply are inseparable, and the classical model therefore is an illusion. Even more so, it is an illusion that is at odds with the very nature and spirit of democracy; for is not this inseparability of input and output one of the greatest virtues of democracy? Is democracy not the political system attempting to link these two together more closely and intimately than any other political system? Does this classical principle of the separability of political input and political output not inevitably create a distance between the two, which, in its turn, inevitably invites the danger that input and output no longer correspond? And if all this does not sound implausible, would that not justify the conclusion that the classical model is a denial of the very idea of all democracy?

Next, romantic political theorists will tend to be political realists and will therefore be little inclined to confuse some ideology—of democracy in this case—with what democracy is in actual historical reality. They will therefore not be content with the observation that the classical model contradicts some ideal of democratic politics. They will also want to demonstrate that democratic *practice* is at odds with the classical model. Murray Edelman has made clear in what respect democratic practice deviates from the classical notion of the separability of political input and political output. One may think here primarily of his thesis according to which "political actions chiefly arouse or satisfy people not by granting or withholding their stable substantive demands but rather by changing the demands and the expectations."[6] Put differently, the output (of political action) codetermines the nature of the input and cannot be separated from it; or, in Edelman's own formulation: "The significant 'outputs' of political activities are not particular public policies labeled as political goals, but rather the creation of political following and supports: i.e., the evocation of arousal or quiescence in mass publics."[7] And, in the second place, the reverse is true as well. For just as political action codetermines the desires of the citizens, the citizens' demands will codetermine the politician's action—a truth that Edelman puts into words by means of the provocative paradox that "political leaders must follow their followers."[8] In summary, if we look at both the ideal and the practice of democracy, then the classical input/output model must be rejected as a technocratic illusion.

But it is unlikely that classical political theorists will be deeply impressed by this kind of argument. They will protest that the romantic political theorists have demonstrated precisely the opposite of what they wanted to prove. For this argumentation, as they will go on to reason, succeeds not so much in demonstrating the *shortcomings* of the input/output model as its *omnipresence* in political reality. For what the romantic political theorist unintentionally showed has been that we will have to apply the model also in cases where we originally had been little inclined to make use of it. Apparently there is a continuous *interaction* or *interchange* between all the actors and factors that are operative in the political domain, and for a correct understanding of this interaction we will have to apply the input/output model even more intensively than hitherto.

An example may clarify the classical political theorist's rejoinder. Think of the situation in which two political parties that differ profoundly from an ideological point of view nevertheless see themselves forced to cooperate in order to prevent worse. One may think here of certain phases in the conflict between labor and capital in Western continental democracies. Such a situation will often give rise to the paradoxical situation that precisely the extremist political "die-hards" of both parties discover themselves to be each other's "objective" allies, to put it in the Marxist jargon of some thirty years ago. For those extremists will be most strongly opposed to compromise and cooperation and they will find the strongest argument for their intransigence in the extremism of their ideological antipodes. So, on the one hand, this presents us with the paradox that precisely the greatest political disagreement is conducive to the realization of a shared political goal. On the other hand, as the classical political theorists will emphasize, in this realization of an unexpectedly shared common political goal, we certainly cannot discern a political *innere Stimme*, as the romantic is apt to do. For the classical input/output model is perfectly well equipped to deal with this paradox. The input of political polarization has caused the output of this rejection of compromise and cooperation desired by the extremists of both parties. In other words, the shared goal of political noncooperation was already latently present in the extremist wings of both parties—and something really "new," something that would, so to speak, transcend what is written in the political scores of the extremists of both parties and that would *not* be reducible to it, did and could not make itself heard. In short, in spite of this surprising paradox of fruitfully cooperating political extremists, we

still safely find ourselves here in the clear and transparent world of classical political rationality.

But precisely this example will also enable the romantic political theorist to demonstrate the deficiency in his classical opponent's position. He
will begin by pointing out that his political conceptions have their natural
biotope in the realm of political conflict—and that, if only for that reason,
the example proposed by the classical political theorist suits him excel-
lently. Just as Schumann's *innere Stimme* was only something that could be
listened to thanks to the oppositions and the complex mutual interferences
of what is played by the right and the left hand, so the political *innere
Stimme* can only come into being thanks to political opposition and conflict. There is no room for this political *innere Stimme* in a society that is
reigned by a universal consensus—whether this consensus actually exists or
has been imposed by brute, totalitarian political force. Romantic political
reality can only be observed, therefore, in a society of political struggle and
conflict. If democracy is the political system aiming at the *juste-milieu* between conflicting political positions,[9] this political *innere Stimme* can be
listened to more often in democracy than in any other political system.

But let us return to the classical political theorist's example and focus now not on the ideological extremists but on those within both parties
who are prepared to compromise and cooperate. It is there that we will,
for the first time, recognize those democratic mechanisms that can properly be accounted for only by the romantic conception of political reality—
which also justifies, by the way, the inference that political renewal can
never be achieved by extremists but only by those who are ready to cooperate with the political opponent. In the first place, we should realize that
this readiness to cooperate will make both parties look for compromise—
and the notion of *compromise* should be clearly distinguished here from
that of *consensus*.

For the latter notion is suggestive of actual ideological agreement;
that is to say, from the perspective of different ideological positions discussion may reveal a set of political views that both parties will consider to
be acceptable or even most rational. In the simplest case consensus will
take the form of an identification of the common denominator of the ideological position of the parties involved. And in more complicated cases
consensus will be a development of this common denominator into ideological directions that both parties had not foreseen when defining their

own ideological positions and that had therefore been left unexplored. But in all cases the ideological conflict is not so much camouflaged, accepted, or momentarily forgotten for the sake of cooperation; conflict really disappears here: where there was previously conflict, consensus now reigns. Obviously consensus will primarily be achieved where ideological differences turn out, on closer inspection, to be much smaller than initially was believed. In sum, in consensus the compatibility of different ideologies is exploited to the full. But precisely for this reason consensus can not produce anything that was not already present in the existing ideologies; all the ingredients for consensus were already part of those ideologies. So even here we are still in the realm of classical political theory.

This process is different from that of compromise, which occurs when two parties agree upon a political option that is explicitly at odds with the desiderata of the different ideologies involved, but both parties are nevertheless willing to take the political responsibility for this option. They recognize that the existence of other parties with other ideologies requires them to accept compromise as an unpleasant but inevitable fact about meaningful political decision making, if the even worse alternative of a total breakdown of the political machine is to be prevented. The paradox of political compromise, therefore, is that, on the one hand, as in the case of consensus, one stands by one's ideological conviction, but, on the other hand, one is prepared to follow a line of political action more or less inimical to that conviction. Hence, it will be obvious that political compromise may produce something that is really *new*, something that was *not yet* present in the existing catalogue of political ideologies. This does not alter the fact that political compromise will always bear the marks or traces of the ideologies contained by that catalogue. And the important conclusion is that, as opposed to consensus, compromise invites the introduction of this political *innere Stimme* in the symphony of democratic politics.

Political compromise enables us, so to speak, to listen to this political *innere Stimme* that was not yet "audible" in ideological conflict but that can indeed be discerned in it *from a later point of view*—the point of view embodied by the political compromise. Only compromise can make us aware of the point of view implicit in previously given political conflict and opposition.[10] Like Schumann's *innere Stimme*, this is a reality that can also *become* a reality. This, then, is the kind of peculiarly ambivalent reality that is indispensable to the proper functioning of democracy—to this political system that cannot live without conflict.

Even more so, the very stability of democracy as such is threatened not by conflict but by consensus and agreement, which, as we saw above, leave no room for the political *innere Stimme.* For, as Edelman puts it, "When statements need not be defended against counterstatements, they are readily changed or inverted."[11] A state and society dominated by consensus is an unstable state and society, since little will be needed to make everybody change their opinion—with all the unpredictable and unpleasant consequences that this may have. By contrast, in a state and society where disagreement is dominant, the pros and cons of the conflicting opinions will be widely discussed and commented on. Under such circumstances public opinion will develop slowly but responsibly, and political disasters that may hurt everybody will be more easy to avoid. A society governed by consensus is a stupid society, given to erratic and counterproductive behavior, whereas the society dominated by struggle and conflict will ordinarily succeed in avoiding the worst follies. As Montesquieu already put it: "In an age of ignorance one has no doubts even if one commits the most serious mistakes; in an enlightened age one trembles even if producing the greatest benefits."[12]

But even more surprising is the typically romanticist political thesis that the conflict between political opinions shores up not only democracy but also those conflicting political opinions themselves. In a manner worthy of Tocqueville, Edelman formulates the insight as follows: "As soon as . . . bits of language circulate in a culture and present themselves for acceptance or rejection, it becomes evident that texts become bulwarks of each other while isolated texts, *unsupported by opposition,* are readily vulnerable to new language."[13] The force of political positions partly lies, paradoxically, in the opposition they will encounter because of the presence of other and rival political positions. It follows that in a democracy the political *innere Stimme* will be easier to discern and that it will play a more beneficial role, to the extent that political positions are more clearly delineated and easier to recognize for all concerned.

Indeed, nobody had a clearer eye for the kind of insight into the nature of democracy and of public debate expounded above than Alexis de Tocqueville. Though no oeuvre resists summary and recapitulation more than Tocqueville's, I may be allowed to indicate one constant in his observations on democracy that is relevant here. Tocqueville always likes to confront his readers with the paradoxes of democracy: he likes to impress on us that democracy often functions for reasons precisely opposite to what we tend to associate with that political system. He says, for example, that democracy is not inclined to revolutionary change but to conservatism, that public debate in a democracy is not a debate in the proper sense of the word but rather a *dialogue des sourds,* that political decision making is not decision making but rather the creative avoidance of it, and that the democratic state does not execute what the people wishes or decides, but that the people decides what the state achieves or tries to achieve.[14] And always the message is that we should not see these paradoxes as signs of a degeneration of democracy but as the conditions of its functioning successfully—though it certainly is true that Tocqueville also fears from democracy several threats to the cause of liberty.

I shall not dwell any longer here on Tocqueville's paradoxes, nor on whether we should always agree with him. Instead I want to point out the congeniality between this kind of paradox and our notion of the political *innere Stimme.* For as generally is the case with paradoxes, Tocqueville's paradoxes also make us aware of an unsuspected political reality that is, in some way or other, hidden or present in our naive discourse about democracy, but that we may only become aware of thanks to the conflicts and paradoxes in that discourse. Paradox is the figure of speech confronting us with these conflicts in our speaking and thinking and that therefore requires us to look at reality itself in order to find our way out of the impasse into which paradox has led us. And *if* we follow this injunction of paradox and actually turn to reality itself, we shall see that what discourse made us believe to be incompatible can peacefully coexist in reality itself. For example, on the basis of what we associate with these words, egoism *seems* to be incompatible with the common interest, but if we may believe Bernard de Mandeville and Adam Smith, in *reality* these two things are in line with each other. In a similar way, Tocqueville often succeeds in demonstrating that what we initially believed to be at odds with the principles of democratic government is, in fact, a condition for its proper functioning.

If we wish to account for these paradoxes of democracy, Machiavelli's perspectivism will prove to be our best point of departure. This viewpoint has its origins in Machiavelli's attack on ethics that many people down to the present day have found so profoundly shocking. The point of

Machiavelli's argument I have in mind here[15] is that in sociopolitical reality there is no perspective or point of view that is uniquely privileged above all others in discovering and defining moral truth. Even more so, not only is there no such Archimedean point of moral truth that would enable us to justify our own moral and political action, it is often exactly *the other* who is in a better position to assess the merits of our action than we are ourselves. "Real" moral truth choses its home rather with the other than with ourselves (and the unsettling fact is that this is true for each determination of what should count as "ourselves"). Hence, paradoxically, it is precisely our respect of the other that requires us to surrender our own moral certainties—and thus any certainty that we might have with regard to how we should properly demonstrate our respect for the other. "Real" moral truth— in short, political truth—is not so much a matter of perky inner moral conviction as a matter of how "the other" perceives "the outside" of our action (regardless of our inner moral convictions that may or may not have inspired it); and we should therefore always consider with the greatest distrust our "Cartesian" inclination to make ethics into a matter of conscience.[16] Moral "Cartesianism" leads us away from "real," essentially *political* moral truth to moral solipsism and the moral complacency of an ethical egocentrism, however sublime the ideals of "Cartesian ethics" may often seem to us at first sight.

But what Machiavelli affirms here about ourselves is obviously just as true for *the other* as it is for ourselves. And this justifies the conclusion that the source of moral (or, rather, political) rectitude cannot be located in ourselves, nor even in others, but instead *in the space between ourselves and others*, so to speak. Much like Schumann's *innere Stimme*, moral and political rectitude can only come into being in the interaction, the interference and conflict between political and ideological convictions with regard to moral and political truth. Next, it is self-evident that democracy, more than any other political system, will have a natural affinity with Machiavelli's perspectivism as described a moment ago. For is democracy not inspired by the belief that political truth can only be the result of the interaction of individuals and groups in a democratic society? The essentially *monological* discourse of ethics is therefore basically at odds with the *dialogue* of democracy, and, hence, the notion of an ethical or moral *foundation* of democracy should be considered a *contradictio in terminis*. Thus, nothing has contributed more importantly to the construction of the po-

litical mentality of democracy than this ill-famed rejection of the pretensions of ethics that we find in Machiavelli's *The Prince*.

POLITICAL STYLE

Several conclusions about the notion of political style follow from the
foregoing. In order to clarify these conclusions, I shall appeal to another less
obvious source within the present context, namely Schiller's essay "Über
naive und sentimentalische Dichtung," of 1796. Schiller distinguishes here
between what he refers to as "naive" and "sentimental poetry." The distinction is defined by him as follows: naive poetry is, above all, an expression of
nature and should also be experienced as such. Put differently, in naive poetry we will find not only an expression of "being that is free, that is, being
which takes its existence out of itself," but also of the *awareness*, or of the
very *idea* of this natural existence that is not in need of anything outside or
beyond itself.[17] And only thanks to this "awareness" or this "idea" are we
able to recognize naive poetry as such and can we be so deeply moved by it:
"We love in it not certain objects, but the idea that they represent."[18]

What exactly is meant by this "idea" may become clearer when we
notice that Schiller links it *expressis verbis* to morality. Why he does so is
suggested by the following comparison proposed by him. We consider the
child to be "naive" and respect its naivete because we believe a call for perfection to be present in the child's naivete. And inevitably every adult like
ourselves has, each of us in a different way, failed to live up to this call for
perfection. Put differently, the child embodies a promise of perfection that
no adult ever succeeded in fulfilling. This is why the child confronts us
with our own moral imperfections and, hence, why the child's naivete has
for the adult this double significance of being a moral appeal and a sign of
his own moral imperfection. Speaking more generally, the naive embodies
a mode of being destined to natural perfection, which is achieved without
artifice and reflection and presented to us like a gift of nature; on the one
hand, it requires us to overcome our imperfections and weaknesses and to
return to this natural naivete; but on the other, precisely by manifesting itself as a requirement, hence as something coming from outside ourselves
and what we naturally are, it makes us deeply aware of the impossibility of
ever satisfying this requirement. There is a kind of double bind in the very
idea of this naive moral perfection: either we possess it, but then we are un-

aware of it, or we have to strive for it, and then we know that we can never achieve it.

And this brings us to sentimental poetry, which is, basically, the kind of poetry originating from this awareness of the immeasurable value of naivete and of what we therefore lost forever by losing it. We now realize that we are no longer part of nature, that we belong to the world of artifice and culture. We feel unhappy about this, and therefore want to get back to nature and begin to ask ourselves how best to achieve this (impossible) goal. The result is "sentimental" poetry. And the contrast between naive and sentimental poetry can therefore be summarized, in Schiller's own words, as follows: "The poet, I said, either *is* nature, or he *strives* for it; the former is the naive, and the latter the sentimental poet."[19]

The crucial difference between the two forms of poetry is that the naive poet has no sense or consciousness of what is alien to him, for it precisely is his grace "to be at home even after having left behind himself what is known and to *extend* nature without *moving beyond* it."[20] The sentimental poet is in a far less comfortable position: finding himself caught in this opposition between nature and culture, he irrevocably is part of culture and yet wants to return to nature. Reality—nature—therefore is to him as much an infinite task as an invincible barrier.[21]

It must strike us how much Schiller's distinction between naive and sentimental poetry is in agreement with Hegel's philosophy of history: the naive is the evident analogue of Hegel's "objective mind" and the sentimental that of the "subjective mind."[22] And if we recall, next, to what extent the dialectics of the objective and the subjective mind is for Hegel the creator of all the political realities that have been realized in the course of world history, this may already give us an inkling of the political dimensions and implications of Schiller's distinction. We therefore need not be surprised that such a distinctly political thinker as Schiller did not hesitate to translate the distinction to the domain of politics. And, indeed, he ends his essay with what is arguably one of the most interesting comments on political realism and idealism that has ever been written. Elsewhere in his essay he discusses "naive" political personalities such as Pope Adrian VI; other examples of naive politicians proposed by Schiller are Julius Caesar and Henry IV of France because they found egg-of-Columbus-like[23] solutions for the political problems of their age.[24] Unfortunately Schiller gave us no examples of "sentimental" politicians. This is to be regretted because—

as we shall see in a moment—political problems preferably present themselves in the domain of the "sentimental."

But more important is the following. Transposed into the domain of politics, the naive is obviously in line with the speculations of natural law philosophy and, more generally, with the conviction that political reality is basically unambiguous, transparent, and thus, in the end, completely fathomable by the naive political theorist and by naive political theory. It may not be easy to do this, and will admittedly require the greatest intellectual sophistication, but if we give our best to this important task, no impenetrable secrets necessarily need remain. In this sense almost all of political theory[25] and contemporary political science is "naive," as this term is understood by Schiller. For on all occasions one is convinced that a point of view, a discourse, a system, or whatever you have, can be found in terms of which the whole of political reality will become transparent to our ratio and our argument.

Compelling in Schiller's analysis, then, is that it already identifies where we should expect a fissure in this allegedly seamless web of political reality of the naive political theorist. For Schiller writes the following about the naive poetic or political genius: "It is modest since the genius will always be a secret to himself."[26] The insight is that it will be impossible to adequately clarify and explain the success of the naive poet within the discourse of naivete itself—it will be inevitable to adopt the discourse of the sentimental if one would try to do so. The whole of Schiller's own argument, or whatever anybody might wish to say about the poetically or the politically naive, is therefore necessarily part of the discourse of the sentimental. The naive is, hence, a category *within* the sentimental; surely, the naive as such can *exist* outside that category, but it cannot be *thought* or *conceptualized* outside the category of the sentimental.

And this brings me to the essence of the argument on political style that is presented in this chapter. For the crucial implication is that the notion of poetic or of political style can have neither meaning nor content for the naive poet, politician, or political theorist. They will experience their poetry, their political action or thought as a direct expression of the way the world is, as a manifestation of the nature of things, as a continuation (*Erweiterung*, as Schiller put it) of it and not as merely one of the many different ways that we may relate to reality. This they would consider an untoward concession to "subjectivity," or even to falsehood. They can only see how nature expresses itself in self-evidence and necessity—and this is to them the sure sign of truth. Only at a later stage, when they have entered into a relationship with themselves and with the world and thereby lost their "naivete" and naive innocence, only then will they realize that their "naive" poetry and political action proceeded from merely one of the many possible perspectives that we may assume with regard to reality. Only after they have become, in a certain sense, "an other," that is to say, a *later* self, only after they thus become able to objectify their former self, may their eyes be opened to their previous style of thinking, writing, and acting (while, at the same time, necessarily remaining blind to their *present* style). And because of this, most people, being little inclined to introspection and self-objectification, will remain in ignorance of the style in which they present themselves to others. In sum, as was the case with Machiavelli's perspectivism described above, our style is primarily something for the *other* to observe; we are typically blind to our own style.[27]

Obviously, all this is even more true for how we relate to others. The gap existing between our naive behavior or self-awareness and the style that we may discern in it from a later perspective, will be the gap normally existing between ourselves and the others (we are "naive" with regard to ourselves and "sentimental" with regard to the others, so to speak). It is natural for the other to see me in the way that I may perhaps come to perceive myself from a later perspective—and vice versa. In short, the characterization of personality in terms of style is what we shall opt for when we consider a personality "from the outside," as it were; and this will be the case as long as we do not feel tempted to relate this behavior to some hidden, deeply-lying sources of the personality, and as long as we remain convinced that all that is relevant in human thought and action simply *is* this "outside."

For several reasons, this should not be seen as some variant of behaviorism. First, whereas behaviorism finds in publicly observable human behavior the foundation for a science of human action, style does not (attempt to) *explain*, it *characterizes*; style does not tell us *why*, but *how* individuals think or act. Second, whereas behaviorism considers human personality to be a kind of black box that will be of no use to us in our effort to explain and to predict human behavior, human personality will be at the focus of our interest when we use the notion of style for the characterization of human behavior. Our conception of an individual's style will be to us a kind of *substitute*, *replacement*, or *model* of that individual's personality, and will be of use to us precisely because it has this function for us. What we see as the person's style will be *what he is like* to us. And I also emphasize this "to us," for when using the notion of style we thereby fully accept the "subjectivity" that is implied by that notion. That is to say, style does not pretend to present us with some deep psychological truths about a human individual's personality that would in principle be acceptable to anybody who is able to speak the language of psychology. Style does away with this monstrous alliance of a generalized, impersonal subject of knowledge with a secret source of truth deeply hidden in some inner sanctuary of the individual—an alliance from which so much contemporary philosophy of action has originated. Style organizes items of human behavior without pretending to bring us to some deeper level allegedly lying behind these items of behavior themselves; for it does this job of organizing behavior in the space *between* the individual human being in question and ourselves, so to speak, and not by moving *beyond* that space into the sphere of a hidden, inner self of that individual.

In this way the use of the notion of style with regard to human action strangely combines a focus on what can publicly be *seen* (as in behaviorism) with an interest in unique individual personality (with all its traditional Cartesian reminiscences). Style therefore presents us with a mix of objectivism and subjectivism in our conception of human behavior that puts it apart from most of contemporary philosophy of action. On the one hand, style is as old as humanity, since it is the category that human individuals have always relied upon in order to make sense of each other's behavior; but on the other, the category is new and revolutionary since philosophy of action has always shunned it on account of its unscientific nature and "superficiality." And, admittedly, the notion of style *is* unscientific and "superficial" in the proper sense of that word, but this is precisely why we need it so much: for in our dealings with other human beings we are interested in what goes on *between* us, so in what is on the *surface* of the behavior of the other, so to speak. We are predominantly interested in what takes place on the *interface* between the other and myself (to use computer terminology) and not in some deep, psychological truths about the other.

This will also make clear where we should draw the boundary between what can and cannot be realized when we have had the wisdom to avail ourselves of the notion of style in our dealings with others—and in politics. With regard to what cannot be realized, where others, as we have seen, experiences themselves "naively" and *nonstylistically*, this naive experience of the self is the limit that our stylistic representation of others and of their behavior will never be able to attain. And with regard to what *can* be achieved by the notion of style, it will give us access to most of what makes culture and politics of significance and of value to us. For what is truly of interest to us in culture and politics is not the objective content of what is naively given to us, not a quasi-Kantian *an sich* of what culture and politics might mean to themselves (supposing that we could make any sense at all of this effort to reach into the *an sich* of culture and of politics), but what becomes accessible to us in terms of the "sentimental" approach of these two domains. As Schiller put it himself: "Naivete has its value in that it may completely grasp the finite, the other [i.e., the sentimental] has this value in the approximation of the infinite."[28]

And we should realize that the difference between nature and the naive, on the one hand, and culture or politics and the sentimental, on the other, cannot be measured on the scale of the relative (in)adequacy of knowledge (i.e., the scale that all our present ideologies of knowledge require us to consider all-decisive). For in a certain sense there *is* no self-knowledge that could function as such an absolute measure of all knowledge and insight: naivete is not a potential object of knowledge to itself in the way that the sentimental can be. Naivete should not be seen as a kind of ideal of knowledge that can only asymptotically be approached in terms of the sentimental: for the domain of the naive *sui generis* lies outside or beyond the reach of (self)reflection. When opposing the naive and the sentimental, Schiller assures us that "only the latter recognizes different degrees and progress," an observation that is both true and misleading. It is misleading in that it invites all these models of scientific knowledge aiming at the approximation of ultimate truth that contemporary philosophy of science has imprinted upon our mind. But here this ultimate truth—the naive—is not a goal to be approximated as much as possible. On the other hand, Schiller's statement is true in the sense that it expresses the insight that the stylistic or aesthetic understanding of the other will depend on the degree of the substitutability of our stylistic characterizations of the other for the other's actual behavior—at least insofar as this behavior is seen from our *own* specific point of view.

We can summarize this as follows. All our knowledge of, grasp of, or insight into sociopolitical reality can be divided into three categories. In the first place there is "naivete" as intended by Schiller: here the self is neither objectified nor thematized; it is experienced—if it is experienced at all—as being a mere continuation of nature and of reality. But, in the second place, the naive self may become the dominant partner in the relationship between the self and nature or reality. And then reflection about nature or reality may become a disguised form of naive self-reflection. Here we have, in Schiller's words, an "extension" (*Erweiterung*) of the self over the nonself; and insofar as we would be prepared to use here the notions of (self)reflection, we should describe this as the peculiar kind of recognition of the self that will be given to one after one has made, unwittingly and unintentionally, the whole of reality into a mirror image of the self. The self can here discern in reality only variants of itself—but it remains unaware of this boundless extension of the self and it can persist in this ignorance since this extension took place under the aegis of a nameless, anonymous, and transcendental self. This is the world of natural law philosophy and of much, though not all, of the social sciences.

But in the third place, there is an attitude toward or an understanding of the world that respects that there is a world alien to us. This is the domain of the sentimental, of the awareness of being an outsider, of being in a relationship to nature or (political) reality without being an integral part of it (as in the naive)—and yet we wish to return to nature and (political) reality. As soon as we enter the domain of the sentimental, we will have decentered ourselves, taken leave of naive self-awareness in both the forms that I described a moment ago. We have now left the "egocentricity" of the naive self that is still so much urged on us by ethics, by Cartesian and Kantian philosophy of mind, and by all its modern successors (think for example, of the highly characteristic "egocentricity" of the Cartesian *cogito*). Now we no longer project ourselves on the world, but reach self-reflection and/or self-awareness via *the other*. We see ourselves as the other will see us (as we ourselves may become aware of the style of our *previous* behavior only at a *later* phase in our life and, hence, from the perspective of that later *alter ego*). In this third, "sentimental" paradigm, not the *self* (or some generalized intersubjective transcendental self) but the *other* is the beginning of all wisdom. This is the paradigm that we encounter in aesthetics and in the writing of history; and the most important instrument it has to offer us is the notion of *style*.

THE POLITICAL STYLES OF DEMOCRACY

In no political system is this stylistic understanding of the other more crucial and indispensable than in representative democracy. As the concept of "representative" democracy already clearly indicates, it is only thanks to how the state "represents" the electorate, and in its turn, how the electorate constructs for itself a "representation" of the state and of politics, that all the mechanisms of a representative democracy start to move and function properly. This typically *aesthetic* notion of "representation" suggests how the notion of democratic style could best be operationalized. For, as may be clear on the basis of the foregoing, the understanding that the electorate and the state mutually have of each other is not "naive," not a form or derivative of socioscientific knowledge, but essentially *stylistic*: the object of political understanding is the *style* of the other, whether of the state or of (groups within) the electorate. And the deliberate stylelessness of "naive," economic and bureaucratic understanding that dominates contemporary political discourse—however useful these discourses may sometimes be— will ultimately result in a blockage of the mechanisms that keep the machine of representative democracy going. An economic or bureaucratic reality will then usurp the place of a political reality of an *innere Stimme*, resulting from the interaction between the "right" and the "left hand" of the represented and of the representative. One of the major problems of contemporary Western democracy is that because of all the clutter of socioscientific data—statistics, bureaucracy, and so on—the electorate and the state simply are no longer able to recognize and understand each other. Only style can guarantee this mutual recognition and understanding—and give us access to "the other" again.

Just as either the right hand or the left hand may be the main contributor to the development of this political *innere Stimme*, so it will also be possible to indicate, on the basis of the foregoing, what must be the primary or elementary political styles in representative democracy (though I hasten to add that this does not as yet imply anything with regard to their relative merits). A distinction made by Schiller proves to be helpful here once again—I am thinking here of his distinction between the elegiac and the satirical style. For Schiller, elegiac poetry and elegiac political style correspond with the naive; they cultivate nature and what is natural at the expense of culture, art, and artificiality. And, as Schiller explicitly points out,[29] the curious paradox is that in this way the natural becomes *idealistic* and the world of art and culture *realistic*: from our present (sentimental) perspective not *culture*, but *nature* presents itself as a shaky and uncertain construction. In this way Schiller nicely and elegantly succeeds in turning Rousseau upside down. Obvious examples of this elegiac and idealistic democratic political style are the idyll[30] of natural law theory and the ideal(s) of direct democracy.

Opposite to the elegiac style, Schiller places satirical poetry, which corresponds with the sentimental: "Satirical is the poet who takes as his subject the estrangement from reality and the opposition between reality and the ideal (the effect both have on the human mind is in each case the same)."[31] In connection to the world of politics we may think here of the political style that is ordinarily called Machiavellistic: in Machiavellism the satire of political action results from the rejection of the ideal as the highest political reality. For this reason we may agree with Robert Hariman when he writes in his recent book on political style that "the *realist* style is the basis of Machiavelli's persuasive success, it has shaped his text's subsequent history of interpretation, and it operates as a powerful mode of comprehension and action in the modern world."[32] And in agreement with Schiller's notion of the satirical as a subcategory of the sentimental, Hariman also situates Machiavelli's endeavor to bring back the idea (i.e., Machiavelli's own high-pitched republicanism) to nature, that is, to political reality.[33] In recent analyses of the comedies that Machiavelli wrote (such as *La Mandragola* [The mandrake]), scholars also attempt to identify in these comedies this same peculiar combination of comedy, satire, and realism that is so much the outstanding feature of his political writings.[34] Hence, where the idyll of the naive political style placed us in the universe of the citizen living in a direct democracy, the satire of the sentimental democratic style has its elective affinity with the democratic politician's dilemmas of what most prudent and effective use he should make of political power.

But more important than the style of naive idyll and that of sentimental satire is how Schiller proposes to subdivide satire. As we shall see in a moment, it is only this subdivision that will give us the style suitable for the political *innere Stimme* of democracy. The distinction that is relevant here is the one between tragic and comic satire. Tragic satire is the style proper for showing how the sheer weight of reality may reduce all human intention, whether good or bad, to dismal, tragic failure. Here the human individual is a mere plaything of social and political reality, unable to exert any autonomous influence upon it. A striking example, according to Schiller, is Tacitus's account of the brute realities of first-century Rome.

But, contrary to what one perhaps would have expected, far more interest and sympathy is displayed by Schiller for comic satire. As will become clear, this is the style that overcomes the one-sidedness of both naive idyll and sentimental satire and that best agrees with the world of political conflict in representative democracy. Schiller gives the following argument in favor of his own preference: "This is why the tragic poet always deals with his subject matter in a practical way, and the comic poet in a theoretical way."[35] The idea is that the tragic poet can safely rely upon the extreme seriousness of the subject matter to captivate the interest of the audience. The comedy writer is without this advantage; success will come in this, if at all, only thanks to the writer's wit, intelligence, inventiveness, and talent to lend to fictive reality authenticity and credibility. It is the writer's handicap "to discover everywhere chance rather than fate" and to have to create a fictive world that is believable to the audience out of the unpromising and pedestrian material that is presented by the goddess of fortune—that is, the goddess of fate and of the unforeseeable but decisive accident. Hence, the challenge the comedy writer has to meet is "to restore spontaneously the unity that had been taken from it by abstraction"[36]—a challenge that is unknown to the tragic poet since this unity is already automatically given by the sublime subject matter.

We may also observe here to what extent the logic of comedy (unlike that of tragedy) agrees with that of representation in general—and with political representation in particular. For crucial to all (political) representation is a similar substitution of the unity (of identity) of the represented for that of its representation.[37] Even more so, this is precisely where the whole use and function of representation must be looked for: representations are "imitations" of reality allowing us to speak about reality in terms of *them*.[38] But since it is a "substitute reality," and not reality itself, representation may make us better aware of certain aspects of reality that remain hidden or difficult to perceive in reality—which is one of the other main merits of representation above reality and (true) description of reality.[39] This is why representation can, in the practice of democratic politics, be so successful and even outright indispensable when we wish to listen to democracy's *in-*

nere Stimme. In sum, Schiller's eulogy of comic satire may help us recognize in what way democracy's *innere Stimme* may present itself to our perception: we can listen to it in the political reality that is created by political representation and in the autonomy that this new reality possesses with regard to the represented.

I therefore heartily agree with the account of democracy given by Combs and Nimmo; more specifically, when they present in their book *The Comedy of Democracy* a number of arguments in favor of the view that the style of democracy is essentially comic. As ordinarily is the case when we attempt to justify stylistic characterizations, these arguments do not permit deductive or logical organization. When we describe style(s), a web of associations is what we should expect. The following elements can be discerned in the mirror image that comedy presents to democracy. Like Schiller, Combs and Nimmo prefer comedy to tragedy, since comedy succeeds in generating its structure out of itself while structure is effortlessly given to tragedy in its subject matter. It is both the burden and the beauty of comedy that it gives us a world without preexisting rules; it is a world that is "un-ruled rather than mis-ruled," as Combs and Nimmo write.[40] The paradox of comedy is that its own order should suggest, as adequately as possible, the *lack* of order existing in reality itself. And Combs and Nimmo therefore also see in Machiavelli's comedies, with their satirical comments on human weakness and stupidity, with their surrender of the tragic dimensions of "cosmic man" in favor of the imperfections of "men in society," their radical openness instead of the closed world of tragedy, their recognition of the role of chance, and their inclination to the subversive and irreverent, as the first announcement of the style of democracy in Western political history.[41] Indeed, the style of democracy is open and ironic, adverse to system and the seriousness of theory—and whoever wishes to impose on democracy a high and sublime goal will try unwittingly to exchange democracy for an aristocracy ruled by the select group of himself and of his own kindred spirits.

But probably the supreme irony of this "comedy of errors" that democracy is lies in the fact that democracy needs this kind of misconception about itself.[42] We need in democracy the tragic dimension of people who take themselves and their political ideals tragically seriously, along with all the misfortunes arising from this. Without this tragic self-awareness of the citizen and the politician, there would be no material that could be fed into the machine of democratic satire. Thus the basis of democracy might well be an incompatibility of the *satire* of that political system itself with the *tragic* political inspiration of the individual citizen and politician. If this makes sense, it would follow that the future of our Western democracies will at least partly depend on our success to carefully uphold this strange and paradoxical balance between tragedy and satire.

In Pauline Westerman's recent study of the miseries of natural law philosophy, she gives an exposition of the conceptual inadequacies of that notion. As she convincingly makes clear, the notion of "natural law" suggests a degree of logical coherence, of conceptual hierarchy and a reducibility to indubitable first principles, that is completely at odds with the plastic and Protean character of sociopolitical reality. She therefore recommends that we make more use of the notion of political style than hitherto has been the case in our theorizing about politics:

An artistic style is not to be seen as a recipe for "how to paint a portrait." The term "style" rather denotes a general way of making or doing things. . . . For instance, the stylistic requirement of unity of time, place and action, which any successful classicist playwright had to meet, was not merely a constraint; it also opened a vast array of possibilities that would otherwise have remained unexplored. Style can be a source of creativity.[43]

We discussed in Chapter 4 the political creativity of democratic politics, and it seems likely that the notion of political style is ideally suited for explaining this creativity.[44] This political creativity preeminently manifests itself in the creation of a new political reality, new in the sense that it transcends the more elementary and primary realities of what is in the minds of the individual participants in the domain of politics. It is a *new* political reality because it is superimposed upon the more concrete reality of already existing political desires, ideologies, administrative habits, or mechanisms[45] whose complex interaction we have tried to elucidate in terms of Schumann's *innere Stimme*. For what is true of Schumann's *innere Stimme* is true as well of this democratic extra, superimposed reality: it cannot be "heard" but it can be "listened to," and this can be done with the same objectivity and accuracy as what is actually "heard."

Precisely because we still find ourselves here in a kind of indeterminate limbo between what is already and what is not yet reality—obviously the kind of limbo in which all creativity will preferably look for its proper home—precisely for this reason, whatever ultimately solidifies into a political reality that will become recognizable to all of us in due time will make here its first entry into the domain of politics. This political *innere Stimme* is therefore the birthplace of all the mechanisms that will keep representative democracy alive. Democracy dies when this political *innere Stimme* is smothered, or when our political ears have become unable or unwilling to listen to it anymore.

If we wish to investigate more closely the peculiar reality of this political *innere Stimme*, the notion of political style will be our best guide. For political style shares with the reality of the political *innere Stimme* the capacity to bridge this so enigmatic and Protean gap between what *is* already and what will *become* political reality. In our contemporary democracies, it is only in terms of political style that the politician may become recognizable at all to the electorate: Buffon's *le style, c'est l'homme même* is preeminently true of how the citizen conceives of the politician. Not political ideology, neither a political program nor political achievement—and it is far from me to belittle these things—but political style, therefore, is the true *trait d'union* between politics and the politician on the one hand and the electorate and the citizen on the other. Political style is the category enabling all the participants of the Schillerian comedy of representative democracy to recognize each other; political style is the domain where the political party and the politician will make their first cautious efforts to redefine their relationship to the electorate or what should, in their view, be seen as beneficial and valuable future public goals.[46]

When a new political reality comes into being it always involves the birth of a new political *style*. Hence, the political theorist avoiding the notion of political style because he thinks the notion too difficult or too cumbersome to use is like somebody who decides that would be it too much of an effort to learn the language which is used by the people among whom he lives.

PART III

DEMOCRATIC THEORY

6

DEMOCRACY AS ANTIFOUNDATIONALISM

In the seventeenth chapter of his *Leviathan*, Thomas Hobbes explains his view of how the state and civil society came into being: "The finall Cause, End, or Designe of men, (who naturally love Liberty, and Dominion over others,) is the introduction of that restraint on themselves, (in which we see them live in a Commonwealth,) is the foresight of their preservation."[1] According to Hobbes, the political order, the state, or "commonwealth," in Hobbes's own terminology, originated from the desire of (self)preservation that he believed to be the first fact about all human psychology. Galilei had shown that the law fundamental to all mechanics is the law of inertia (according to which all bodies persist in their movement unless some outside force is exerted upon them). Hobbes believed that this law of the overriding human desire of self-preservation plays, or rather ought to play, a similar role in the science of politics. For Hobbes, this was a quasi-Cartesian first principle from which could be derived all human behavior and, more importantly to him, the science of politics teaching us how to construct the Commonwealth.

More specifically, if all human endeavor aims at self-preservation (or can ultimately be related to this desire), then the state or Commonwealth should see as its primary task to guarantee the personal safety of the citizen. Hobbes's life in a time of religious civil war and his unusual preoccupation with his own personal safety further contributed to his conviction that self-preservation is where all politics begins and ends.[2] Consequently, as Hobbes continues his argument, "the only way to erect such a Common Power, as may be able to defend them [i.e., the citizens] from the invasion of Forraigners, and the injuries of others . . . is to conferre all their power and strength upon one Man, or upon one Assembly of Men, that may reduce their Wills, by plurality of voices, unto one Will."[3]

In sum, there is a clearly identifiable *foundation* of the state or the "Commonwealth": self-preservation. And from this first principle we can proceed by logical argument to the state, its power and its prerogatives. Next, the "absoluteness" of the foundation of the state must have its self-evident counterpart in the no less absolute power that Hobbes grants to the state. Hobbes's absolute certainty about the origins of the state and the certainty of his argument resist any doubt about the absoluteness of the state's power. For since nothing is lost or added on the trajectory of Hobbes's argument from its origin to the state itself, the state must be just as absolute as its foundation. Thus came into being the Leviathan, "that mortall God," to which the citizen surrendered all his independence and political autonomy: "I authorize and give up my right of governing myselfe, to this Man, or Assembly of Men, on the condition, that you give up thy Right to him, and authorize all his Actions in like Manner."[4]

Hobbes is rightly seen as the father of all modern(ist) political thought. It is certainly true that later political theorists, such as Locke, Rousseau, Kant, the contract theorists of the seventeenth and the eighteenth centuries in general, and theorists like Hegel or Marx often presented us with conclusions differing dramatically from those of Hobbes. Nevertheless, there remains one fundamental point of agreement: their arguments all have their point of departure in some conception of what should be considered the origin, basis or—to use the right word in this context—*foundation* of the political order, whether this foundation is found in self-preservation (as in Hobbes and Spinoza), in freedom (Locke), reason (Rousseau, Kant), or history (Hegel, Marx). And from this foundation they then deduce, in one way or another, the requirements of the good, just, or free political order. Their political theories can therefore be called "foundationalist" in the sense that in all of them a certain principle, an aspect of the citizen or of the social or political order, is conceived as the *foundation* of these theories that enables the political theorist both to explain the political order and to develop proposals for how it should be improved in terms of the proposed foundation.

The same is still true of most, if not all, contemporary political philosophy. Most contemporary political philosophy centers around the debate between the liberals (and the libertarians) on the one hand and the communitarians on the other. That Rawls's profoundly influential liberal political theory as expounded in his *Theory of Justice* (1971), with its celebration of a sovereign Kantian practical reason and its proud claims of being "strictly deductive" and of presenting a "moral geometry,"[5] is foundationalist will surprise few people—despite Rorty's protests.[6] And a great part of contemporary political thought—think of the many writings by Ronald Dworkin, Bruce Ackerman, or Brian Barry—continues to build on the foundationalist thought projected in Rawls's famous book. And we should not be tempted to believe that the kind of critique of Rawls developed by the communitarians automatically implied a rejection of foundationalism as well. For, as Shapiro convincingly demonstrated, Rawls's communitarian enemies, who criticized him for not situating the human individual in a historical, moral, and political context, remained just as much foundationalists as Rawls himself. For them, Aristotelian or Hegelian conceptions of what it is to be a citizen function as the foundation of the political order.[7] Both sects, the liberals (and libertarians such as Robert Nozick) and the communitarians, find their foundational principle in the human individual, though they may differ about how the human individual should be defined. The liberals and the libertarians operate with a completely ahistorical and asociological definition of the human individual and are criticized accordingly by the communitarians. But though we have every reason to prefer the more realistic definition of the human individual of the communitarians to that given by the liberals, the form of both their arguments is fundamentally still the same as the one that structured Hobbes's *Leviathan*. Hence, wherever the participants on this debate may differ, all are foundationalists because of their belief that without foundational principles political philosophy is impossible.

And this obviously raises the question of the possibility of an antifoundationalist political philosophy—for which Machiavelli is obviously a good point of departure. We need only think of Machiavelli's attack on ethics as the foundation of politics, of his conception of politics as a game that we must play with the goddess of Fortune—with ourselves as the stakes of this most dangerous and orderless game, in order to see this. Indeed, the whole point of Machiavelli's political thought is to inculcate the ineluctable truth that each foundation one might consider for politics will, sooner or later, turn out to be quicksand. Hence, for Machiavelli, the really interesting question precisely is how to do politics in the absence of any certain and reliable foundation for our political calculations. This is, as Machiavelli emphasized over and over again, what history teaches us. Moreover, what Machiavelli also derived from history was the recognition of the representationalism inherent in all human (inter)action and, especially, in politics. The representations that we have of each other—and not some fixed and reassuringly intersubjective reality lying behind or beyond these representations—will at all times determine what we shall see as the appropriate thing to do in politics. This automatically brings us to the aestheticism that is shared by history and politics. The aestheticism of history announces itself in the fact that we can only know the past in the form of representations of the past; and the aestheticism of politics makes itself felt in our awareness that the *innere Stimme* of how we represent each other constitutes the so typically kaleidoscopic nature of political reality. This aestheticism, so strikingly shared by politics and history, will inevitably mean the end to all foundationalist dreams for the two of them. For in the country where aestheticism holds sway, foundationalist rules have even less chances of survival than a polar bear in a tropical forest. No less an authority than Kant (and was ever a philosopher more motivated to find rules for all domains of intellectual activity than Kant?) was unequivocal about this "antifoundationalism" of aesthetics:

The concept of beautiful art does not permit the judgment upon the beauty of a product to be derived from any rule which has a concept as its determining ground, and therefore has as its basis a concept of the way in which the product is possible. Therefore beautiful art cannot devise itself the rule according to which it can bring about its product.[8]

What more could the antifoundationalist hope for from the history of philosophy? Taking into account, then, the aestheticism of a political philosophy having history as its point of departure, we can expect that Machiavelli's political philosophy may give us an idea of what an antifoundationalist political philosophy might look like. So let us return to Machiavelli.

THE ORIGINALITY OF MACHIAVELLI

Forty years ago, Isaiah Berlin devoted a long essay to what he referred to as "the originality of Machiavelli."[9] Berlin's point of departure in this brilliant essay was the question of why the spectrum of interpretations of Machiavelli's writings is so much wider than is the case of almost any other great political theorist. Berlin correctly observes that this extreme diversity of interpretations could not possibly be explained by the complexity of Machiavelli's writings or by the obscurity of his style. For no political theorist ever wrote clearer and more transparent prose than Machiavelli.

The explanation instead, ventures Berlin, is that precisely this exceptional clarity makes Machiavelli's text into a mirror in which commentators finds themselves mirrored rather than the author's intentions. When we think we see Machiavelli, in other words, we in fact see ourselves. And if this is true, of course, the observed extraordinarily wide spectrum of Machiavelli interpretations need no longer surprise us. Elaborating this mirror metaphor, one might go on to say that because of its extraordinary message, Machiavelli's *The Prince* more than any other text in the history of political thought pits us squarely face to face with our *own* often unnoticed political and ethical presuppositions. Hence, if you wish to know what kind of political personality you are, read *The Prince* and you will find out. And it follows that what so many commentators from the sixteenth century down to the present day find objectionable[10] in *The Prince* will be our surest guide to the nature of the political presuppositions we all apparently share.

Here is how Berlin effectively identifies these most fundamental and most universally shared presuppositions:

What Machiavelli institutes is something that cuts deeper still—a differentiation between two incompatible ideals of life, and therefore two moralities. One is the morality of the pagan world: its values are courage, vigour, fortitude in adversity, public achievement, order, discipline, happiness, strength, justice and above all the assertion of one's proper claims and the power needed to secure their satisfaction. . . . Against this moral universe stands in the first and foremost place Christian morality.[11]

Later on, Berlin places this observation in a wider framework. He then argues that Machiavelli contests our tacit and most widely shared political presuppositions by his recognition that "there is more than one world, and more than one set of virtues: and confusion between them is disastrous."[12] That is to say, the reality in which we have to act contains *both* these moralities; and it is for that very reason a radically *broken* reality consisting of components that are not so much *incompatible*, as Berlin says himself—for this would still presuppose a shared background necessary for establishing this incompatibility—but rather *incommensurable*. Both pagan and Christian morality will have their own validity under certain circumstances, but there is *no* third ethical language that is neutral with regard to both and to which both can be reduced and in terms of which their conflict can satisfactorily be settled.

Machiavelli knew that the true tragedy about our collective existence is that ideals that we all (rightly) love, revere, and wish to realize as much possible—ideals such as freedom, equality, justice, reasonableness—are more often than not in conflict with each other and that you cannot have one of these ideals without having to sacrifice another. The pantheon of our most lofty political ideals is divided against itself. For example, as Tocqueville would so strikingly demonstrate three centuries later, whoever loves freedom must acquiesce in inequality and whoever loves equality will have to live with infringements upon freedom.[13] And there exists no (third) supreme political virtue that would enable us to definitely settle this hopeless and unending conflict of freedom and equality. They truly are incommensurable. Even more so, the worst political crimes that were committed in this century have often been excused because it was naively believed that the realization of one political virtue, for example equality, would automatically entail the realization of those other sublime virtues of our political pantheon (such as justice or freedom). Indeed, if twentieth-century intellectuals so often served the cause of totalitarianisms, their errors ordinarily had their origins in the embrace of this naive, though admittedly quite natural belief in the ultimate commensurability of all desirable political ideals.

But we need not think here exclusively of the Sartres, the Foucaults (or the Merleau-Pontys and the Le Roy Laduries during a certain phase in their intellectual careers). For most Western intellectuals never questioned the commensurability thesis and always accepted it as a matter of course. Certainly Western intellectuals were aware that such a thing exists as Machiavelli's conception of *raison d'état*, opposing these two (or more) conceptions of the collective good mentioned by Berlin. But, with the possible exception of some of the more perceptive historians (history is the domain where this incommensurability of values is often demonstrated *ad oculos*), they never incorporated it in their *Weltanschauung*. It remained to them much like a foreign language that has been taught us but that we will never be able to speak like a native speaker and in which we never really feel quite at home. The insight was relegated to that storehouse of regrettable certainties whose existence we know about but that we visit as rarely as possible. This may explain why Machiavelli's insight into the brokenness of political reality may seem to most people a fairly trivial and uninteresting truth but that one nevertheless tries to ignore or to dismiss out of hand.

Since few things in the world of the mind are more interesting than this kind of unpleasant and ignored certainty, it will pay to elaborate here Machiavelli's and Berlin's notion of the brokenness of political reality. The true significance and scope of Machiavelli's and Berlin's thesis will only become clear if we are prepared to recognize that it runs counter to almost all of the history of foundationalist Western political thought. As we observed in the previous section, however much foundationalist political theorists like Hobbes, Locke, Kant, Hegel, Marx, and Rawls or Habermas (to include two of our present-day heroes) may differ from each other, they all believe that there is such a thing as a "political reality," with the all-too-often unnoticed *monistic* implications suggested by that term. Their political world is, fundamentally, an *un*broken world, and it owes its unity and coherence to foundational principles such as self-preservation, (dialectical) reason, history, justice, "communicative action," and so on. I hasten to add that these monistic conceptions do not in the least exclude the recognition of the existence of political conflict and struggle: one need only remember Hegel or Marx. But even in their dialectical systems, political reality is fundamentally monistic, because "history," or "dialectical reason" or the "class struggle" in the end encompasses all these conflicts and struggles within one grand and overarching synthesis.

Even more so, foundationalist political systems may well go as far and take struggle and conflict as their very "foundation" and see precisely *there* the monism of political reality. This was the case in Carl Schmitt's ill-famed *Der Begriff des Politischen* (the concept of the political),[14] where the *ius belli* is presented as the foundation not merely of the international political order, but also of civil society. Hence, conflict, division, and struggle are the ultimate *foundation* of Schmitt's political theory, and we need not be surprised by the demonization of politics resulting from this conception of political reality. So, harmony is not necessarily part of how the foundationalist sees social and political reality.

In order to distinguish the adherents of Machiavelli's paradigm of the brokenness of political reality from their foundationalist opponents it may be worthwhile to elaborate this a little further by comparing Machiavelli to Schmitt. When Machiavelli argues for the brokenness of the political domain and openly accepts all the implications of strife, conflict, and struggle that go with that, he is not saying, like Schmitt, that strife, conflict, and struggle are its ultimate *source* and *foundation*. He is saying, rather, that these constitute a permanently present *aspect* of politics. And this is a subtle, though absolutely crucial difference, the difference between the pessimistic view that *all* is evil in life (Schmitt's position) and the more realistic view that evil will always be *part* of our life (which is Machiavelli's position). Or, speaking metaphorically, this is the difference between believing that conflict is the foundation of marriage (Schmitt) or believing that it merely is an inevitable *part* of it (Machiavelli).[15] The indisputable fact that we shall always have to fight in order to realize our political goals and ideals does not imply that fight and struggle are *themselves* the central issue in all politics. Or, to formulate it in the terms that have been used in this section: if the incommensurability of our political ideals invites a continuous fight between them, this fact does not elevate political fight to the status of being a new and extrapolitical ideal. This is the kind of political metaphysics of which Schmitt was guilty in his *The Concept of the Political*: the conflict between political goals and ideals was transformed there into an extra- (and most undesirable) political ideal. But this foundationalist political beard badly needs to be shaven off by Occam's razor.

FOUNDATIONALISM AND ETHICS

I want to emphasize the dangers of this almost universal political foundationalism. Political foundationalism has proven to be a rich and inexhaustible source of political irresponsibility and has often induced political theorists to support even the most objectionable regimes in the history of mankind. And this is not difficult to explain. For if totalitarianism is not implausibly defined as the attempt to reduce the complex variety of political reality to a few simple principles, its elective affinity with foundationalism need not surprise us. J. L. Talmon's, Karl Popper's, or Friedrich von Hayek's critique of totalitarianism and of those natural law philosophies and speculative philosophies of history from which totalitarianism originated, need only be recalled in this context.[16] They showed that the crimes of totalitarianism predictably resulted from these systems' hostility toward all that resisted an easy reduction to foundationalist principles: the physical elimination of the offending (groups of) individuals being the easiest way to effectively achieve this reduction.

Obviously, I do not wish to imply that such utterly respectable theorists like Kant, Bentham, Rawls, or Habermas have actually contributed to the abject cause of totalitarianism. Even the merest hint in that direction would be a ridiculous and most perverse distortion of their political thought and hurt the accuser far more than the accused. What I am saying is that these systems are often insufficiently secured against the totalitarian temptation and customarily succeed in avoiding this temptation only at the price of inconsistency, irrelevance, or a candid confession of inapplicability. Take the Rawls of *A Theory of Justice*: only thanks to the pronounced normativity of the theory of justice proposed there and thanks to his sovereign disregard for how his theory should be put into practice can he evade an embrace of the outrightly tyrannic state that the realization of his political program would inevitably require. Only because he so openly speaks the discourse of normativity can he avoid getting entangled in the kind of problems occasioned by the brokenness of political reality that authors such as Machiavelli see as central to the politician's concerns. For the discourse of normativity creates around itself a reassuringly rationalist and monological[17] pseudo reality without all the unexpected, unpleasant, and painful paradoxes in which the brokenness of political reality presents itself to us.

Speaking more generally, ethics is the field of gravity that is generated by the black hole of practical irrelevance, into which so many high-pitched political systems have already disappeared. Ethics is or seems to be so much the easiest and securest way to political "truth" but is, precisely because of this, without any real value in our search of political truth. The situation is strikingly similar to what Popper had in mind with his well-known attack on the logical-positivist thesis that probability is our criterion for scientific truth. For, as Popper argued against the logical positivists, if we accept this criterion, statements like "Tomorrow it will rain, or it will not rain tomorrow" are the very acme of scientific truth, since whatever happens tomorrow will not disconfirm this statement. Clearly, as Popper went on to say, statements like these are of no help if we wish to get the kind of useful information about actual reality that science has always been so good at providing.

And so it is with ethics. Ethics teaches us (with Kant) that we ought not to steal, or (with Rorty) that we should avoid cruelty, and so on. But all this is as true as it is useless (and vice versa). No sane and sensible person would wish or has ever wished to deny such normative claims. Such claims belong to the realm of what Aristotle described as "philosophical wisdom"—and we saw in Chapter 2 how idle the problems of philosophical wisdom are if compared to those of practical wisdom. For example, what should we do when ethical norms, such as freedom and equality, conflict? Or when democracy is threatened in a country where democracy has always been the mask for corruption, nepotism, and violence? Or when in some young African country political violence seems to be the only alternative to the nation's disintegration? Should we then be content to show which of the two (or more) conflicting values should take precedence over the other(s) and add with Kantian resignation: *fiat iustitia pereat mundus*? Should we then try to spell out the nature of the conflict in terms of some more fundamental value, in the hope that this more fundamental value will show us the way out of the conflict? Or should we simply add some more abstract ethical argument by focusing on the conflict of values? But little is to be expected from approaches like these. For as both historians and politicians know, if we are confronted with dilemmas like these everything will depend so much on context and actual detail that values more or less disappear behind the problem of their application to context and to actual detail. Such was, again, the essence of Burke's (Machiavellian) argument against the French revolutionaries as expounded in Chapter 2: "practical wisdom" will swallow here all of "political wisdom," to use Aristotle's terminology. When confronted with such dilemmas, pure and historically undiluted ethics will forever be caught in paradoxes; and it is therefore practical wisdom, the *phroonesis* of the (Machiavellian) politician that will then be all-decisive and from which the best outcome only is to be expected. Ethics will then ordinarily make things worse rather than better.

In sum, the sad fact about (the political uses of) ethics is that the more we will all agree about the rationality of an (ethical) argument, the less its political value and significance will be. This is not to say that political decisions should be included in the domain of the *arcanum imperii,* discussed in Chapter 1; hence to a sphere lying outside rational argument. My claim is, rather, that in politics *another* way of thinking supersedes ethical argument—and I hope to be able to say something useful about this in the remainder of this chapter.

FOUNDATIONALISM, ANTIFOUNDATIONALISM, AND DEMOCRACY

It will be worthwhile to relate the foregoing argument against (foundationalist) ethics to Rorty's thesis of the antifoundationalism of democracy. I am thinking here of Rorty's essay entitled "The Priority of Democracy to Philosophy," which, thanks to the quality and exceptionally wide scope of its argument, I consider to be one of the most important contributions to contemporary political thought that have been written in the past few decades. Rorty develops his position in the form of a commentary on Rawls's later writings, where, according to Rorty, Rawls successfully distances himself from the foundationalism that one might still discern in his *Theory of Justice*. Rorty follows Rawls when the latter argues that "philosophy as the search for truth about an independent metaphysical and moral order cannot . . . provide a workable and shared basis for a political conception of justice in a democratic society." We should, therefore, confine ourselves to collecting "such settled convictions as the belief in religious toleration and the rejection of slavery" and then try to "organize" the moral intuitions "implicit in these convictions into a coherent conception of justice."[18] Or, as Rawls is quoted elsewhere by Rorty in his essay:

> Justice as fairness is a political conception in part because it starts from within a certain political tradition. We hope that this conception of justice may at least be supported by what we may call "overlapping consensus," that is, by a consensus that includes all the opposing philosophical and religious doctrines likely to persist and to gain adherents in a more or less just constitutional democratic society.[19]

The crucial idea is that politics and political justice need not and even should not pronounce on the philosophical and metaphysical foundations of our moral and political convictions, but be content to accept them for what they are and then organize them into a conception of justice more or less acceptable to all of us. Of course, this should not in the least prevent us from speculating about these philosophical and metaphysical foundations, but such speculation is, as Rorty emphasizes, an essentially "private" affair that does not belong to the sphere of politics in the proper sense of the word. It follows that as citizens and as social theorists we can afford to be indifferent to philosophical disagreements about the moral or ethical "foundations" of the social and political order. In this way a neat separation is effected between the philosophical effort to define the moral foundations of the political order on the one hand and the functioning of this order on the other. And about the latter we can say, that "truth, viewed in the Platonic way, as the grasp of what Rawls calls 'an order antecedent to and given to us', is simply not relevant to democratic politics. So philosophy, as the explanation of the relation between such an order and human nature, is not relevant either. When the two come into conflict, democracy takes precedence over philosophy."[20] Hence, what is wrong with looking for ethical, or more generally, philosophical foundations of democratic political practice. Clearly, Rorty's argument shows at least a certain parallelism with Machiavelli's and Berlin's thesis of the brokenness of political reality.

I find Rorty's conclusions both convincing and satisfactory. Nevertheless, two problems remain. A first problem has already been mentioned by Rorty himself. For it might be objected (as he writes at the end of his essay) that this division of labor between philosophy and politics will again require some philosophical justification and that would give back to philosophy all its foundational prerogatives. In connection with this objection, Rorty argues that (1) such philosophical justifications necessarily rely upon some conception of the human self, and (2) his (and Rawls's) minimal description of the task of democratic politics can do without such conceptions of the self. We may grant to Rorty the second thesis, but it is less obvious that only a conception of the self can supply the link between philosophy and politics; perhaps, but this would require some extra argument. Besides, the many foundationalist political theorists who see it as their main task to give a philosophical justification of the kind of political order they cherish will probably argue that Rorty's division of labor between philosophy and politics begs the question at precisely the point that is crucial to the whole enterprise of political philosophy. For, they will protest, if a conception of the human self would really prove to be an unreliable foundation of politics, this should only be taken as an indication that the desired foundation of politics is to be looked for elsewhere—for example, in some basic fact(s) about human society or in history.

Leaving aside what may be said about these issues, there is another, and probably more interesting, problem with Rorty's (and Rawls's) division of labor between philosophy and democratic politics. In setting the stage for his argument, Rorty quotes Rawls as saying that we need a conception of political justice that will "allow for a diversity of doctrines and the plurality of conflicting, and indeed incommensurable conceptions of the good affirmed by the members of existing democratic societies."[21] The individual citizens of a democratic society will most often cherish incommensurable political ideals and, as Rawls and Rorty argue, it is essentially a political and not a philosophical problem of how to deal with this datum.

We may agree with them about this, but a new and more difficult problem will present itself when we are confronted, not with the incommensurability between *A*'s and *B*'s political opinions, but with the incommensurability of political ideals themselves. To begin with, it should be observed that we should carefully distinguish between a conflict of political opinions on the one hand and a conflict of political ideals on the other. Opinions have no existence without the people who hold them, whereas political ideals live a wholly autonomous life in the realm of logic. We cannot properly speak about opinions without taking into account how the people holding them deal with them, that is, how they interpret them, how they relate them to the other opinions they have, or what relative importance they will grant to them. All these (practical) aspects are absent from political ideals themselves: a political ideal is a mere abstract theoretical claim—and logic decides about what we can and cannot do with political ideals. More specifically, you can have a democratic decision procedure about opinions; but such decision procedures are just as impossible with regard to political ideals as we could democratize the debate about scientific truth.

So, as soon as we have to do with pure political ideals, we can no longer rely upon democratic political procedures in order to iron things out in a politically decent way. It follows that if you have a really difficult political problem that you wish to solve, and if you do not know how to get beyond the paradoxes it poses, you should try to couch it in the discourse of opinion rather than in that of political ideals. If your problem has the form of a conflict of political ideals, your only hope is that you may be mistaken when thinking that there really is a conflict, for if there truly is a conflict, you can only fight it out and see who is strongest. Sheer physical strength will then be decisive, and you simply have no other arbiter. In this sense logic and sheer physical strength belong, strangely enough, to one and the same world; namely the world where we lack humble opinion in order to take the pressure off. As soon as political logic is victorious over opinion, civil war is at hand. However, no such appeal to violence—as will be inevitable in the case of a conflict of political ideals—is called for in case of a conflict of opinion. For you can do business with opinions, an opinion merely is what it means to you—and such a relaxed attitude is impossible with logic, and, hence, with political ideals. You may then find that you do not really care so much about a specific political ideal (and it is only the discourse of opinion that permits you to make such a discovery at all), so that you are willing to surrender this ideal to somebody else who feels far more strongly about it, even though you remain convinced that you were completely right when believing in this ideal. But you are prepared to give away this ideal only on the condition that the other may, under certain circumstances, display the same generosity to you. And what initially divided you may then unite you: for this display of generosity by both of you will then sow the seeds of trust and of mutual confidence in the relationship between the two of you.

So it always is far easier and certainly far more productive to deal with persons having incommensurable political opinions than with those incommensurable political opinions (or ideals) themselves; and it may well be argued that it has precisely been one of the outstanding successes of democracy to translate incommensurability from the latter context to the so much more manageable former one. Put differently, democracy should not primarily be seen, perhaps, as the political system involving the whole nation in the process of public decision making, but the political system transforming political ideals into political opinions, more exactly, into persons with opinions—for, in fact, this has been its truly unique and epochal discovery and why it has been so much more successful in assuring civil peace than any other political system.

But at the level of the incommensurability of political ideals themselves—one may think of, for example, of the incommensurability of freedom and equality that was mentioned above—political problems will therefore stubbornly remain "philosophical" in Rorty's sense of the word. And the weakness of Rorty's argument is to identify the conflict between political ideals with the conflict between persons. However—to take again this example—the conflict between equality and freedom may present itself with no less urgency to one and the same *individual* politician, as it may divide the *group* of all the adherents of equality and that other *group* of the adherents of freedom. But in the former case democratic decision procedures will be of no avail.

It should be observed, furthermore, that political problems seem to have a regrettable preference for this quasi-"philosophical" level. Rorty already emphasized himself that Rawls's argument originated from his preoccupation with toleration. Indeed, Rawls's and Rorty's proposal to take political disagreement out of the hands of philosophers and theologians and to entrust them to democratic procedures is a most welcome and ingenious invitation to tolerance. But tolerance has to do with the freedom that we allow to other people to think or to do certain things, hence with the *removal* of certain issues from the political agenda rather than with *making certain decisions* about issues of political urgency (such as the issue of what is, under the present circumstances, the right balance between freedom and equality). Speaking more generally, Rawls's and Rorty's argument is most convincing where we begin to turn our backs to politics, rather than when the politician really has to cut the Gordian knot of some nasty political dilemma. It must have been the memory of the toleration issue mentioned just now that tempted both Rawls and Rorty to turn their backs on political decision making in this way.

Philosophy is both more and less a part of doing politics than is suggested by Rawls's and Rorty's division of labor between the two. Philosophy is more prominent in politics since dilemmas such as the equality/freedom paradox invite or even oblige us in actual political practice to look at them from a quasi-philosophical perspective. Because of the incommensurability of the two political ideals, Rawls's hope of achieving "overlapping consensus" is doomed to failure from the very outset. And perhaps it is the very heart of politics to put us face to face with this kind of refractory problem that simply does not seem to permit rational solutions and that, in this way, confronts us with that brokenness of political reality that Machiavelli and Berlin indicated.

On the other hand, philosophy is further removed from politics than suggested by Rawls and Rorty. For the achievement of an "overlapping consensus," the attempt to achieve an optimum integration of the politically relevant elements in existing philosophical and religious doctrines, is for two reasons a not very realistic account of the politician's job. In the first place, this account seems to overintellectualize politics and thereby to eliminate from politics something that is absolutely central to it. As we shall see in greater detail in Chapter 8, politics aims not at consensus but at compromise. And it belongs to the nature of political compromise that political (philosophical or religious) disagreements are simply taken for what they are, and that one therefore tries to invent some kind of political *juste-milieu* with which most parties can more or less live. Though politicians may try to convince the electorate of the correctness of their opinions, they will rarely do that with each other. This is not because they consider each other to be blockheaded dogmatists inaccessible to rational argument but because they know that they are not expected to do just this sort of thing: it is their task to negotiate the best compromise *on the basis* of existing political disagreement while *not* blurring political disagreement in the process. In the second place, Rawls and Rorty's conception of the task of the politician is too passivist; the politician does not consider political (or philosophical and religious) disagreement with the same detachment that we expect from the historian. For politicians are always and inevitably partisans in political debate and should be so in order to guide politics in the direction desired by them and their political friends. So the regime of the philosophical and the political is in actual political practice different from the division of labor between them proposed by Rawls and Rorty.

However, all this does not undermine Rawls's and Rorty's arguments; rather, it lends extra force to them. For if the upshot of their argument is an attack on the search for foundations and an adhortation to "stay on the surface, philosophically speaking" in political practice (as Rorty himself put it), the suggestion of the foregoing is, rather, that we simply *cannot but stay on the surface.* There simply is no other possibility. This is the lesson we may learn from Machiavelli's and Berlin's thesis of the brokenness of political reality. For this thesis entails that the search for philosophical foundations— as embodied in some ethical or political general theory pretending to offer us such foundations—will sooner or later always confront us with unsolvable dilemmas. And then the "surface" of conflict is all that is left to us; there is no "depth" anymore. In disciplines like logic and mathematics (and perhaps some of the sciences) foundations may give us certainty. However, in disciplines like politics and history it is the other way round: here certainty has an affinity with the surface while dissolving into paradoxes and contradictions as soon as we attempt to move toward abstraction and depth.

Pascal already distinguished between *l'esprit fin* and *l'esprit géomètre.*

The difference is that the "foundational" principles of the latter require us to abstract from daily reality, but as soon as we have done so, they will demonstrate themselves with great clarity: for *l'esprit géomètre*, "principles are self-evident, but removed from common sense, so that it requires an effort to turn our gaze in the right direction: but if you look in the right direction, these principles cannot fail to be seen." With regard to *l'esprit fin* it is the other way round: here all the relevant principles lie on the surface of daily reality, they are obvious and easily perceivable to anybody, and the only capacity required is to see them all, but precisely this is very difficult since we always tend to miss some of these things even though they lie on the surface of daily life: "With the *l'esprit de finesse* the principles are part of common usage and before the eyes of anybody. You need not turn your gaze in a certain direction, nor to do violence to yourself; it's merely a matter of having good eyes, but *this* is essential, for these principles are so variegated and in such great number, that it is impossible not to fail to see some of them."[22] And this is how things are in political practice and in the writing of history.

In sum, we must agree with the later Rawls and with Rorty that politics is not foundational. But their argument to that effect has its shortcomings insofar as it still insufficiently demarcates the domain of philosophy from that of politics. Especially in the case of Rorty, there is the tendency to tie the distinction between politics and philosophy to the distinction between public and private life. But this parallelism is not without its problems, as we have seen. For the brokenness of political reality may sometimes confront us with a tragic dimension of human existence that must affect us also as human individuals and stimulate our inclination to "philosophical" reflection. On the other hand, in political compromise the fruits of private, philosophical reflection will be dealt with as if they were mere commodities.[23] Thus, the political sphere brutally invades the sphere of private philosophical inquiry. It need not surprise us, therefore, that this incomplete parallelism also invites Rorty sometimes to sin against his own division of labor between politics and philosophy—as is the case when at the end of his essay he counters *political* opponents of constitutional democracy, such as Loyola and Nietzsche, by means of a *philosophical* argument.[24] Hence, we will agree with Rawls's and Rorty's antifoundationalism, but we had better exchange their arguments for the more effective ones that we may find in Machiavelli's and Berlin's insight into the brokenness of political reality.

THE NETWORK, THE EXPERT, AND
REPRESENTATIVE DEMOCRACY

General predictions about the future of the nation-state are impossible.[1] Admittedly, at present no realistic scenario is conceivable that would
lead to the end of the United States or Japan as an independent nation-
state. On the other hand, though not likely, it is not completely unthinkable that the process of European integration will ultimately result in the
erosion of proud and old nation-states like France or Germany and in
their gradual absorption into a new European community.[2] It is dispu-
table, however, whether even such an unlikely development would really
be a decisive argument against the future viability of the nation-state. For
European integration could well be interpreted, of course, as the effort to
create a *new* nation-state that is expected to be a more successful nation-
state than its individual predecessors. Such a development should then be
seen as proof of the remarkable resilience rather than of the obsoleteness
of the nation-state. Similarly, the creation of the Dutch Republic, in the
sixteenth century, out of the seven individual provinces preceding it was a
phenomenon characteristic of that period of nation building rather than
an exception to it. In sum, the phenomenon of political integration (on
whatever scale) is by no means a decisive argument against the durability
of the nation-state.

But recently a number of more compelling arguments against the future viability of the nation-state have been made. All these arguments have
in common the idea of a "displacement of politics," that is, the idea that

the kind of decisions that will shape our future lives are no longer made on a national level and by national governments, but in myriad less conspicuous places such as in the boards of great companies, the laboratories of scientists, or the complex and fragmented interaction between state and civil society. Politics has moved away from the center that it traditionally had in parliament or congress and has, so to speak, been scattered throughout society.[3] Furthermore, because of globalization these fragments have now been thrown about all over the globe: it may well be that decisions made by the board of some national bank, or of a company in a country you never visited or even know of, or the introduction of some new technology invented in some remote part of the world will affect you more directly than many of the decisions of your own national government. In this view, politics has repeated the same movement from integrated center to fragmented periphery that postmodernists have always seen as the common denominator of all developments in contemporary culture. And the conclusion would have to be that politics should abandon its traditional pretension to be the forum where decisions are reached about our collective future; the thesis of the "displacement of politics" leads, in this way, to the even more radical thesis of the "end of politics." Thus, the postmodernist diagnosis of contemporary politics would, paradoxically, coincide with the old, typically modernist Saint-Simonian ideal of the replacement of *le gouvernement des hommes* by *l'administration des choses*. The whole complicated political machinery of representative democracy, as it developed in the course of two centuries, would thus have been unmasked by these contemporary developments as a by now atavistic irrelevancy that may well satisfy our illusionistic desire that collective decisions are still possible and do still matter, but that is completely out of touch with these new and essentially apolitical or postpolitical realities.

A striking example of this kind of argument against the future viability of the (democratic) nation-state was formulated some years ago by Jean-Marie Guéhenno in his much discussed *La Fin de la démocratie*.[4] Guéhenno begins with the unexceptionable observation that our criteria for measuring political power and success have dramatically changed in recent decades. Political power and success no longer have their condition in the mastery over as large as possible a part of territory but in the participation in a "network."[5] His argument can be summarized as follows.

Until the end of the Cold War, or even until the sudden and unexpected demise of the Soviet regimes after 1989, the paradigm of political power, as old as the pharaohs, was the possession of and power over as many countries and people as possible. But with the ultimate triumph of economics over all its rival foundations of political power, the possession of countries and people became a precarious and counterproductive political aspiration. It is illustrative that the West made no very serious, and certainly no very enthusiastic, effort to fill the political vacuum that came into being after the collapse of the Soviet Union; the proposal to extend NATO to the East—though done in the end—was widely resisted on the basis of the sensible consideration that the risks of this extension of political responsibility would in all likelihood outweigh its gains. And, speaking more generally, it is now generally recognized that the possession of (and responsibility for) economically less developed countries is a handicap rather than an advantage. Until quite recently, nations always wanted to integrate as large as possible part of the world within the sphere of their political influence—and this aspiration was the cause of their many (imperialist) wars. But by now this geographical fixation has almost completely disappeared. In this way we now seem to have reached the nearly complete opposite of imperialist colonialism: no contemporary decent Western democracy would be willing to reassume responsibility of one of its former colonies even if offered as a kind of political present to it: the present would undoubtedly prove to be a bottomless pit for its economic and political capital. Far greater gains are to be expected from the perfection of its own economic strengths than from (re)gaining possession of an economically weaker country. One need only remember here how much Germany, that otherwise so formidable economic locomotive, is still groggy from the absorption of the former German Democratic Republic. And this is also why nobody cares about Africa anymore.

Far more important therefore, according to Guéhenno, is the extent to which a nation—or, rather, its citizens—has access to and is active in international economic, financial, scientific, or technological networks. A network (*réseau*) consists of a number of persons or corporate bodies succeeding in dominating or even monopolizing for themselves an area of civil society in nonhierarchic cooperation thanks to their excellent and unchallenged expertise in this specific area. Though the network always aims at exclusiveness, it is completely open as far as participation is concerned: anybody having the required expertise can or is even eagerly invited and expected to join it. The network therefore is a paradoxical combination of extreme openness and extreme closure. Characteristically, Guéhenno clarifies his conception of the network with reference to the decision-making process in Japanese companies. Crucial there, as he points out, is the absence of a central and supreme decision-making body and of a clearly hierarchically structured debate preparing decisions. What exists, rather, is an "empty center" (of which the Japanese emperor is the image and prototype), while decision making is embedded in a complex system of mutual dependencies.[6] It is worthwhile to point out at this stage that the elective affinities of the network and the Japanese paradigm of political power strongly suggest the weaknesses of the network and its fundamental incapacity to adequately replace traditional centers of decision making either on the scale of a company or on that of a whole nation. For is not Japan's all too apparent failure to solve the economic and political problems facing it for more than a decade a decisive and eloquent argument against the network as a new and more up-to-date model or paradigm of (political) power?

Then follows the decisive step in Guéhenno's argument. For he goes on to compare the network with (representative) democracy. The comparison makes sense because the network (as we saw a moment ago) is no less egalitarian and no less effective in the generation and distribution of power than is (representative) democracy—or perhaps it is even more so. Consequently, it is Guéhenno's view that nothing that used to be done by representative democracy could not be done better and more efficiently by the network. Indeed, we had better start liking the network, since, whatever our opinions about it may be, it will certainly supersede democracy as we know it. For the network cuts right across all the political, institutional, and organizational textures of traditional democracy as it developed within the framework of the nation-state. The network is supra- or infranational; it eludes the grasp of the nation-state and its decisions. Or, if the nation-state attempts to interfere with the workings of the network, the damage it thereby does to itself will in most cases exceed the damage that it does to the network.

Next, the fragmentation of each problem presenting itself via the network, the subtle process of the countless "microdecisions" by means of which the network, so to speak, "digests" a new problem, are both alien and superior to the centrally organized decision making by the nation-state. Opposite to the supple and quasi-biological way of functioning of the network we have the rigid, quasi-physical functioning of the democratic nation-state.[7] And simply phrasing it in this way makes it abundantly clear once again which of these two forms of democracy is superior to the other. In one word, in the Darwinian struggle of different forms of government a new and immensely successful mutation has recently come into being—and whoever tries to ignore its presence will inevitably find himself on the side of the losers in history.

THE NETWORK AND ITS DISCONTENTS

For a proper evaluation of Guéhenno's thesis, our best point of departure will be one of his own metaphors for the network: "To take another image, one could compare the network to the human brain, where the connections between neurons is achieved by billions of electrical impulses functioning all the better to the extent that the neurons are surrounded by a perfectly homogeneous environment. In a society in which power has become 'relational', social 'conductivity' has become essential."[8] As is so often the case in sociopolitical reality, an appropriate metaphor is a better guarantee for stimulating new insight than a thorough and penetrating analysis. To be more specific, it is precisely this metaphor that will enable us to become aware of the strengths and weaknesses of the network as described by Guéhenno. On the one hand, this image of the network as myriad neurons permitting an infinity of potential fruitful contacts will deeply enhance our respect for the subtlety of the network. On the other, it must strike us that Guéhenno reduces here the functioning of the human brain to what happens at the level of neurophysiology while leaving out of his account the level of conscious human thought. The suggestion of his metaphor is, therefore, that in the network "thought" does not really transcend or go beyond the network's functioning (as a quasi brain). From this perspective there is something peculiarly "brainless" about the network-as-brain: Guéhenno's network-brain is reduced to its functioning at microlevel while the (macro)-dimension of thought and of consciousness does not seem to have anywhere its proper analogue in his use of the metaphor. Consequently, the suggestion is that Guéhenno's networks may function at this microlevel better than any previous human institution but that it is unable to "think," that is, to think about itself, about the world outside itself and about its relationship to the outside world. The world of the network—such is the suggestion of the metaphor—is a world that is wholly enclosed within itself: these networks are exclusively interested in their own (optimum) performance, but do not worry about their relationship to other networks, or, speaking more generally, to anything taking place outside themselves. The network is essentially "solipsistic" and remains therefore strangely blind to what is outside itself in spite of its capacity to develop a tremendous and irresistible power in one quite specific area of civil society.[9]

This insight into the nature of the network takes on an extra and paradoxical characteristic in light of the extreme vulnerability that Guéhenno himself also claims for the network: "If a strong force makes itself felt at some point of its delicate texture, the texture will immediately be torn apart."[10] For example, the immense power of the supremely successful financial network may be broken from one day to the next if national states were to follow the advice to take certain steps in that direction by economists like Milton Friedman and Jeffrey Sachs.[11] And this vulnerability is all the more remarkable since it is primarily a vulnerability for adverse social and economic conditions that have been generated by the network itself—as also is exemplified by the financial network and its tendency to produce effects that hurt itself. Particularly instructive here is Guéhenno's speculation at the end of his book that at some point in the future ecological problems may mean the end of our trust in the network and force us to recognize that a *political* intervention will be necessary again: "The ecologist movement, unlike the defenders of the environment preceding it, refuses to make man into the measure of all things and is in search of the principles of an order going beyond ourselves."[12] The network's solipsism makes it insensitive to this kind of principle transcending its own logic and only thanks to a *political* decision can these principles be introduced into our decision-making procedures. And it may well be the very impact of the network on the environment that will invite or even oblige politics to reassert itself to the detriment of the network. The networks somehow involved in the exploitation of our environment have, so to speak, an innate tendency to fall victim to their own allergies or autoimmune diseases; they seem to secrete what can result in their own demise.

The solipsism of the network may introduce us to features that it may share with older and better known social or political structures and where these conflict with (representative) democracy in a way requiring our attention in the present context. Our thinking about networks *avant la lettre* will call to mind the world of scholars and universities. Especially communities of scholars all working within one domain of scholarly research will in all relevant aspects satisfy Guéhenno's description of the network as given above. The community of experts in a field like economics, medicine, or psychology present us with this combination of closure, openness, and the inward gaze that is so characteristic of the network. Hence, the age of the network also is the age of the expert.

SLAMA ON THE AGE OF THE EXPERT

In his bleak account of contemporary representative democracy, Alain-Gérard Slama attempts to show how much it suffered from the advent of the expert in politics. Since Daniel Bell's *End of Ideology* of more then forty years ago, it has been pointed out again and again that science and technocracy may help us to solve urgent social and political problems. For example, the anticonception pill could help to simply eliminate most of the problems caused by overpopulation in some African and Asian countries; new and better techniques of agriculture may be quite successful in the struggle against poverty and the social problems accompanying it. And econometry may show who is right and who is wrong in the traditional ideological debate about government spending that used to oppose the political left to the political right. Though it should be added to this last example that for a long time econometrists themselves were no less divided about this issue than politicians (and the ideologies represented by them) had always been since the social question entered the political agenda one and a half centuries ago. If, by now, the political right seems to have won this last debate, this is due less to the cogency of the arguments of anti–government-spending econometrists than to the fact that politicians gradually recognized that government spending simply did not produce the results so eagerly expected from it. Hence, hard economic realities rather than econometric theories put an end to this specific ideological debate (for the time being, at least). But perhaps we need econometrists to tell us what economic realities are. Be that as it may, no reasonable observer of our time would wish to deny that there is much truth in Bell's thesis of the neutralizing or depoliticizing effects of science and technology.

But Slama's thesis is a different and more subtle one. He wants to make clear that the expert does not put a rigorous end to political debate but rather achieves its dislocation and perversion. We may acquiesce in or even be happy with Bell's technocratic prophecies, but those suggested by Slama should really worry us. For a correct assessment of Slama's thesis of the dislocation of politics by the expert and of its extent, we should observe that the public use of the expert is mainly restricted to the private sphere. At least this is where they are most effective and have most authority. The prototypical expert is, we may well presume, the medical specialist taking care of our health, which is the private preoccupation par excellence. Hence, according to Slama, the (political) regime of the expert had to result in a strong emphasis on the private, at the expense of the public sphere, in an ascendency of negative over positive freedom, and, above all, in a strong fixation on those typical expert's problems as are related to issues of health, safety, and insurance. The result is that political problems tend become the kind of problems that an insurance company has to deal with.[13] And just as an insurance company only insures risks without having either the capacity or the pretension to do anything about these risks themselves, so the state seems to have gradually abandoned its pretensions to effectively guide society on its way to the future. Indeed, the state seems to have become a huge insurance company insuring us against risks too dangerous for other, private insurance companies, while political debate has been reduced to a debate about the amount of the policy to be paid and how best to distribute its payment over civil society as a whole. The result is an ironic disproportion between the size of the state and the aims it sets itself: we pay more to the state than ever before in history, but less than ever do its actions make any real difference to the kind of world in which we live. Even more so, the state deliberately tries to make itself as invisible as possible and insofar as political decisions are still reached at all they seem to just "happen" (in the same way that changes in the weather just happen) instead of being the result of a public and political debate.[14] All volunteerism has disappeared from politics: our future has somehow been fixed already by some anonymous force, and politics has no other function than to accustom us to this future.

Slama makes us aware, furthermore, of the paradoxical intimacy of expert opinion and moral or ethical judgment. We are naturally inclined to model their relationship on the *is* versus *ought* dichotomy. We believe that the expert speaks the discourse of the *is* and is the paradigmatically impartial observer of how things simply *are*, whereas the moralist focuses on the different question of how the world ought to be. Obviously, one cannot deny that there is or at least has been much truth in this so natural and apparently unobjectionable picture. But according to Slama contemporary moralism is no longer an "involved" moralism; it is no longer inspired by the belief that moral conviction might make a difference to how the world fares. On the contrary, moral conviction has become the accomplice of the sciences and of the expertises of the *is* by restricting itself to a comment *ex post facto*. Contemporary moralism originates in the desire "to get things dispatched in good conscience," and the expert would be only too happy to be as helpful as possible in satisfying this desire. And indeed, who else but the moralist would or could still speak after the expert has presented to us his indisputable views and recommendations? Nothing more is left to us then besides the self-satisfaction of the moral judgment after the expert has been as successful as always in taking an issue beyond the horizon of us all. We recognize that the world is how the expert tells us that it is, congratulate ourselves with our self-righteous moral judgment of the world—and breathe a resigned sigh. Hence, to the degree that our society became ever more complicated and ever more the domain of the expert, it became an ever more attractive option to proudly advertise one's noncommittal moral superiority.

Slama reminds us in this context of Milgram's famous experiment in which ordinary people proved to be prepared to inflict on other people electric shocks that would have killed them if it were not just an experiment. As Slama insists, the truly interesting thing about the experiment was that the reluctance to inflict any further shocks increased tremendously as soon as the participants in the experiment were left to themselves and each other to discuss the experiment. But as long as the experts were around they tended to ignore their moral inhibitions and to go along with the experts in their recommendations not to worry too much about them.[15] The lesson to be learned from the Milgram's experiment, according to Slama, is that it will rarely be difficult for the expert to corrupt our moral judgment and that in practice therefore the distance between technocratic knowledge—the *is*—and moral judgment—the *ought*—is far smaller than we like to believe.[16] In our age of the network and of the expert, moralism is easily led astray in the tension between fact and value. Hence Slama's slogan "Who wants to be an angel will come out as a beast," and, self-evidently, the provocative title of his book.

THE BROKENNESS OF THE POLITICAL DOMAIN

We are naturally inclined to value concord, union, and consensus in politics: for does not all politics aim at the reconciliation of conflict and at the replacement of disorder and disunion by order and union? And is this not also why we are naturally inclined to expect great benefits from the efforts of the expert? For the expert speaks the language that may bring together conflicting parties; his expert knowledge is, essentially, an *impartial* knowledge enabling him to transcend the narrow partiality of conflicting political parties. The expert unites what was "broken" and in disunion; and his whole effort consists in the development of the potentially unificatory (expert) language making all (political) positions commensurable and reconcilable. This is where the appeal of the expert originates, and that of the network in which the experts have organized themselves.

From this point of view Machiavelli's eulogy on conflict and disunion is of all the more interest: it exemplifies a style of political thought wholly at odds with that of the expert and the network as discussed above. The network and the expert abhor (political) conflict, whereas Machiavelli sees in conflict the preservation of freedom and of political and social success. For example, regarding Rome's amazing rise to power Machiavelli writes:

> I say that to me it appears that those who damn the tumults between the nobles and the plebs blame those things that were the first cause of keeping Rome free; and that they consider the noises and the cries that would arise in such tumults more than the good effects that they engendered. They do not consider that in every republic there are two diverse humors, that of the people and that of the great, *and that all the laws that are made in favor of freedom arise from their disunion,* as can easily be seen to have occurred in Rome.[17]

The explanation Machiavelli gives for his counterintuitive praise of conflict and disunion is that good laws are those that are satisfactory to most people, and one can only decide in favor of what is satisfactory to most people on the condition that free rein is left to the people's ambition and that people are left relatively free to express their desires. And doing so will naturally and inevitably sow the seeds of discord, struggle, and tumult in a republic. But these tumults are beneficial, for only they can make it clearly felt what the desires of the people are and thus how the well-being of the republic can best be realized. "The desires of free people are rarely pernicious to freedom because they arise either from being oppressed or from suspicion that they may be oppressed,"[18] as Machiavelli writes in a statement that may well be considered the first plea in favor of modern, representative democracy in history.

We may discern in Machiavelli's statement such a plea in favor of representative democracy (decried so much by Guéhenno as an outmoded political model) if we relate it to two other arguments in his writings. In the first place, Machiavelli sees the people who govern and the people who are governed—the nobles and the ignobles in his terminology—as inspired by a different political desire:

Without doubt, if one considers the end of the nobles and of the ignobles, one will see great desire to dominate in the former, and in the latter only desire not to be dominated; and, in consequence, a greater will to live free, being less able to hope to usurp it than are the great. So that when those who are popular are posted as the guard of freedom, it is reasonable that they have more care for it, and since they are not able to seize it, they do not permit others to seize it.[19]

And it is the balance of these two desires that is the condition and guarantee for good government and the people's freedom. From the desire not to be dominated originates the people's freedom, and the desire to dominate makes even the noble into a partisan of the people's freedom, for he knows that others will soon be taking his place if he does not sufficiently care about it. It follows from Machiavelli's account that freedom should not exclusively be located in or associated with either the nobles or the people; freedom rather requires a specific form of *interaction* between the two and can only come into being *between* them instead of having its exclusive locus in the people (as the believers in popular sovereignty always argue).

This insight can be elaborated further of we think of the following passage from the dedication to Lorenzo de Medici with which Machiavelli begins his infamous *The Prince*:

Nor I hope will it be considered presumptuous for a man of low and humble status to dare discuss and lay down the law about how princes should rule; because just as men who are sketching the landscape put themselves down in the plain to study the nature of the mountains and the highlands, and so to study the low-lying land they put themselves high on the mountains, so, to comprehend fully the nature of the people, one must be a prince, and to comprehend fully the nature of princes one must be an ordinary citizen.[20]

This aesthetic metaphor of the relationship between the prince and the people adds a new and extra dimension to what was said a moment ago. We observed that the prince and the people need each other for the cause of freedom; here a metaphorical explanation is given of this mutual dependence. For it is Machiavelli's *perspectivist* thesis here that such self-knowledge as the people (or the prince) may have will prove to be insufficient in order to guarantee freedom and good government. It is only the people's and the prince's *other*—the prince and the people, respectively—that are capable of such knowledge and insight. Self-knowledge is characteristically insufficient in politics (where everything that is of interest happens *between* us and the other and not in the domain that is the potential object of self-knowledge).

Of specific interest in this aesthetic metaphor is that it so much emphasizes the irreducibility of these two different perspectives. There is no common background to these two perspectives that would enable us to translate the insights gained from the former into insights to be expected from the latter. For any two perspectives on something there is not a third perspective from which these two can be derived; nor can any perspective—that is, seeing something from a certain point of view—be dissolved in two or more other perspectives that would be constitutive of the original one. Perspectives are unique and indivisible; so, though perspectives may, on the one hand seem to introduce us into the realm of abstraction, on the other, we reach rock bottom with them. We cannot move onto some still deeper level functioning as a perspective's foundation; we cannot look through a perspective in order to discover there something more fundamental than it. In this sense perspectives are no less real to us than reality itself. Perspectives are the atoms of the (political) universe of representation. It is here that we must necessarily stop and where we encounter what simply is the given. This is why, both in the case of art and of politics, reality should preferably be defined in terms of representation. In art reality should not be identified with the physical being of what is represented but with the perspectives generated by representation. And so it is in politics. Political reality is not to be identified with citizens, institutions, and so on, as these may exist prior to and independent from processes of representation; only if citizens, institutions, political parties, and the rest develop representations of each other, only if they start seeing each other from a certain perspective, only then will a platform of interaction emerge that can properly be said to be political reality. So political reality can only come into being after the notion of representation has, in one way or another, been given constitutional form in a nation or state. And we should therefore praise and honor representative democracy, since it so obviously is the system of government that is most successful in giving actual constitutional form to the requirements of representation. And, similarly, we should be weary of all attempts to devise general rules or some kind of general background that would enable us to move quasi-automatically and unproblematically from the represented to its representation in the sphere of politics or in that of art.

This, then, is where the real threat for democracy lies in the age of the network and of the expert. For the discourse of the expert, the discourse that has to be used if one seriously wishes to qualify as a member of the network, is as distinct from the language of politics and representation as the diagram or statistics from the work of art. Of course, one may well believe that the diagram and statistics are our more reliable and more sophisticated successor to the clumsy paintings of a previous age—and a similar view could be upheld for politics. But if this view becomes generally accepted, and if our social world becomes structured accordingly, this would inevitably mean the end of politics and of freedom.

8

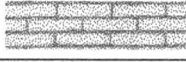

COMPROMISE AND POLITICAL CREATIVITY

Good riddance, one might say after having listened to the argument expounded in the previous chapter. Why shouldn't we be happy to exchange the inefficiency and the messiness of democratic politics for the scientific precision that we may expect from the network and the expert? We need only recall, so the argument might go on, the many disasters occasioned by ideologically inspired economic politics. Shouldn't we be content that we presently have these financial networks spanning all of the globe and now functioning not so much as a mere definition of economic reality, but as economic reality itself? Not only would political interference with the reality embodied by this network be bad politics, it would be tantamount to an explicit denial of what reality simply *is* like. So would it not seem that the network and the expert are, for better or worse, simply our destiny; would it not be quixotic, if not outright suicidal, to fail to comply with their requirements?

THE NECESSITY OF POLITICS

In order to deal with this question, we had best start with the observation that the domain of action of the network is far more narrowly circumscribed than that of better known and more traditional power structures. No contrast could be greater than that between, for example, the amoebic, formless, and unstructured exercise of power of the feudal state and the very precisely defined range of action of the financial network. The network and the expert's knowledge are like a microscope: an extremely thin slice of reality is perceived with unparalleled clarity and precision, but everything outside it has become blurred or outright invisible. Because of this almost myopic focus on such restricted and limited areas of social reality, the totality of the networks, when taken together, resembles an archipelago rather than a united continent. There is no supernetwork uniting all the networks within itself. Self-evidently, this is where the network most conspicuously fails if compared to representation. For achieving this kind of unity is precisely what we have representation for. It may be that representation is less successful than the network in identifying the elements that are to be welded together in a representation; but the network is wholly incapable of the operation of representation. Our dilemma as human, or rather, as political beings may be that we shall always have to choose somehow between either an exact grasp of the detail or a conception of the whole. We will lose the whole when opting for the former and the exact detail when we prefer the latter option. And there is no way to combine the strengths of both in a view of the world that both respects the detail and is all encompassing. So our only alternative is to decide for each individual case where we should situate the narrow optimum between these two mutually exclusive options. The talent for finding this optimum is what distinguishes good politicians and historians from their less gifted colleagues.

The implication of this state of affairs is that a political center in which the social realities that have been created by the networks are harmonized and integrated will be just as necessary—if not even more so—than when democracy still had the more mundane and better-known task of reconciling the warring ideologies and interests of its citizens. For it may well be that the citizens of a previous dispensation were more aware of their adversaries than the networks are of each other. The latter really tend to be, and to behave, like Leibniz's "windowless monads." And where no "invisible hand" took care of the social and political conflicts that kept nineteenth- and twentieth-century democracies politically divided, we have no a priori certainty that the networks will all nicely cooperate to achieve the *bonum commune*. On the contrary, as we all know by now, the activities of the medical, pharmacological, financial, agricultural, or technological networks can all generate unintended side-effects that may often be far from harmless. And there is no automatic pilot that we can absolutely rely upon to take care of these side-effects and of how these side-effects might, in their turn, interact with each other. Politics therefore is an activity that we can never relinquish as the sad burden of previous generations not yet possessing our (post)modernist instruments for achieving the just and well-ordered society. Guéhenno may have been right in making us aware of the challenge to representative democracy that is embodied by the network. But such challenges should urge us to refine and adapt representative democracy to the requirements of a new age rather than to abandon it. We will still need politics in order to legislate the Umwelt in which the networks and the experts will function.

This brings me to a further and more fundamental consideration. When we compare the advantages of the expert and the network, on the one hand, and representative democracy, on the other, we had best associate the former with "truth" and the latter with "the organization of truth." Self-evidently, it is science, and the technological application of scientific truth and knowledge, to which the network and the expert owe both their authority and the aura of efficacy and efficiency. The state in a representative democracy, however, is a *representation* of the electorate, and its functioning is therefore determined by using the logic of representation to focus on how truth had best be organized into a coherent and self-consistent whole. Let me explain this.

In order to appreciate this difference between *truth* and the *organization of truth* we had best look at historical representation (more generally, as is discussed in my *Historical Representation*, historical writing is the discipline in which the logic of representation most clearly manifests itself). Truth certainly is an important category in historical representation: the historian "representing" the past is expected to respect the truth about the past (just as the portrait painter is expected to present us with a good likeness of the sitter). Nevertheless, truth is not the decisive criterion in historical representation. For, as I have argued elsewhere,[1] representations are, essentially, metaphorical proposals for how to see or how to perceive a certain part of reality. And these metaphorical proposals are proposals for how to best organize truths as expressed by the individual singular statements that may or may not be part of a historical representation of the past. As has often been argued, historical representation is essentially a matter of *selection*, a matter of making up one's mind about what true statements one will include in one's historical narrative, and which statements will, in the end, have to be left out because they are not illuminating. Historians can make many more true statements about the past than they ultimately decide to do; and when they make up their minds about this they select those and only those true statements that will together produce the "picture" or "image" of the past that is favored by them.

The crucial fact then is the following. It is certainly true that good arguments can be given for or against such metaphorical proposals and that their pros and cons can be rationally discussed. We need only think of historical debate. However, of proposals we can say that they are sensible, fruitful, helpful, and thought-provoking (or not), but not that they are either true or false. For it would be nonsensical and meaningless to speak of "true" or "false" proposals. It follows, first, that representation deals with the "organization of truth" rather than truth itself, and second, that the problem of representation cannot be reduced to the problem of truth.

If we try to grasp where these representational proposals go beyond truth and falsehood, the notion of aesthetic creativity will be, once again, our best guide. The aesthetic creativity of the artist articulates itself in his capacity to make us look at the world in a *new* way; as Oscar Wilde once put it, great art is not a copy of the world, but makes reality imitate art. One may think here of how we tend to have a different experience of a wooded landscape in which we are wandering after having just visited a picture gallery with landscapes by Ruisdael, Hackaert, or van Everdingen. If we experience the landscape in a new way, this is not because we now have discovered new truths about trees and forest tracks; Ruisdael's paintings show nothing that might make us doubt the truths that we already knew about this kind of thing. We simply look at the same things in a new and different way and thus respond to the aesthetic creativity of the painter. All this is even more obviously so in the case of historical representation: saying true things about the past is undoubtedly where all historical writing begins, but this simply is not enough. As I suggested a moment ago, the historian has the task to tell us the *right* truths about the past; we know that the nature of historical representations and their plausibility depend less on whether historians always succeeded in saying true things about the past or not than on what true things they decided to tell us in their story. And it is at this level of the selection of what kind of historical truths require our attention that the historian's creativity announces itself.

All this can be translated to the domain of politics and make us aware of the political creativity of representative democracy. It is, in this context, of specific interest that we can make two apparently contradictory statements about the relationship between the represented and its representation. In the first place, we can say that the represented is more specific than its representation, since *this* representation is just one element out of the class of all possible representations of this represented. But we can also argue the other way around and say that the representation is more general than what it represents, since each representation abstracts in one way or another from the totality of properties that the represented possesses. In this respect, the representation can be compared to concepts like house, tree, or dog that also are more general than the individual houses, trees, and dogs that are categorized by them. Hence, however paradoxical this may seem to be, we must conclude that the representation is both more specific and more general than what it represents. Put differently, the representation has a regime of the general and of the specific differing from that which we shall find at the level of the represented.

Now, if political problems ordinarily concern the relationship between the individual (interest) and the general (interest)—and who could deny that this is the common denominator of almost all political problems?—it follows that (political) representation offers us the possibility of rephrasing or redefining political problems in new ways. In the transition from the represented, or the electorate, to its representation, the political party, the state, and so on we somewhere pass this "aesthetic gap" mentioned above so that a new regime in the relationship between the individual and the general may announce itself. And it may well be that what seemed to be hopelessly irreconcilable at the level of the represented *can* be reconciled at the level of its representation. Hence, political representation enables us to creatively redefine the political landscape and to discover solutions for our political problems that we would never have had access to if our perspective had remained exclusively tied to the level of truth and knowledge.

This is why representative democracy may draw from a rich source of political creativity that is inaccessible to the network and the expert—without, as I hasten to add, implying either a rejection or a disparagement of the expert's category of truth. The network and the expert function on the level of *knowledge*, whereas representative democracy functions on that of the *organization of knowledge*. And as we saw above, the writing of history demonstrates that the transition from the former to the latter level does not automatically place us beyond what can rationally be discussed and decided. Representation and the reliance on (political) representation is by no means an irresponsible jump into the irrational. So let us make use of the rich possibilities presented to us by political representation and avoid restricting our political scope to the truth and knowledge presented by the expert and the network. Indeed, with the organization of truth by representation we will find ourselves at a higher level than that of truth itself: hence, the more the social and political problems of our time are occasioned by the actions of the expert and of the network and by the unintended consequences resulting from them, the more we will need political representation.

CONSENSUS AND COMPROMISE

It might be worthwhile to be more specific about what the foregoing meditations about political creativity may mean for actual political practice. More specifically, what mechanisms in the complicated machinery of representative democracy stimulate political creativity most? What areas of political practice make the strongest appeal to political creativity? I shall argue in this section that political compromise is the best answer to this question. And this need not surprise us. For in the previous section we associated political creativity with representation and, next, representation with the organization of knowledge rather than with knowledge itself. And since compromise is an organization of (components of) political truths rather than the justification of political truth itself, we may expect it to have an elective affinity with political creativity. The politician formulating the most satisfactory and lasting compromise in a political conflict is the political "artist" par excellence.

This can best be elucidated by opposing the notions of (political) consensus and compromise, since, as we will see below, compromise stimulates political creativity, whereas consensus kills it. Rawls has recently analyzed the notion of political consensus and investigated what possibilities for political problem solving can be expected from it. He believes that consensus may help us to diminish or even to solve political conflict and to achieve a "stable" political order respecting the political rights of its members. Or, as Rawls formulates the problem himself: "How is it possible that there can be a stable and just society whose free and equal citizens are deeply divided by conflicting and even incommensurable religious, philosophical and moral doctrines?"[2] Rawls's main suggestion in connection with this problem is that such conflicts should not be decided by going down to the "foundations" of these doctrines. Doing so, as Rawls most plausibly comments, would make things only worse because the deeper you go, the wider the gap will become between these doctrines. Insofar as agreement can be achieved at all, we may expect it to be realizable "on the surface," so to speak, rather than on the deeper-lying level of moral, philosophical, or religious foundations. Or, to put it in more practical terms, though it is utterly unlikely that a Calvinist and a Kantian will ever succeed in convincing each other of the truth of their opinions, it may well be that they will discover (perhaps to their own surprise) far less disagreement with regard to how each of them translates beliefs into actual public behavior. "From the outside" it will often not be easy to distinguish the Calvinist from the Kantian, though the difference becomes manifest as soon as each of them starts talking about "inner" moral and religious convictions. Rawls wants to exploit this most fortunate fact as much as possible in order to ease potential conflict. And, surely, Rorty was right in discerning here a move toward antifoundationalism that we would not have expected from the author of *A Theory of Justice*.

What we should do, he suggests, is to take as our point of departure the place where agreement happens to exist and to try, next, to expand the domain of agreement as far as possible from there:

Since we seek an agreed basis of public justification in matters of justice, and since no political agreement on those disputed questions can reasonably be expected, *we turn instead to the fundamental ideas we seem to share* through the political culture. From these ideas we try to work out a political conception of justice congruent with our considered convictions on due reflection. Once this is done, citizens may within their comprehensive doctrines regard the political conception of justice as true, or as reasonable, whatever their view allows.[3]

Hence, we start with these "comprehensive doctrines" (such as Calvinism, Kantianism, and so on) and investigate, next, where in practice they can peacefully coexist; then we use this shared component as (1) a basis for reaching further agreement, and (2) as an argument *within* each such a "comprehensive doctrine" to convince its adherents of adopting it as an expression of political justice. The procedure thus is "horizontal" rather than "vertical," to put it metaphorically. This, then, is what Rawls refers to as the procedure of "overlapping consensus."

There is much to be applauded in this notion of an overlapping consensus. Above all, it undoubtedly provides us with the most effective and painless procedure for achieving political agreement. Moreover, as Rawls emphasizes himself, the procedure does not require us to abandon the philosophical, moral, or religious doctrines we happen to cherish, while at the same time allowing us to discover common ground with our doctrinal adversaries. So whenever political conflict can be settled in this way, we should not hesitate for a moment to use the most welcome opportunities offered to us by this Rawlsian procedure.

But at the same time we may have our doubts. I will mention two problems. In the first place, there may well be "comprehensive doctrines" (such as theocracy, orthodox Muhammadanism, Maoism, or variants of anarchism) that by their very nature are opposed to the procedure. For example, an orthodox Muslim is not likely to be prepared to abandon the Koran as our supreme legislator for the blessings to be expected from Rawls's overlapping consensus. Of course, Rawls recognized this problem and tried to get around it by admitting that the procedure will only work in a community of "reasonable" citizens, that is, citizens who are willing to provisionally bracket those parts of their "comprehensive doctrines" that will not fit in the machinery of the overlapping consensus. But this is less than satisfactory. For, by excluding the theocrats, the Maoists, and others, we will have excluded precisely those categories of citizens that we would most wish to involve in the procedures of overlapping consensus. Hence, the procedure as described by Rawls seems to presuppose precisely that kind of "public reasonableness" that it recommends to us. There is, therefore, an odor of circularity around Rawls's notion of overlapping consensus that will be difficult to dispel.

But there is a more interesting and more complex problem. When Rawls speaks of "overlapping *consensus*," he means exactly what he says: its aim truly is the overcoming of initial disagreement by reaching *shared* opinions (about political justice). Where disagreement continues, overlapping consensus is helpless. And, as Rawls concedes himself, quite substantial areas of political conflict may thus be outside the reach of overlapping consensus: "Thus, if the liberal conceptions correctly framed from fundamental ideas of a democratic public culture are supported by and encourage deeply conflicting political and economic interests, and if there be no way of designing a constitutional regime so as to overcome that, a full overlapping consensus cannot, it seems, be achieved."[4] And one might now skeptically add that politicians ordinarily are confronted with such "deeply conflicting political and economic interests" and that it is precisely their job to reconcile somehow these interests in the absence of "a constitutional regime" (whatever that might, in practice, be in this context) telling them how to do so. So, much in the way that we observed a moment ago, precisely when things truly become interesting and critical from the perspective of actual political practice, the procedure of overlapping consensus leaves us empty-handed.

THE LIMITATIONS OF POLITICAL CONSENSUS

We may well ask ourselves how to explain Rawls's disappearance in the theoretical mists of practical irrelevance. His own writings are our best guide here. For we cannot fail to be struck by his contempt for a notion closely related to consensus, though essentially different, namely the notion of compromise. Instead of "compromise," Rawls speaks of a *modus vivendi*, and there can be no doubt about his very low esteem of it. For example, Rawls is at pains to make clear that his overlapping consensus is not something as base and objectionable as a *modus vivendi*. He has two equally interesting arguments for upholding the distinction. In the first place, as opposed to a *modus vivendi*, the overlapping consensus has a moral status and "can be affirmed on moral grounds." Secondly, and closely related to the former argument, a *modus vivendi* is "merely a consensus on accepting certain authorities, or on complying with certain institutional arrangements, founded on a convergence of self- or group interests."[5] However, as opposed to this depreciation of the compromise, or the *modus vivendi*, in favor of consensus, all the more surprisingly Rawls upholds the (historical and/or logical) priority of the former to the latter. For when he asks himself the question "How might a constitutional consensus come about?" he proffers the following answer:

Suppose that at a certain time, because of various historical events and contingencies, certain liberal principles of justice are accepted as a mere *modus vivendi*, and are incorporated into existing political institutions. This acceptance has come about, let us say, in much the same way as the acceptance of the principle of toleration came about as a modus vivendi following the Reformation: at first reluctantly, but nevertheless as providing the only workable alternative to endless and destructive civil strife.[6]

So, it all *begins* with a *modus vivendi* and then, only at some later stage, this *modus vivendi* may become codified in terms of the moral rules as expressed by some overlapping consensus. Hence, without compromise no consensus; and even on Rawls's own terms it seems to follow that *history precedes ethics*, that compromise is more fundamental than consensus, and that the conflict of interests is prior to how any settlement of this conflict is codified by means of a conception of political justice. In thus privileging history to ethics, one is not guilty of the naturalistic or causalistic fallacy in the sense of attempting to morally justify mere historical contingency. The accusation of naturalism would be correct if *compromise* were legitimated in terms of historical contingency and causality. But I have merely been saying that a conception of Rawlsian *political justice* legitimated a certain outcome of a certain historical conflict (of interests). And this is the legitimation of a compromise and not of the contingent historical circumstances from which compromise arose (which would make one guilty of the naturalistic fallacy).

Besides, Rawls's argument about overlapping consensus as the foundation of a conception of political justice—whatever opinion one may have of this argument—must be situated on the trajectory from compromise or *modus vivendi* to conceptions of political justice and *not* on that from historical contingency to compromise. Obviously, the whole purpose of Rawls's argument is to give a moral basis and support to (an already existing) compromise. Or, to put it differently, apparently there are two domains of rationality involved in all this. In the first place, there is the practical rationality to which people (or their political leaders) appeal in order to avoid disastrous consequences of political conflict and in order to construct some kind of compromise as the lesser of evils. Next, one may invoke "Rawlsian" political rationality in order to demonstrate to all the partisans reconciled by the compromise why the compromise in question is a defensible and rational one from their own, respective, partisan point of view—or from that of their own "comprehensive doctrines," to use Rawls's terminology.

Putting it this way will leave no doubt as to which of these two rationalities is truly decisive in the creation of a free, liberal, and democratic political society—and we can only be amazed by Rawls's preference for a rationality merely codifying what has come into being already. Undoubtedly part of the explanation is the "prudish contempt" of interests and compromise that den Hartogh correctly observed in the writings of Rawls and many contemporary Anglo-Saxon political philosophers[7]—a prudery, as Govert den Hartogh goes on to say, that has its dangers. For, in contrast to compromise, consensus à la Rawls resists the bargaining of political principles in the sense that I might be prepared to grant you your principle P_1 (though I remain firmly opposed to it) on the condition that you are willing to grant me my principle P_2, because I prefer a political reality containing both principles to one containing neither. For within the framework of Rawlsian overlapping consensus, we could only do business as long as we can be sure that we still find ourselves on common ground.[8]

Certainly there are areas where Rawls's prudishness is justified. Basic political principles concerning issues such as toleration, freedom of thought, or civil freedom may never be given away in exchange for economic or financial advantages. Speaking generally, as long we are thinking of what we have come to see as the citizen's basic *rights*,[9] it is true that we have no room for compromise. But, with the exception of debates about issues such as abortion or euthanasia, this is a small or negligible part of actual political debate (though, of course, the importance of this kind of issue is inversely proportional to their frequency in the political history of a nation). Normally, however, political debate and decision making concern problems such as whether one should invest more money in education or in national defense; how much money should be invested in the country's infrastructure; whether one had best fight crime by more police or by programs for the social integration of dropouts (or by adopting both strategies); how to react to the damage done to the environment by industry and transportation systems; or a host of economic issues such as whether the state should or should not stimulate the economy, in what stage improvements in social security might become counterproductive, how best to fight unemployment, and so on. None of these questions permits translation in the terms of "rights" and political justice and each attempt to do so would effectively prevent any workable solution to them.

At this stage several comments should be made about this apparent elective affinity between Rawls's model of the overlapping consensus and the vocabulary of political rights. To begin with, as we all know, this was the kind of political language that was also predominant in seventeenth- and eighteenth-century natural law philosophy. For a double reason, this was, for the political philosopher of those days, the most appropriate philosophical vocabulary to use. In the first place, in order to protect the citizen against potential encroachments on civil liberties by the absolute monarch or a despotic state, no instrument could be more effective than a philosophically convincing deduction of human rights. The struggle with the absolute monarch predominantly was a struggle about toleration, freedom of opinion, free assemblage, due process of law, and similar issues; and these were all political desiderata that naturally could best be formulated in terms of *rights*. Or, to phrase it historically, such (natural) rights would offer a better safeguard of these civil liberties than the haphazard and inconsistent protection of both individuals and associations as were embodied in the privileges, traditions, or simple agreement of feudalism's legal order. In the second place, and no less importantly, we should realize that before the nineteenth century few people saw the state as a politically creative institution. This was not a matter of political conviction or of a protoliberal belief in the minimal state. Apart from foreign policy or fighting a war, the state was expected to do little more than to take a few decisions in the field of legislation and administration, decisions that would not require much time and effort and that would touch only the surface of society. The "makeability" of society is a postrevolutionary idea, and the notion of a politically creative state and the amount of state interference that we have now all become used to would be just as strange to our eighteenth-century ancestors as Renaissance perspective would have been to a Giotto or Cimabue.

This, then, is one of the problems that one may have with Rawls's notion of the overlapping consensus and, more generally, with the whole of his conception of politics. Both are not so much wrong as irrelevant from the perspective of the kind of society in which we live at the start of the new millennium. Rawls is a most interesting discussion partner of seventeenth-century theorists such as Thomasius, Locke, or Bayle—but not of a later generation of political philosophers that has theorized about the highly complex and continuously changing political order that has come into being since the Industrial Revolution and about its moral and political implications.

One might object that an up-to-date and philosophically satisfying vindication of our civil liberties as has been put forward by Rawls and similar contemporary political theorists is at best a permanent necessity and at worst an innocuous irrelevance. But this view might be too optimistic. For Rawls's political vocabulary all too easily invites us to conceive in terms of rights political issues that should be approached differently. Especially from a European point of view, the main trouble with the public domain in the United States is its near to complete juridification (so rightly regretted by Francis Fukuyama in his recent book on trust):[10] it seems that the judiciary has gradually acquired in the United States a most unhealthy predominance over the legislative and the executive powers and has brutally invaded areas of public decision making where it does not belong and can only do damage. There is in the United States a strong inclination to translate all politics into terms of rights and to see law as the paradigm of all politics. One may well conjecture that to the extent that Rawls's writings did have any practical effect, they have been a contribution to this most questionable development. And we may certainly expect trouble for a society attempting to settle juridically issues that are essentially political. For such a society may be expected to willfully blind itself to its most urgent problems. In order to recognize this, it will be helpful, once again, to contrast interests with rights. There is no legislation for interests, though after a conflict of interests has been observed (such as between capital and labor), legislation may be produced for dealing with the conflict. Interests are, so to speak, rights *in statu nascendi*. Hence, much, if not all, that is from a political point of view new, unexpected, unforeseen, and unforeseeable in the development of a society will initially present itself in terms of interests and emphatically not in terms of rights and of the law case. So if one focuses on rights instead of on (the conflict of) interests, one will have cut through the ties linking social and political reality to political practice, and an unpractical political philosophy will be the result. One may even go one step further and emphasize how necessary and indispensable these conflicts of interests may often be: for it is only thanks to the existence of conflict that we may become aware that there is something wrong in society that needs to be remedied by public decision making. The conflict of interests gives us access to the nature of social and political reality and without it we are blind, politically speaking. The vocabulary of rights does not give us this access to social reality: it only exemplifies or expresses a certain conception of social reality without testing it in the way that typically happens when interests conflict.

From that perspective we also have every reason to be suspicious of Rawls's repeated insistence on the need of founding a "stable society" by his method of the overlapping consensus. To be sure, it would be both wrong and inappropriate to see in this insistence a covert concession to

conservatism—for we cannot doubt for a moment Rawls's sincere preference of political justice to the reign of the forces of inertia—the danger is,
rather, that the effort to "stabilize" society by means of rights and the demands of political justice will isolate legislation and public decision making from both political reality and from what are our civil society's real
needs and interests. In sum, ethical and/or juridical formalism alienates us
from actual political content and may ultimately result in either the irrelevance of politics or in an unhealthy polarization of state and civil society.

THE POLITICAL CREATIVITY OF COMPROMISE

And this brings me to a last comment on Rawls's conception of the
overlapping consensus; I wish to enumerate the advantages of compromise
to consensus. In the first place, compromise brings us much closer to what
actually happens in the practice of politics than consensus. It is, to quote
Burke,

a very great mistake to imagine that mankind follows up practically any speculative
principle, either of government or of freedom, as far as it will go in actual argument
or logical illation. All government, indeed every human benefit and enjoyment,
every virtue, and every prudent act, is founded on compromise and barter. We balance inconveniences, we give and take; we remit some rights, that we may enjoy
others; and we choose to be happy citizens rather than subtle disputants.[11]

Second, as was argued in Chapter 5, compromise requires us both to
respect the presence of our opponents in spite of their adherence to political principles that we may reject and their and our own willingness to fulfill our part of the agreement, however disagreeable this may be to us. In
this way compromise will inculcate in us the virtues of tolerance, of the respect of others and their moral autonomy, of trusting others, of living up
to one's pledges, and of knowing how to successfully participate in a pluralist society.[12] Compromise even more powerfully contributes to these
virtues than consensus, since consensus (especially in Rawls's conception
of it) does not force us to leave the domain of what is rational and justifiable in our own eyes: consensus may at most effect a shift in the center of
gravity of our political universe but does not require us (in the way compromise does) to move outside it. Hence, compromise involves us more
deeply and in a more existential way in society and in the complex web of

interhuman relationships than consensus. Compromise socializes, whereas consensus leaves us the separate individual that we were.

Third, it is often argued that compromise is at odds with ethical integrity. As Benjamin has pointed out, compromise is often considered to be characteristic of the "moral chameleon" and a sign of opportunism, self-deception, and hypocrisy,[13] if not worse.[14] But, as he goes on to say (with Thomas Nagel), though there may admittedly be some truth in this view in certain cases, compromise will not ordinarily, and certainly not necessarily, be opposed to moral integrity. The accusation only makes sense if one conceives of the moral order as a kind of quasi-mathematical system deductively based on indisputable first principles. But mature individual citizens participating in a mature political culture will know that the complexity and the paradoxes of social and political life resist such a simplistic conception of moral truth.[15] Therefore, the individual who is willing to seriously consider alternative views of what should be done, and to risk his own views in discussion and compromise with others, is morally a more respectable person than the person who sees in compromise a betrayal of moral truth. And the argument is even more pressing if we recall the argument of the previous chapter that conflicts of ideological and moral standards are by no means restricted to the situation where one (group of) individual(s) is opposed to another (group of) individual(s). Moral and ideological conflict may just as well manifest itself in the mind of one and the same individual; and in such cases the necessity to find the best compromise between incommensurable values may be no less urgent than if (groups of) individuals find themselves in moral conflict. Certainly in such cases we will have a greater moral respect for the individual who courageously engages in this most unsettling kind of inner conflict than the individual who believes to have ready-made answers for all of them.

Lastly, and most importantly, in our comparison of consensus and compromise, we should realize that consensus represents the static rather than the dynamic aspect of politics and political decision making and that precisely for this reason a greater contribution to the practice of politics is to be expected from compromise than from consensus. Certainly, Rawls's argument about overlapping consensus admirably makes clear that achieving consensus is far from easy and that consensus truly is what we need when it comes to our most basic rights and freedoms. I am not belittling the significance of overlapping consensus and of the domain where it is operative. But these rights and freedoms define the limits of the state's actions and interventions instead of suggesting what the state might creatively do *within* these limits. Rawls is interested in the *foundation* (*pace* Rorty) of a political order in terms of constitutional rights and freedoms but not in what can or should be *constructed* on this foundation. Rawls's overlapping consensus has its natural affinity with constitutional issues rather than with the kind of political dilemma of actual political practice where compromise is the only way out—dilemmas, that is, arising from the conflict of interests and ideologies in civil society and that, together with the compromises resulting from them, determine the political realities of a country and its civil society. And though these dilemmas and compromises may sometimes concern fairly trivial issues, they may on other occasions be no less fundamental than the rights and freedoms discussed by Rawls. For, as I have argued in Chapter 4,[16] representative democracy in continental Europe even originated from the recognition of politicians (of the post-1815 period) that consensus was wholly unattainable, that political decisions had yet to be reached in spite of this, and that compromise would be the only way to do so.[17] Or, to put it more forcefully, continental representative democracy was the political system specially devised for allowing compromise between political adversaries lacking sufficient common ground for consensus. Historically, compromise and representative democracy are most intimately linked. Overlapping consensus, however, is possible without a specific constitution (such as representative government); a debating club or the forum of political philosophers may be a more appropriate platform for achieving consensus than representative government with its open and unrestrained embrace of political conflict. Even more so, political representation will presumably hinder rather than further the kind of rationalist political discussion that Rawls has in mind.

The decisive difference between consensus and compromise is, in the present context, that the latter may be a solid basis for cooperation even if consensus is unattainable—whereas, whether we like it or not, "in politics we have to *act*," as Carens so neatly put it.[18] Thus it may bridge political gaps that consensus will never be able to bridge. And there is an even more interesting difference between consensus and compromise. Consensus is essentially conservative (and hence, not creative) in the sense that it cannot bring about something that is not already present in the position of the contending political parties (though, of course, the realization of the overlap in the position of these parties in terms of legislation may introduce something that is new in political reality). However, precisely because co-operation may be the politician's fate even if no consensus can be realized, compromise may force the politician to enter upon new and hitherto unexplored paths.[19]

If no greatest common denominator of political points of view can be identified as the basis for a Rawlsian overlapping consensus, a political position will have to be developed that is essentially "new." There are two reasons for this. In the first place, since the old political positions offered no basis for political cooperation, only a new one can be expected to function as such. In the second, to the extent that the previous political position of a political party would still remain visible in the compromise, this may be explained as a victory of one of these political parties over the other(s) and thus dangerously weaken the support for the compromise. Hence, the "newer" and the more creative the compromise is, the more strongly it will be supported by all parties involved in the compromise. To put it dramatically, in political compromise all parties have to make into their own final position as *much* as possible what was in their original position as *little* as possible. Needless to say, this should not be understood as an injunction to betray as much as possible one's original position. For doing so would be political suicide. The emphasis is, rather, on a *metamorphosis* of one's original position—a metamorphosis consisting in the combination of remaining as close as possible to one's original position with the greatest possible transformation of that original position. In this way, a new political world can come into being, "dialectically" transcending old positions and oppositions. Carens describes this politically creative dimension of compromise as follows: in the process of achieving compromise "a party may gain new insight into ways in which goals and preferences of the other may be combined with his own and may be able to propose *entirely new options that had not occurred to either party before and that would not emerge from a simple trial-and-error process.* The more complex the problem, the more likely it seems that the most integrative solution will emerge from this kind of creative thinking."[20] So the most complex problems are, paradoxically, our best guides for the improvement of society; and the absence of such complex problems will inevitably invite its degeneration.

And so it is. Whereas consensus puts us in a world in which time has no role to play, compromise places us in the world of history and of the unintended consequences of our thinking and actions, whereby something may be brought about that was not yet present in our conscious desires and intentions. Perhaps no example more perfectly exemplifies the benefits of compromise than the welfare state as it came into being in several countries on the European continent after World War II. The struggle between capital and labor was ended by means of the compromise of the welfare state that ensured the material well-being of Europe's industrial proletariat, while at the same time leaving intact the essence of capitalist production. And the welfare state was explicitly or implicitly present in neither capitalist nor socialist ideology. It was essentially a *new* idea and even opposed to both capitalist rationality and socialist ideology. And if the welfare state and social security are better developed in continental than in Anglo-Saxon democracies, this surely is partly due to the fact that the coalition governments of the European continent put a greater premium on compromise than their Anglo-Saxon counterparts. And it certainly is no coincidence that the eulogy of consensus extensively discussed in this chapter was written not by a European but by an Anglo-Saxon political philosopher.

In this chapter I have sketched the main advantages of compromise over consensus. The list certainly is not exhaustive. For example, compromise will also compel the parties involved to a new testing of their political views against what political reality is like: for only on the basis of such testing can they expect to arrive at a balanced view of what may and what should not be surrendered to the opponent in this process of the metamorphosis of one's original position into a political compromise. Furthermore, insofar as compromise tends to create new political realities, it will be indispensable to see how these new realities fit together with the existing ones. The advantage of compromise over consensus is, from this perspective, that it will give us a politics that is closest to and interested in what political reality actually is like. Second, the negotiation of a compromise and its justification to political friends and allies requires discussion and will thus stimulate the interest in politics and in political decision making. Furthermore, the results of political negotiations, insofar as these deviate from an original political position, will have to be explained and defended to the rank and file of a political party. And this will further contribute to the nation's political involvement and to the effort to ensure that political decisions have the widest possible support. A nation used to political compromise is a politically mature nation and politics will die in a society content with consensus. Third, compromise does not require political parties to abandon their own original position. The negotiation of a political compromise is not an exercise in the discovery of political or ideological truth (though under certain circumstances and in certain of its phases this may be part of the procedure); it simply is an exploration of where agreement can be attained. The coalition of a socialist and a liberalist party[21] does not require these two parties to abandon their socialist and liberal ideologies; though it may be expected that political cooperation will stimulate a better understanding of one's political opponent and more sympathy for his political ideology. This strongly furthers the cause of tolerance; whereas consensus is inherently intolerant since it requires one to inculcate one's own political values as much as possible in others. One need only be reminded, in this context, of how "political reeducation" was commonly used by totalitarian regimes such as Mao's China to deal with political opponents. Consensus tends to give to political debate the aura of a debate about political truth, where compromise does not aim at the discovery of truth but merely at cooperation. A truly liberal society should therefore prefer compromise to consensus.

But there are, admittedly, disadvantages as well. The negotiation of a compromise may be either so difficult, or the willingness to compromise may be so great, that the negotiation of compromises acquires an autonomy of its own. It may then become more important to achieve a compromise, whatever its nature and content, than to guarantee its appropriateness to existing political reality. A permanent danger is, furthermore, that precisely this metamorphosis of original political views required by compromise may inspire in the electorate a distrust of or even disgust with politics. Next, since we have a greater commitment to the truth than to a transitory political compromise, compromise may invite political indifference. And political indifference will inevitably mean the death of all democratic politics. It is most reassuring from this perspective that political indifference—though certainly on the increase in continental democracies—has not yet attained the proportions that can be observed in the United States.

Taking together, the advantages and the disadvantages of both consensus and of compromise, we may conclude the following. The decisive advantage of the kind of representative democracy we have in the West over rival models of power, as embodied by the network and the expert, is its unparalleled capacity for creating new and original solutions for existing political problems. Certainly, the expert and the network may introduce dramatic and even revolutionary changes in our individual lives and on a social level. We need only think of the information revolution, the media, or our contemporary global economy. But because of the solipsism that we attributed above to the network and the expert, they are not a suitable forum for achieving political solutions. Their creativity is merely technological but not political. Once again, this does not mean that the revolutionary changes that may be brought about by the network and the expert have no political consequences. Quite the contrary. But from the perspective of the network and the expert, these are essentially the unintended consequences of their activities. Hence, the paradox is that the more the network and the expert succeed in changing our lives and society in general, the more we will need politics in order to see whether these changes are beneficial or not, how they interact with each other, what new social realities are created by them and how the state had best react to these new realities in order to harmonize them with the interests of all citizens. In short, the merely *technological* creativity of the network and of the expert puts an extra premium on the creativity of *politics* and of the *politician*. The age of the network and of the expert is by no means the end of politics: it makes "the primacy of politics" even more urgent than before.

The new social realities created by the network generate a whole set of new problems; for example, to what extent different segments of society may or may not be expected to participate in the new economic order and what to do about those who will lag behind; the long-term impact of technological innovations such as in biogenetics; the dangers of "asset inflation" occasioned by the financial network; the diminishing returns in terms of life expectancy to be awaited from further investments in medical care; and so on. Only politics is adequately equipped to deal with such issues. Only (national) politics can place these urgent problems within a wider context and relate them to developments elsewhere and to achieve a responsible weighing of the interests of all parties involved. And it is only representative democracy that may guarantee that the people who make the truly important decisions are accountable for them to the whole nation.

But above all, thanks to its aestheticism, representative democracy possesses the creativity to translate a counterproductive conflict of social developments and of interests into a new synthesis transcending, in a quasi-

Hegelian way, previous conflicts and oppositions. It may be true that some democracies may be expected to be more successful here than others—in Chapter 4 we have compared Anglo-Saxon and continental democracies from this perspective—but we can be certain that without representative democracy we shall be unable to face the challenges of the future. It is all the more regrettable that contemporary democracies, both Anglo-Saxon and continental, show so few signs of being sufficiently aware of the nature of these challenges.

9

RESPECT

In the three preceding chapters, (Machiavelli's) political perspectivism, political aestheticism, and the thesis of the brokenness of political reality and pluralism were opposed to (traditional) foundationalist political philosophy as defined in Chapter 6. In this chapter I wish to argue that no political system is more in agreement with political perspectivism and better respects our acknowledgment of it than representative democracy. Political systems such as theocracy, absolute monarchy, aristocracy, or direct democracy have always been justified by means of foundationalist argument. And our tendency to look also for a foundationalist justification of representative democracy shows that we have not yet completely freed ourselves from these older political traditions. But since Rorty's thesis of the priority of democracy to philosophy (as expounded in Chapter 6) we now know that we should refuse this heritage from our collective past.

This also suggests where we had best look if we wish to discover the intrinsic weaknesses of the theoretical justifications of these older political systems. Our insight into the brokenness of political reality tells us that these justifications will always, somewhere, and somehow, break down if only one penetrates "deeply" enough into them, that their theoretical foundations will eventually reach down to a level where reliable foundations are no longer available, where all kinds of unexpected subterranean landslides are occasioned by this brokenness of political reality. For example, think of how the foundations of Christian theocracy will fall apart as soon as we reach the level of that conflict between the virtue of justice and that of Christian love of one's neighbor that already so fascinated Jules Michelet.[1]

But absolute monarchy, democracy's immediate predecessor, provides us with an even more instructive example. Think of Hobbes's argument in favor of absolute monarchy as rendered at the beginning of Chapter 6. After having heard Hobbes out, we might well formulate the following objection. If all the individual citizens surrender their freedom to the state or "commonwealth," it by no means follows automatically that the "Man" or "Assembly of Men" benefiting from their willingness to do so is numerically different from these individual citizens. Hobbes's absolutism follows not necessarily from his sketch of how the political order came into being but from his presupposing and surreptitiously introducing a *new* entity (the absolute monarch of a later phase) to whom all these individual freedoms were entrusted. But this new entity is an obvious candidate for Occam's razor, an ontological redundancy that Rousseau would understandably protest against a century later. For on the basis of much the same foundations as had been used by Hobbes, Rousseau could argue that the sum of all these *individual* freedoms would nevertheless remain in the possession of the *collectivity* of the citizens. What each individual citizen had given away is returned to the collectivity at a later stage, so to speak. This is, of course, from an ontological point of view the more economic and clean argument. Anyway, we see illustrated here how on one and the same foundational basis such completely different political systems as that of Hobbes and Rousseau can be built. Incommensurability can be retraced here to different interpretations of exactly the same foundational basis. It required a mere little push somewhere along the long trajectory from political foundation to conclusion to steer Hobbes's argument in favor of absolute monarchy in the direction of its near to complete opposite, that of Rousseauist direct democracy.

Representative democracy, on the other hand, is not built on the shaky basis of foundationalist political argument—and this is what sets it so much apart from the many other political systems that we know from history. This obviously invites the question of what theoretical account should be given of representative democracy if this political system differs so much from all others. And, obviously, such a theoretical account could not possibly take the form of a theoretical foundation or justification of democracy—for that would mean an unwarranted return to foundation-alism again. My focus will thus not be on how representative democracy can be justified foundationally, but on how this best known but least understood of all political systems works and on what enables it to do the work that it does.

MACHIAVELLIST PERSPECTIVISM

Once again, it is best to start with Machiavelli. For in the previous section foundationalism was attacked in the name of the Machiavellian thesis of the brokenness of political reality. It seems natural, therefore, to expect from a closer investigation of his writings the illumination that we need in order to come to a better understanding of representative democracy. Turning to Machiavelli for a better understanding of democracy will certainly raise many eyebrows. Perhaps some readers will have been willing, albeit reluctantly, to go along with Machiavelli's thesis about the brokenness of political reality—especially since a contemporary political saint like Sir Isaiah Berlin agreed here with Machiavelli. But to present a self-confessed apologist of political crime and tyranny like Machiavelli as a theorist who can teach us something about (representative) democracy that we did not yet know seems definitely to be carrying things too far. Or, to give to this criticism a more workable and constructive form, granted that there is this opposition between most of political thought on the one hand and Machiavelli on the other, should we then not for precisely this reason prefer the former because this tradition may well be, after all, the lesser evil? Should not precisely this opposition compel us to perfect the founda-tionalist justification of representative democracy as much as we can, instead of joining the most doubtful company of Machiavelli. Certainly, doing so seems to be exchanging the Devil for Beelzebub.

I hope to make clear below how the thesis of the brokenness of the political world automatically brings us into the political climate of repre-sentative democracy. Most illustrative is here the dedication of *The Prince*, where Machiavelli presents the surprising argument that the prince may sometimes understand the people better than the people understands itself, and vice versa, quoted already in full in Chapter 7.[2] For just as valleys can best be painted from the perspective of a mountain ridge and mountain ridges from the perspective of the valleys, so the people has a better understanding of the nature of princes than princes themselves, and the prince a better understanding of the people than the people itself. The suggestion of Machiavelli's optical metaphor for political understanding obviously is that all political thought and action is *perspectivist* and originates not in a submersion in the object of understanding but in the discovery of the most appropriate perspective from which it should be *looked at.*

Three comments may clarify Machiavelli's conceptions. First, this "perspectivist view" generates a distance between—and not a conflation of—the political agent and the object of interest, which explains Machiavelli's most amazing suggestion that others often understand us better than we do ourselves, and vice versa. In politics, understanding only can come into being thanks to the aesthetic distance that separates a represented (either people or prince) from its representation (in the mind of either the prince or the people)—from which it follows that representation is the notion central to all politics. Without representation, no politics. Self-knowledge—where this aesthetic distance is absent—therefore keeps us outside the realm of politics. Moreover, to elaborate on Machiavelli's optical metaphor, we can properly appreciate a painting not when we keep it right under our noses but only when we look at it from an appropriate distance. And so it is in politics (and perhaps in most of social life as well): we are too close to ourselves to be able to understand ourselves. It is only "the other" who has the distance required for understanding. Or, to put all this differently, in politics, everything of interest takes place on the trajectory between ourselves and others, while all that precedes or goes beyond this trajectory is of no political interest. Second, this is what connects Machiavelli's perspectivism to historical insight: we know that historical insight and the historical perspective often enable the historian to understand the meaning of human action better than the historical agents in question themselves. Not surprisingly, it can be argued that modern historical consciousness was born from the writings of Machiavelli and those of his younger friend and kindred spirit, the politician and historian Francesco Guicciardini.[3] For the tragedy of sixteenth-century Italy effected in their minds a (traumatic) dissociation between how they had experienced this tragedy as participants in it and how they attempted to explain the tragedy. And thanks to this profound tension, thanks to the distance and the friction between these two perspectives, their sense of history could come into being. Third, and most importantly, this perspectivism certainly is no accidental peculiarity of Machiavelli's views. It has its deep roots in the Renaissance and Machiavellian *Weltanschauung* that opposed *virtù* to the whims of the goddess Fortuna and in the awareness that in politics there is room not for truth or falsity but only for criteria like prudence, tact, appropriateness, and good sense—in short, for what is the right *perspective* for successful political thought and action. For just as there is no neutral background that is shared by all perspectives, so there is no background for establishing truth and falsity. Obviously, this can be read as a reformulation of the rejection of political foundationalism expounded above.

This may also explain where Machiavelli's perspectivism goes beyond and should not be reduced to what is customarily defined in contemporary political science as "pluralism." Not unlike Machiavelli, pluralists such as Robert Dahl focus on the notion of political power and, once again, much as in Machiavelli's perspectivism they argue for "the existence of many power centres, diverse and fragmented interests and the marked propensity of one group to offset the power of another."[4] The difference, however, is that pluralism is a theory *about* perspectivism and therefore not (Machiavellist) perspectivism *itself*; that is, it asks itself how the assumption of perspectivistically inspired political action may help us explain what happens in political reality. In this way, it is no less foundationalist than the variants of foundationalism discussed above. But this kind of socioscientific question was not the question that inspired Machiavellian perspectivism: Machiavelli is concerned with political decision making and action, and not with how perspectivistically inspired decision making and action may help us *explain* what goes in political reality. Pluralism objectifies perspectivism, so to speak, and in doing so takes away the perspectivist tension between seer and seen that is so much the heart of all perspectivism.

Put differently, by proposing a single model for explaining political action, pluralism undoes, once again, the brokenness of political reality that is perspectivism's most cherished and original insight; by relating perspectivism not to action itself, but to the question what model to use for explaining it, the Machiavellian thesis of the brokenness of political reality is exchanged once again for monistic unity—in this case that of a foundationalist social science. And one might say that where Schmitt (whom we mentioned above) saw in perspectivism the *foundation* of political action, and where pluralism sees perspectivism as the foundation of *political science*, both Schmitt and pluralism must be distinguished from the Machiavellian position according to which political action *itself* is perspectivist.

It may well be that the distinction made just now between pluralism and the Machiavellian thesis of brokenness will be considered a mere technical subtlety having no other purpose than to save Machiavelli's "originality" and to protect it against an inglorious submersion in pluralism and Schmitt's political philosophy. In order to refute such a playing down of the difference between pluralism and the Machiavellist thesis, I now wish to insist that their difference runs parallel to that between the social sciences (pluralism) and historical writing (the counterpart of Machiavellianism). And it will need no further clarification that *this* distinction is by no means an irrelevant subtlety.[5] Elsewhere I have related the perspectivism of historical writing to the claim that the historical text essentially is a proposal for how to look at a specific part of the past.[6] Since they essentially are *proposals* (of which we could not possibly say that they are either true or false in the strict sense of these words), historical texts do not embody a specific cognitive claim—as undoubtedly is the case with the findings of the social sciences, such as political science. The historical text is aestheticist since, just as in painting, its success predominantly depends on whether the historian has found a suitable perspective from which to propose a view of the past. For example, should we see the French Revolution from a Marxist point of view, or should we prefer the point of view that Tocqueville had recommended? Historical debate, therefore, is primarily a debate about what is the most "fruitful" or "appropriate" point of view from which we should see the past (and the optical metaphor is taken quite literally here). Needless to say, we encounter here the same optical metaphor that had so powerfully been used by Machiavelli in the dedication of *The Prince*. What both Machiavelli's metaphor and historical writing have in common—and what is crucial to perspectivism—is that all depends on how the subject is positioned in relation to the object. In perspectivism—think of Machiavelli's metaphor—all the decisive emphasis is on the trajectory *between* the subject and the object, and not so much on the object itself. And so it is in historical writing.

This presents us with another way to contrast perspectivism with foundationalism—and thus historical writing with the social sciences. In perspectivism the relationship between subject and object is open, variable, and changeable—and the uses that are made of this indeterminacy are what primarily interests us both in politics and in historical writing. Foundationalism, on the contrary, is the attempt to fix this relationship for once and forever, and it is the epistemological investigation of the conditions of true belief from which this fixation is expected.

PERSPECTIVISM AND HISTORISM

It must strike us that perspectivism harbors, at least potentially, a particularly strong argument in favor of democracy, insofar as democracy is associated with the recognition of the uniqueness of the individual, and how could this recognition be better acknowledged than by perspectivism's claim that there is no common, foundationalist denominator of all the citizens' perspectives? In this way, perspectivism undoubtedly presents us with a better and stronger defense of democracy than the typically Enlightened foundationalist argument deriving democracy, in one way or another, from the essential equality of human individuals or from some other general aspect of the individual. I do not contest that these Enlightened foundationalist arguments have served their intended or unintended purpose: nobody could wish to deny the importance of the Enlightenment's contribution to the cause of democracy. Nevertheless, insofar as the respect of the human individual is a central element in democratic orthodoxy, this respect has a stronger support in perspectivism than in Enlightened universalism. And this difference between perspectivism and Enlightened foundationalism as ensign-bearers of democracy is all the more of practical interest in the light of postmodernist argument (as given by Berel Lang or Zygmunt Bauman)[7] that relates totalitarianism to Enlightened universalism. There certainly is more than a kernel of truth in the postmodernist analysis that the universalism of the Enlightenment foreshadowed totalitarianism by its lack of sympathy for what escapes the general rule of reason. While on the one hand this universalism gave us the equality of all citizens and the rule of law, the *Rechtsstaat*, on the other it stimulated a deep resentment against all that, for one reason or other, was difficult to fit into the dictates of universalist reason.[8]

I would like to pursue a little further this game of questioning (and reversing) the reputation of intellectual movements from the perspective of their contribution to (representative) democracy. If the Enlightenment is generally granted the honor of having given us democracy, it is no less generally agreed that historism is intrinsically antidemocratic. Several strands can be discerned in this line of reasoning. In the first place, it is argued that historism has been the heir of Machiavellian *raison d'état* thinking, and that *raison d'état* thinking urges us to identify with rulers, kings, and diplomats and thus to eschew the democratic perspective. The first part of the claim is undoubtedly correct: a self-professed historist such as Friedrich Meinecke wrote a whole book to demonstrate the continuity between *raison d'état* thinking and historism.[9] But the second part certainly is incorrect, since it by no means follows that the substitution of the kings and emperors of the *ancien régime* by our contemporary democratically chosen leaders would automatically rule out *raison d'état* as the politician's political compass. Democratically chosen leaders can sometimes be just as ruthless as their aristocratic and absolutist predecessors. There simply is no incompatibility between *raison d'état* thinking and democracy.[10] In the second place, it has been pointed out that historism, because of its conservatism, posed a serious threat to the (revolutionary) ideology of nascent democracy. But we need only think of Marx to realize that historism can just as well be revolutionary as conservative or reactionary. Who could doubt the historism of Marx's conception of history? Certainly most nineteenth-century historists happened to be political conservative, but the inference from this indisputable fact to the alleged inevitable conservatism of historism is a matter of sociological contingency rather than of theoretical necessity. Thirdly, and most importantly, historism was accused of historical relativism and, hence, of an incapacity to adhere firmly to moral standards in circumstances requiring us to do so. More specifically, in postwar German historiography there is a near to unanimous consensus that the historist heritage fatally weakened the moral defenses of German historians and intellectuals against the criminal policies of the Nazis. And the customary inference is that this may at least partly explain why the horrors of the Nazi regime became possible in the country where historism had won its most resounding victories.[11] It is this third criticism of historism that I shall focus on in the remainder of this chapter. Just as the *communis opinion* about the Enlightenment is only part of the whole truth, so it might well be with historist relativism. In order to substantiate this claim, I shall argue below that historist perspectivism entails a (democratic) respect of others rather than a relativist indifference to them, and that this is one of the more attractive features of historism, insufficiently recognized until now.

A first indication of the contribution by historism to such democratic values offers itself when we ask ourselves how historist perspectivism was translated into historical practice. Since in historist perspectivism all depends on finding the most appropriate perspective from which the past ought to be seen, nothing was allowed to interfere with the difficult and subtle process of identifying that perspective. More specifically, initially historism was a sustained attack on how Enlightenment values and self-complacency about the achievement of these values tended to curtail the freedom of movement of historical perspective. At a later stage all sorts of historical, cultural, religious, and metaphysical determinations were seen to threaten perspectivist freedom and were condemned for that reason. And at the end of this route lay Gadamer's attack on historical epistemology that had until then succeeded to escape this historist onslaught on the limitations of perspectivist freedom. Since Gadamer, the historist can only establish that there are certain traditions in how historical perspective has been defined—think of Gadamer's notion of *Wirkungsgeschichte*—but there is nothing, no longer even a historical epistemology, that may guide the historian's perspective. In this way, the *ne plus ultra* of objectivism, the urge to leave the past as it was (i.e., untainted by even "epistemological prejudice"), is paradoxically combined with the requirement of a complete freedom for the historian's perspective—on the face of it, the *ne plus ultra* of subjectivism. Not the epistemological regimentation of perspectivism but a quasi-anarchic freedom of movement is now the guarantee of historical "truth" and objectivity. Historical objectivity demands a complete openness of the historian to the subject matter, and this requires, in its turn, the abandonment of all "foundationalism" as understood in this book.

RESPECT

But even more important in the present context is the following. The requirement of this complete openness of historians in their relationship to their subject matter was codified in Ranke's famous "Jede Epoche ist unmittelbar zu Gott" (Each epoch is immediate to God), in which God's perspective is presented as the embodiment of the historian's perspectivist freedom. The intuition is, apparently, that God's point of view becomes accessible to us to the extent that we succeed in overcoming all moralist, historical, epistemological, and other determination of historical insight. This is an intriguing idea, and we had, perhaps, best rely on the notion of historical experience in order to flesh it out.[12] But within the scope of this chapter another aspect of Ranke's famous dictum is of more interest. As far as I know, de Boer was the first to draw our attention to the universalism of Ranke's statement. Perhaps this universalism always went unheeded since the statement was exclusively interpreted as emphasizing the unicity and the individuality of a historical period. Nevertheless, Ranke explicitly speaks of *jede*, of *each* historical period: *each* historical period must be unconditionally respected by the historian and be studied accordingly. Our respect of the value peculiar to a period should not be restricted to that one period only, but embrace the whole sequence of periods that we have learned to discern in our past.

The universalism of the Enlightenment and the respect for individuality that is so typical of historism are thus most happily combined with each other. It could succeed in achieving this remarkable feat because it began by taking seriously the Enlightenment belief in a universal moral truth, but observed, next, the lack of respect for the individuality of historical periods resulting from the Enlightenment program, and it could thus conclude that *respect* is the only universalist value that could be rescued from the shipwreck of Enlightenment universalism. "Respect" had to be the outcome since (1) the projection of Enlightenment values "universally" stimulated this lack of respect (so that it required a mere reversal of the Enlightenment's "universal" error in order to produce respect as the new universalist value); and (2) "respect" satisfied the historist minimum condition for a universalist value of respecting the incommensurability between historical periods. In this way historism truly was only possible thanks to, and after, Enlightenment universalism; in this way, moreover, historism is not a radical negation or antithesis of the Enlightenment, but, once again, its perfection. And the value of respect is what we have gained by moving from the Enlightenment to its completion in historism. When we follow de Boer in his proposal to translate Ranke's dictum to the domain of human individuals and their interaction, the result is a more complete and forceful plea for the respect of the human individual than is given by Enlightenment universalism.[13] For the foundationalism of natural law philosophies demanded a respect of only those aspects of the human individual that fitted within the foundationalist account of human nature. Hobbes required the state to respect and guarantee the individual's safety, and could require *only* this, because the desire of safety was the foundation of his political system. His political philosophy left no room for the state's obligation to care about, for example, the citizen's education and intellectual development. This parameter simply was not in his system. On the contrary, each aspect of the human individual can, in principle, be part of a historist list of the state's obligations with regard to its citizens. Thanks to the historist focus on individuality, on the integral individuality (of a historical period or of the human individual, if we follow de Boer) nothing is a priori excluded from the range of the historist's value of respect.

Two remarks must be added for a correct understanding of the historist theory of the respect we owe to the human individual. In the first place, one might begin by complimenting the historist for achieving this synthesis of the Enlightenment and historism, but then point out that a high price will have to be paid for this. The price to be paid is, so one might go on, that the introduction of the very notion of the integral human individual (as opposed to the foundationalist's invariably truncated human individual) in our argument will prove to be an open invitation to totalitarianism. For where do we find, or encounter this integral human individual? It's not something that we can come across, like that house over there, or the dog of our neighbor. In fact, it will at all times be a construction, a conception of what we take to be the integral human being. But, as the history of the past century shows, however high-minded such conceptions may be, in practice they are far from innocent. For as soon as the powers that be accept such a conception we may expect them to yield to the temptation to enforce it upon the citizen. All the old Rousseauist mechanisms of "forcing the citizen to be free" will then be put into motion; and the present American war on smoking and on drugs demonstrates that these dangers are far from being illusionary even in a still essentially liberal society. In agreement with the common wisdom in political philosophy it will be argued that the only effective brake upon this totalitarian seduction is a completely antimetaphysical conception of the human individual, carefully refraining from pronouncements on the so-called integral human being. In sum, all that we might expect from the intersection of the Enlightenment and historism will be lost again as soon as we embrace this so dangerous notion of the integral human individual.

However, the historist may successfully counter this objection with the simple but decisive observation that respect is at stake in his argument and that totalitarian encroachments on the citizen are therefore ruled out by the very nature of the historist argument and of the value in question. In fact, no virtue is more conspicuously absent in totalitarian thought than that of respect.

In the second place, should we not restrict the historist argument to the sphere of private life and prefer Enlightenment foundationalism for the public sphere, the sphere in which the state has to act? But if seen as an extension or radicalization of Enlightenment notions of the obligations of the state toward the citizen, the distinction between the private and the public sphere is irrelevant to it. Self-evidently, this does not mean that the distinction *as such* would be irrelevant (from the historist point of view). The implication merely is that the distinction does not follow from it and therefore requires an independent justification. And when the distinction (admittedly) almost automatically follows from foundationalist Enlightenment argument, this should, perhaps, be seen as its shortcoming rather than as one of its charms. For these two things *really* are different. There is no a priori reason to believe that the distinction between where the state should and should not respect the individual citizen runs parallel to that between the private and the public. Think, once again, of education: education is part of the *public* sphere and an aspect of the *individual's* life that the state, in our contemporary conception of the state's tasks, is supposed to (actively) *respect.*

But does the historist's respect of the integral human individual not also require the state to respect the criminal, and hence merely to try to understand him instead of punishing him for his criminal behavior? And is it not part of the logic of the historist argument that seeing an individual as a whole in which his history, his life, his psychology, and so on are integrated, will ultimately invite an attitude of *tout comprendre c'est tout pardonner*? In the same vein it has often been argued that the respect that the historist should demonstrate for each historical period will also require him to "respect" such abject regimes as Nazism or Soviet communism. More specifically, does not the historicization of the Nazis, for example, invite a wholly untoward attitude of forgiveness? For can we go on holding Christopher Browning's family fathers responsible for the incredible atrocities committed by them after these have been explained historically? This question has been put on the historian's agenda with a renewed urgency in the recent debate about the Browning-Goldhagen controversy.[14] There are two strands in arguments like these, which need to be disentangled. In the first place there is the old philosophical problem of how the explanation of human behavior affects our notions of freedom and moral responsibility. This is not the place to deal with this old and extremely complicated problem. Suffice it to say here that the issue not only arises with regard to historism, but is occasioned by all history and all historical writing claiming to be able to explain human behavior. So whoever fears the relativist implications of historicization should not reserve his wrath for historism only, but place *all* of historical writing under a moral interdict.

However, precisely historism is less helpless against this accusation of moral indifference than other variants of historical writing. Recall that historism requires us to cultivate the virtue of respect for historical periods, cultures, or religions that may seem at first sight alien, strange, and incommensurable with our own. Needless to say, it was the complete disregard of precisely this supremely historist value with which the crime committed by the Nazis began. No historist who takes historism seriously can subscribe to anti-Semitism. Let us turn, finally, to the problem of criminal behavior that was mentioned above. Certainly, the state, the judge, must "respect" criminals by hearing them out, by trying to understand what made them commit their crimes, by granting them due process of law, and so on. But this is all that is needed, also within the historist argument, since going beyond this and to surrender to the attitude of *tout comprendre c'est tout pardonner* would testify to a lack of respect of the legal order or of the (safety of the) citizens that have been or could in the future be hurt by the criminal's actions. Though not necessarily so, the virtue of respect can be no less even-handed than its cognate virtue of justice.

In sum, "respect" is the value that is given to us in return for the historist historicization of the world, and this value is an adequate compensation for the dangers that we may, rightly or mistakenly, expect from historicization. Moreover, it is a value especially "valuable" in and for democracy, insofar as democracy is par excellence the political system requiring us to respect our fellow citizens, whatever their background may be. In this way, there is an elective affinity between historism and democracy, and it need not surprise us that both came into being under the same historical circumstances.

MONADOLOGY AND DEMOCRATIC PERSPECTIVISM

The historist theory of historical representation can render us another service. Historians like Friedrich Meinecke or Ernst Cassirer have pointed out how much the historist's notion of historical individuality owes to Leibniz's monadology. When historists wanted to attack and discredit the universalism so typical of in all Enlightenment thought, they looked for a philosophical system elevating individuality above generality or universality. Leibniz's monadology proved to be the best weapon in their fight with the Enlightenment. Here the right arguments could be found in order to prove that "the individual is ineffable" and that individuality precedes generality.

According to Leibniz, the universe is constituted by individual monads that correspond more or less to the objects contained by the world as we know it; here, no clash with universalist Enlightenment thought was to be expected. But such a conflict arose when Leibniz went on to argue that these monads were "windowless." The idea is, roughly, that it is only an illusion when we believe that we perceive other things outside ourselves (i.e., outside the individual monads that we are), certain regularities determining their behavior, and so on. We should conceive of the individual monad, rather, as an individual looking within the privacy of a strictly private cinema to a film of what seems to take place outside this cinema. But the individual monad is "windowless," in the sense that he can not have a look outside this private cinema, to which he is condemned, and see what takes place in "the real world," so to speak. So if I believe that something takes place in a reality outside myself, this is only because the life program (the film that I am looking at, as it were) of the monad that I am, causes me presently to be in a mental state that makes me think so.

Whatever the attractions or oddities of Leibnizian monadology may be, there is a big problem that it will have to deal with in some way or other. The problem is this. When different monads have certain perceptions of what seems to take place in a reality outside themselves, such perceptions have a surprising tendency to correspond and to reinforce each other. When *I* see a table in this room, *you* are likely to perceive this table there as well. Obviously, Leibniz's thesis of the windowlessness of the monads makes this difficult to explain. For why should the film that *I* am looking at in *my* private cinema correspond so completely to what *you* see in the privacy of *your* cinema? Leibniz had a rather brutal solution for this difficult problem. He began with the axiom that God, when creating the world (or, rather, the totality of individual monads), had wanted to realize the best and most perfect world. In order to realize this aim, God had to figure out how the life programs of all the individual monads would have to be, down to the last detail, so that they would all completely correspond with each other and achieve this best and most perfect world. So it is thanks to God's decision to realize a perfect world that all a monad's perceptions of a world outside itself cohere and are in perfect harmony with the perceptions of all other monads of this outside world. This is Leibniz's thesis of the *harmonie préétablie*. Needless to say, the actual realization of this "preestablished harmony" required an amount of calculation of which only God is capable. And this is why Leibniz could use the immense problems occasioned by his monadology to his own advantage by presenting them as the measure of both God's goodness when creating the best of all possible worlds and of His unimaginable computational talent for correctly figuring out how to realize this most perfect world. This truly is what is called making a virtue out of a necessity.

Anyway, whatever one may think of Leibniz's monadological speculations, in the present context it is worthwhile to have a close look at the optical metaphor that Leibniz used himself to explain his monadology. The metaphor in question is as follows:

Just as the same city viewed from different sides appears to be different and to be, as it were, multiplied in perspectives, so the infinite multitude of simple substances (or monads), which seem to be so many different universes, are nevertheless only the perspectives of a single universe according to the different points of view of each monad. . . . Now this mutual connection or accommodation of all created things to each other, and of each to all the rest, causes each simple substance to have relations which express all the others and consequently to be a perpetual living mirror of the universe.[15]

Now, what is of so much interest in this metaphor is the suggestion that we do not have the city first and only then look at it from different perspectives. This is, of course, our natural, and commonsensical way of thinking. But within Leibnizian monadology this picture is completely reversed. For there we have, first, different perspectives, as embodied by the monads perceiving (or believing to perceive) the city. And, next, to the extent that all these perspectives cohere, the city can be said to exist and not to be an idle illusion. Hence, and this is what Leibnizian monadology is all about, it is not so that we first have a universe with all the individual things (or monads, if you prefer) contained by it and, only next, the perspectives from which these things or monads perceive each other. It is precisely the other way around. You first have the monads (whose nature and life programs should all be perspectively defined, as is required by monadological ontology), and only then, only afterward, will you have some kind of universe that they all seem to inhabit and that may arise out of the mutual interaction of their perspectives. The universe is here *derived* from the individual monads, from individuality, and does not *precede* them.

Elsewhere I have argued that Leibnizian monadology is the kind of metaphysics ideally suited to the world of history and of historical writing.[16] If Leibniz's monadology may well seem the absurdest system ever devised by a philosopher to account for the world of houses, trees, chairs, or human beings, and for how we perceive these objects, it is ideally suited to an account of the "objects" inhabiting the worlds of culture and history. But Leibnizian monadology can also contribute to a better understanding of democracy and of where that political system differs from others. We can think of Leibniz's monads as the individual citizens of a democracy and of the state as the level where their perspectives mutually interact and may achieve a (partial) harmony. Of course, I shall be the first to admit that this is an incredibly crude and clumsy model of democracy. Nevertheless, it does capture most of the essential differences between democracy and other political systems.

First, as Leibniz emphasizes, "the nature of the monad being to represent,"[17] the nature or substance of a monad, is determined by what it sees of the universe from its own specific and unique perspective. This is in agreement with the Machiavellian thesis of the brokenness of political reality (and it must strike us that Machiavelli defended his thesis with much the same optical metaphor as the one used by Leibniz), which is nowhere more manifest than in antifoundationalist representative democracy. Second, the uniqueness of each individual citizen (and the necessity to *respect* this uniqueness) is unassailable insofar as it is related to the monad's perspective. For each change in perspective would automatically give us another monad; individuality and perspective are indissolubly tied together. Third, Leibniz's "preestablished harmony" has its obvious counterpart in democracy's political aim of achieving an optimum compromise of the political vantage points of all the individual (monadological) citizens. Just as the notion or idea of Leibniz's city may gradually arise out of a comparison of all monadological perspectives, so the notion or idea of the common good, which both "respects" all individual perspectives and yet creates something new out of this (i.e., this notion of the city), may arise out of the interaction of all these perspectives. When this fusion of perspective is reached in politics, we speak of political compromise. Obviously, perspectivist harmony can only be partial in politics, since there is no God with His superhuman capacity for calculation to achieve a political *harmonie préétablie.* So the distinction between the private and the public (or the political) is a reflection of man's imperfection, if compared with God, and therefore very well protected against totalitarian attempts to do away with it.

But of even more importance within the present context is the following. This chapter has mainly been an attack on political foundationalism in the name of Machiavellianist perspectivism. The question then arises of how deep are the differences between these two political positions, between foundationalism and a perspectivist political aestheticism (from which most is to be expected for a proper understanding of democracy), and what philosophical means can best be used to express those differences. The foregoing suggests that the discussion between political foundationalism and its perspectivist opponent can best be conducted in terms of a discussion about the advantages of Leibnizian monadology, compared with traditional metaphysics and epistemology when both are applied to the sphere of politics. And the decisive advantage of Leibnizian monadology is that here the (political) universe does not *precede* individual monads but is a *product* of them. Here the priority of the citizen to the state is better protected than in any other (foundationalist) political ontology.[18] We should therefore turn to Leibniz if we wish to spell out in detail what it means to subscribe to Rorty's thesis of "the priority of democracy to philosophy."

Most of contemporary political philosophy and political science is foundationalist, as defined above. Certainly many good things can and should be said about foundationalist political philosophy. The essential shortcoming of foundationalism, however, is that it cannot account for the theory and practice of representative democracy. For as authors like Talmon and Popper have suggested, foundationalism has an inbred tendency to yield to the totalitarian temptation. And if, fortunately, in most cases it effectively resisted this temptation, this was thanks to its methodological individualism and the aversion to a strong state caused by this methodology, rather than by an open-minded analysis of the state and of the functioning of representative democracy. Civil liberties and the small state were the most welcome trophies obtained by methodological individualism in its struggle with its own alter ego, that is, with the universalist pretensions of foundationalist political philosophy.

We must be grateful to foundationalist political philosophy for its many contributions to the causes of equality, civil freedom, justice, and responsible government. Its weakness has been, however, a lack of understanding of the workings of representative democracy. Representative democracy is a far more subtle, sophisticated, and therefore also a far more vulnerable political system than we tend to believe. In this chapter I have tried to show that the acceptance of Machiavelli's and Berlin's thesis of the brokenness of political reality is the indispensable first step toward a satisfactory understanding of representative democracy. Next, I have tried to elaborate this insight into the nature of representative democracy. To that end I have discussed perspectivism, the elective affinities of representative democracy and historism, and "respect" as the supreme virtue of representative democracy.

We have no reasons to worry about those elements of representative democracy that we have inherited from the Enlightenment, foundationalist tradition. Freedom, toleration, the rights of minorities, the *Rechtsstaat* are less threatened than ever before in most contemporary Western democracies. But there is less reason for satisfaction, let alone for optimism about the elements of representative democracy that were discussed in this chapter. The brokenness of political reality, the uses, and even necessity of political conflict, the indispensable role of political parties in the expression of political conflict, the political creativity of compromise (which was discussed in Chapter 8), the dilemmas of decision making in actual political practice—all these things are not only rarely discussed in (contemporary) political philosophy but even tend to disappear from political practice itself. The political machinery of representative democracy seems to have become an obsolete irrelevance in our contemporary societies; science, technology, and the network now all seem far better equipped to deal with our collective problems than representative democracy. In Chapter 4 we saw what adverse consequences we must fear from the impending death of politics. For I remain convinced that we cannot do without representative democracy; I therefore cannot share the equanimity of many about the falling apart of the mechanisms of representative democracy.

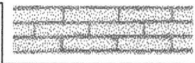

EPILOGUE

If traditionally the philosopher's subjects are said to be the true, the good, and the beautiful, the first two have always been most intensively discussed. The beautiful we associate with art; and though nobody will deny what art can mean to us, most people will agree that, if necessary, we can do without art but not without what we may expect from the investigation of the true and the good. "Truth" will provide us with the necessities of life, and the good ensures that the behavior of our fellow human beings will not be a constant threat to us (nor our own to them, for that matter). Art may beautify the ugliness of life, but as such it is a lie and a flight from reality rather than a key to the secrets of the world and of ourselves. From Plato to Rousseau and beyond, many philosophers have held such disconsolate opinions about aesthetics.

The main purpose of this book has been to suggest where this dismissive attitude toward aesthetics is profoundly wrong. For the significance of aesthetics exceeds by far the analysis of artistic excellence. Aesthetics is part of our lives and permeates all kinds of human activity that at first sight seem to have no relationship with aesthetics. In the introduction to my *Historical Representation*,[1] I discussed Wolfgang Welsch's notion of "transversal reason," the kind of reason he associated, following Kant in this, with aesthetics.[2] Welsch attributed to aesthetic transversal reason the capacity of transcending "local" variants of rationality, such as "cognitive, ethical, aesthetic, religious or technical" rationality. These rationalities share no common ground; they are *incommensurable* with each other and therefore do not permit the transition from one to another on their own terms only. Nevertheless, such transitions become possible thanks to transversal reason: for it possesses the unique capacity of dealing with incommensurability.

The notion of (aesthetic) representation may clarify how the challenges of incommensurability can be met. And this should not surprise us. For the historian presents us with representations of the past, and such representations do indeed achieve, with more or less success, a unity or an integration within one coherent whole of developments on domains that are incommensurable with each other. For example, the historian may present us with a coherent picture of the cognitive, ethical, aesthetic, religious, or technical preoccupations of a period, and may then freely move from one domain to another and show how what happened on one domain can meaningfully be related to what took place elsewhere.

If we ask ourselves how representation may enable us to do this, the answer is that the unique contribution of representation (and of aesthetics in general) is that it involves the knowing subject. For the synthesis effected by representation is an implicit adhortation to readers of a historical account to place themselves on, or, rather, to *identify* themselves with a certain point of view. The self is activated by representation in a way that would mean the end of objective knowledge and of description. Representation adds the idea of the point of view to that of objective knowledge. And from the point of view recommended by a representation, suddenly a common ground can be discerned for domains that seemed, hitherto, completely unrelated and incommensurable. For example, at first sight seventeenth-century rationalist philosophy and absolutism will have nothing in common for us. But then the historian may suggest the point of view of the transcendental ego, of a self that withdraws from the world but only in order to get a firmer hold of it. And this point of view makes us aware of what the Cartesian self, doubting all knowledge only in order to gain access to absolutely certain knowledge, has in common with Louis XIV withdrawing from the bustle of Paris to Versailles in order to confirm his absolutist mastery of France. Incommensurability will remain as long as we focus on seventeenth-century epistemology and political practice themselves. We may ponder these two domains as long as we wish and penetrate into them as deeply as we can—but this will never result in the intellectual illumination that may follow when adopting the point of view the historian has recommended to us.

It is true that this identification with the point of view suggested by the historian will not always affect our personal identity very deeply. It will remain relatively outside of our personality, and the identification is only partial and temporary. Nevertheless, becoming acquainted with the possibility of many such points of view will add, each time, a new, though tiny stone to the mosaic of our personality. And in the end this cannot fail to have its effect on the kind of person that we are. So much was emphasized already by nineteenth-century German theorists recognizing, in the footsteps of Humboldt, how historical learning may contribute to *Bildung*. Literally, the word *Bildung* means "formation"—here the formation of our personality—a connotation that is lost in its English equivalent, "edification." We become a different person by reading history and this is thanks to how representations, albeit locally, may contribute to the formation of our personal identity. For what is our identity, after all, other than a Protean and loosely stitched-together set of points of view?

And no less indispensable is representation in the realm of politics. We tend to restrict the political uses of the notion to how political parties or politicians may represent the electorate. And since representation is the heart of representative democracy, we shall not easily overlook the importance of political representation. But representation is more omnipresent in politics. For we have politics for no other reason than that it enables us to deal in a more or less responsible way with the paradoxes and the incommensurabilities that constitute social reality. And it is thanks to representation that the politician may succeed in rising above the chaos of these incommensurabilities. In this way, political representation is the symbol of all politics; and if only because of this, we cannot praise representative democracy enough. For it has made the symbol of all politics into its very heart.

REFERENCE MATTER

NOTES

INTRODUCTION

1. Thucydides, *History of the Peloponnesian War*, in M. I. Finley, *The Portable Greek Historians* (Harmondsworth, Eng., 1959), 231.

2. For a history of this topic, see Koselleck's classic *Historia Magistra Vitae: Über die Auflösung des Topos im Horizont neuzeitlich bewegter Geschichte*, in R. Koselleck, *Vergangene Zukunft: Zur Semantik geschichtlicher Zeiten* (Frankfurt am Main, 1979), 38–67.

3. N. Machiavelli, *Discourses on Livy*, trans. H. C. Mansfield and N. Tarcov (Chicago, 1996), 85.

4. See the second section of Chapter 6 for a discussion of Berlin's comments on Machiavelli.

CHAPTER 1: *History and Political Theory*

1. One may think here, for example, of G. H. Sabine, *A History of Political Theory* (London, 1968); M. Prélot, *Histoire des idées politiques* (Paris, 1970); W. Theimer, *Geschichte der politischen Ideen* (Bern, 1955); L. Arnhart, *Political Questions* (New York, 1987); L. Straus and G. Cropsey, *History of Political Theory* (Chicago, 1963); L. Macfarlan, *Modern Political Theory* (Oxford, 1970); J. Plamenatz, *Man and Society*, 2 vols. (London, 1963); D. D. Rafael, *Problems of Political Philosophy* (London, 1976); J. S. McClelland, *A History of Western Political Thought* (London, 1996); B. Readhead, ed., *From Plato to Nato* (London, 1984). All translations in this book are my own unless quoted from secondary literature or otherwise cited.

2. On Strauss's work and influence, see T. L. Pangle, ed., *The Rebirth of Classical Rationalism* (Chicago, 1990).

3. L. Strauss, *Natural Right and History* (1950; repr. Chicago, 1968), 9.

4. Ibid., 29.

5. In Chapter 2 of my *Historical Representation* (Stanford, Calif., 2001), I show what is wrong with this argument and how to avoid relativism in a political theory that takes history as its point of departure.

6. Quoted in A. Seifert, *Cognitio historica: Die Geschichte als Namengeberin der frühneuzeitlichen Empirie* (Berlin, 1976), 185–86.

7. It was a "vorwissenschaftliche, wirklichkeitsnahe Sacherkenntnis." See ibid., 10, 29.

8. Examples of this, apart from what has been said just now, are history as *narratio rei gesta, vera narratio, cognitio quod est, sensata cognitio, cognitio aliorum sensibus, nuda facta notitia,* and *cognitio ex datis,* respectively.

9. "Wahrscheinlichkeit heisst wenn ich fremde Empfindungen unvolkommen erkenne." Quoted in Seifert, *Cognitio historica,* 159.

10. Though historical theory (*historice,* in Vossius's terminology) did have the status of being a science: "As we have been saying, although the writing of history is neither a science nor art, and hence no discipline at all, seeing things historically is an art, since it involves an appeal to universals" (quoted in ibid., 20). Wickenden attributes to Vossius a conception of history that is far closer to contemporary conceptions. See N. Wickenden, *G. J. Vossius and the Humanist Conception of History* (Assen, Neth., 1993), 66–72, 82–88. We should take into account, however, that Wickenden tries to bring Vossius as close as possible to contemporary conceptions of historical theory.

11. H. Grotius, *De iure belli ac pacis* (Amsterdam, 1720), xxii: "Primum mihi cura haec fuit, ut eorum quae ad ius naturae pertinent probationes referrem ad notiones quasdam tam certas, ut eas negare nemo possit, nisi sibi vim inferat. Principia enim eius iuris, si modo animum recte advertas, per se patent atque evidentia sunt, ferme ad modum eorum quae sensibus externis percipimus."

12. Ibid., xxv: "For I emphasize that it has been my intention to abstract from singular facts when writing about law just as mathematics investigates figures without considering actual objects."

13. L. Gossman, *French Society and Culture: A Background for Eighteenth-Century Literature* (Englewood Cliffs, N.J., 1974); A. H. Horowitz, *Rousseau, Nature, and History* (Toronto, 1986). Characteristic of Rousseau's ambivalent attitude toward history is the strange place of the *Contrat social* in the whole of his oeuvre. Whereas the two *Discourses* explain how the course of actual history had distorted human nature, the completely a- or antihistorist *Contrat social* has no other purpose than to legitimate (an extreme degree of) socialization under certain, well-defined conditions. Hence, history is needed for a correct understanding of existing society, whereas all the "obstacles" of history have to be removed if we wish to realize the societal "transparency" of the good of society. Of course, I'm using here the metaphors proposed by J. Starobinski in his brilliant *Jean-Jacques Rousseau: La Transparence et l'obstacle* (Paris, 1971).

14. G. W. F. Hegel, *Vorlesungen über die Philosophie der Weltgeschichte,* 4 vols.; vol. 1, *Die Vernunft in der Geschichte* (Hamburg, 1955), 28, 29.

15. L. von Ranke, *The Theory and Practice of History,* ed. G. G. Iggers and K. von Moltke (Indianapolis, 1973), 25–51.

16. N. Machiavelli, *Discourses on Livy*, trans. H. C. Mansfield and N. Tarcov (Chicago, 1996), 83–84.

17. P. S. Donaldson, *Machiavelli and Mystery of State* (Cambridge, Eng., 1992), 10, 123, 200.

18. E. Kantorowicz, "Mysteries of State: An Absolutist Concept and Its Medieval Origins," *Harvard Theological Review* 48, no. 1 (1955): 65–93.

19. Ibid.

20. Quoted in Donaldson, *Machiavelli and Mystery of State*, 114.

21. G. Naudé, *Considérations politiques sur les coups d'Etat*, intro. and notes Françoise Charles-Daubert (1639; facsimile, Hildesheim, Ger., 1993), 65–66. The verses at the end are from Horace, *Epistles*, 1.16.60.

22. The association with the sublime is all the more appropriate since Naudé compares his coups d'etat with natural phenomena such as the appearance of comets, storm surges, earthquakes, or the eruptions of vulcanoes that are ordinarily seen as the prototypical manifestations of the sublime. See Naudé, *Considérations politiques*, 78.

23. See, for example, E. Burke, *A Philosophical Enquiry into the Origin of Our Ideas of the Sublime and the Beautiful* (Oxford, 1990), 121–22.

24. N. Machiavelli, *The Prince*, trans. Q. Skinner (Bungay, Eng., 1961), 99.

25. Naudé, *Considérations politiques*, 76.

26. Donaldson, *Machiavelli and Mystery of State*, 174.

27. Of course, Machiavelli had already discovered some Machiavellianisms in the Old Testament; see, for example, *The Prince*, chap. 26, or *Discourses on Livy*, bk. 1, chaps. 4, 9, 26.

28. For Naudé's relationship to the *libertins érudits* and their risque theological speculations, see the huge but disappointing R. Pintard, *Le Libertinage érudit dans la première moitié du XVIIme siècle* (Paris, 1943), 156ff.

29. Donaldson, *Machiavelli and Mystery of State*, 197.

30. Naudé, *Considérations politiques*, 40.

31. F. Meinecke, *Idee der Staatsräson in der neueren Geschichte* (1924; repr. Munich, 1976), 237.

32. Another way of dealing with this problem has famously been proposed by Leo Strauss and his followers. Strauss argues that Machiavelli's text is a secret mirroring the secrecy of the *arcana imperii* themselves.

> As the friend or father of new modes and orders, he is often of necessity the enemy of the old modes and orders, and therewith the enemy of his readers who would not have to learn from him if they were not adherents of the old modes and orders. Machiavelli's action is a kind of warfare. Some things which he says about strategy and tactics in ordinary warfare apply strategy and tactics in what we may call his spiritual warfare.

See L. Strauss, *Thoughts on Machiavelli* (London, 1958), 35. For a defense by one of Strauss's most faithful disciples against his many detractors, see H. C. Mansfield, *Machiavelli's Virtue* (Chicago, 1996), chap. 9.

33. See, for example, B. Graciàn, *Obras completas*, ed. A. del Hoyo (Madrid, 1967), cxxxi.

34. This is where these modern natural law philosophies so much differ from their contemporary variants, which, whether liberal or communitarian, tend to take a so much more optimistic view of the human individual (or normatively demand such a view).

35. The crucial contribution of Dutch seventeenth-century political thought to this "naturalization" of Machiavellianism in natural law philosophy is shown in Blom, *Morality and Causality in Politics: The Rise of Naturalism in Dutch Seventeenth-Century Political Thought* (Ridderkerk, Neth., 1995).

36. Just as less than a century later Bernard de Mandeville would shock the world (again) by pointing out what Christian duties can paradoxically be served by selfishness and egoism.

37. Naudé, *Considérations politiques*, 202.

38. M. Stolleis, "Machiavellismus und Staatsräson," in Stolleis, ed., *Hermann Conring (1606–1681): Beiträge zu Leben und Werk* (Berlin, 1983), 181.

39. N. Hammerstein, "Die Historie bei Conring," in Stolleis, ed., *Hermann Conring*, 223.

40. Ibid., 221.

41. Ibid., 219.

42. A. van Deursen, *Geschiedenis en toekomstverwachting* (Kampen, Neth., 1971), 9.

43. Ibid. See also A. Seifert, "Staatenkunde: Eine neue Disziplin und ihr wissenschaftstheoretischer Ort," in N. Rassem and J. Stagl, eds., *Statistik und Staatsbeschreibung in der Neuzeit* (Paderborn, Ger., 1980).

44. Quoted in Meinecke, *Idee der Staatsräson*, 455.

45. Ibid., 453.

46. L. von Ranke, *Sämmtliche Werke*, vol. 24, *Abhandlungen und Versuche* (Leipzig, Ger., 1872), 288–89.

47. L. von Ranke, "Anhang über Machiavell," in Ranke, *Sämmtliche Werke*, 54 vols. (Leipzig, Ger., 1874), 34: 151–74.

CHAPTER 2: *Edmund Burke*

1. For this issue, see G. A. Reisch, "Chaos, History, and Narrative," *History and Theory* 30 (1991): 1–21; and D. N. McCloskey, "History, Differential Equations, and the Problem of Narration," *History and Theory* 30 (1991): 21–37. The standard example is always the butterfly in China causing a hurricane in the United States.

2. This is, by the way, the lady who so famously aroused Rousseau sexually while spanking him.

3. J. Starobinski, *Jean-Jacques Rousseau: La Transparence et l'obstacle* (Paris, 1971), 18–19.

4. Ibid., 19.

5. See F. Meinecke, *Die Entstehung des Historismus* (Munich, 1965), 270.

6. E. Burke, *The Works of Edmund Burke*, 12 vols.; vol. 4, *An Appeal from the New to the Old Whigs* (Boston, 1866), 176.

7. Ibid., 165.

8. And he might even be prepared to concede to Rousseau that history is the tragic spectacle of human injustice and iniquity. But, as Burke argued in his *Vindication*, one may "confess all these things, yet plead the necessity of political institutions, weak and wicked as they are." See E. Burke, *The Works of Edmund Burke*, vol. 1, *A Vindication of Natural Society*, 65.

9. E. Burke, *The Works of Edmund Burke*, vol. 3, *Reflections on the Revolution in France*, 346.

10. "This is why the prejudices of the individual historian have a far greater scope than his pronouncements about the past." And in the section following this claim, Gadamer expounds the role of "prejudice as a condition of historical understanding." See H. G. Gadamer, *Wahrheit und Methode* (Tübingen, Ger., 1960), 261.

11. For an exposition of the relevant weaknesses of Gadamer's argument, see my *Exploraties: Politieke filosofie*, 3 vols.; vol. 2, *De macht van representatie* (Kampen, Neth., 1996), 226 ff.

12. It may well be that Burke—who, as the author of *A Philosophical Enquiry into the Origin of Our Ideas of the Sublime and the Beautiful*, was so much more fascinated by the obscurity of the sublime than by the clarity of the beautiful—unwittingly carried over his aesthetics to his politics here.

13. Quoted in L. Strauss, *Natural Right and History* (Chicago, 1968), 301.

14. Burke, *Reflections on the Revolution in France*, 296.

15. Ibid., 345–46.

16. And it certainly is a most surprising fact about *Wahrheit und Methode* that its careful and so immensely erudite author never pays any attention to Burke.

17. As I show in chapter 1 of *Historical Representation* (Stanford, Calif., 2001), this is the kind of question that belongs to the heart of all historical writing.

18. I. Kant, "Über den Gemeinspruch: Das mag in der Theorie richtig sein, taugt aber nicht für die Praxis, in Kant, *Kleinere Schriften zur Geschichtsphilosophie, Ethik und Politik* (Hamburg, 1973), 85.

19. Let us agree with the prevailing opinion according to which the correspondence theory of truth gives the correct definition of the meaning of the word "true" (i.e., a statement is true, if and only if it corresponds to a certain state of affairs in reality). It follows from this definition that truth and falsity can only be established if the distinction between language and reality presents us with no difficulties. For if *such* difficulties would arise it would *ex definitione* have become impossible to use the correspondence theory of truth. So if one accepts the correspondence theory, one is automatically obliged also to accept this clear demarca-

tion line between language and reality and vice versa—hence, precisely that distinction which is put into question within the regime of wisdom versus folly.

20. Burke, *Reflections on the Revolution in France*, 443.

21. In the very first sentence of Erasmus's *Praise of Folly* Erasmus explicitly states that it is precisely the fools who hate folly most.

22. See chapter 3 of the *Praise of Folly*. With regard to the last part of this essay, it is of interest to note the Aristotelian link between wisdom and happiness suggested here by Erasmus.

23. As Foucault unusually succinctly puts it: "If there is such a thing as reason, we can only find it in the continuous movement between wisdom and folly and in the awareness of their reciprocity and of their impossible mutual dependence." See M. Foucault, *Histoire de la folie à l'âge classique* (Paris, 1972), 44.

24. Quoted in ibid., 47.

25. Burke, *Appeal from the New to the Old Whigs*, 188.

26. And Burke even goes on to argue that in proportion that rights may seem to us metaphysically true, they must be morally and politically false. See Burke, *Reflections on the Revolution in France*, 313, and Strauss, *Natural Right and History*, 307, 310.

27. Burke, *Reflections on the Revolution in France*, 274.

28. Ibid., 311. Or, as Tocqueville once succinctly put it: in politics "Nothing is more improductive to the mind than an abstract idea." See A. de Tocqueville, *Democracy in America*, 2 vols. (New York, 1945), 2: 243.

29. Burke, *Reflections on the Revolution in France*, 311.

30. C. Schmitt, *The Concept of the Political* (Chicago, 1997), 35.

31. Burke, *Reflections on the Revolution in France*, 313.

32. One may regret that nowhere in his writings does Burke discuss the legitimacy of the Dutch revolt against Philip II of Spain. On the other hand, one cannot fail to notice his amazingly dispassionate view of the Civil War and Burke's not unsympathetic assessment of Cromwell, described by him as that "great bad man of the old stamp" (see ibid., 294).

33. Ibid., 308.

34. E. Burke, "Letter to a Member of the National Assembly," in *The Works of Edmund Burke*, 4: 41.

35. For an absurd exaggeration of these disasters, to which Burke is typically prone, see Burke's *Vindication of Natural Society* (24 ff.), where he calculates the number of people murdered in the whole of history and, in his enthusiasm in this enterprise, loses from sight that the calculated number even exceeds his estimate of the total number of people who have lived since the days of Adam.

36. Burke, *Reflections on the Revolution in France*, 418.

37. Ibid.

38. As early as 1793 Friedrich von Gentz, that very influential conservative thinker of post-Napoleonic Germany, published a German translation of the *Re-*

flections. For an exposition of Burke's reception in Germany, see F. Meinecke, *Weltbürgertum und Nationalstaat* (Munich, 1919), 135 ff. Characteristic is Novalis's wisecrack: "Many antirevolutionary books were written in favor of the revolution. Burke wrote a revolutionary book against the revolution." See Novalis (pseudonym of Friedrich Leopold von Hardenberg), *Blüthenstaub*, 2 vols. (Heidelberg, 1953), 1: 340.

39. In order to avoid the most unfortunate confusion that the word "historism" so often gives rise to in Anglo-Saxon countries, I emphasize that I use that word here not in Popper's sense, but as referring to the view of history and of historical writing that is ordinarily associated with the names of Ranke or Humboldt.

40. "It is universally acknowledged that there is a great uniformity among the actions of men, in all nations and ages, and that human nature remains still the same, in its principles and operations. The same motives always produce the same actions. The same events follow the same causes." See D. Hume, *Enquiries Concerning Human Understanding and Concerning the Principles of Morals*, ed. L. A. Selby-Bigge (Oxford, 1972), 83.

41. Of course, this is a reckless simplification of a far more complex phenomenon. Since Meinecke's book on the origins of historism, the historist tendencies in many Enlightenment authors, from Leibniz to Herder, have often been pointed out.

42. The nature of Burke's traditionalism manifests itself most clearly in his conception of the history of the English constitution; though there is continuous change, change has, for Burke, always the connotation of adaptation, and never that of "organic" growth, in the sense of a development, or of an unfolding of what was potentially already present. It is here that I would side with Mrs. Welcker and against Meinecke. Discussing Burke, Meinecke writes:

> Burke's conception of history represents the highest stage of traditionalism, especially since he was not so much interested in a careful devotion to the institutions, customs, prejudices, etc., that we have inherited from the past. What mainly interested him, instead, was the moral inner life pervading them all (like the blood of a living organism) and that made them grow together into the members and organs of one political and social organism.

See F. Meinecke, *Die Entstehung des Historismus* (1936; reprint, Munich, 1965), 277. But this historist organicism is, as Mrs. Welcker demonstrates, explicitly rejected by Burke himself; she quotes Burke when writing that "these analogies between bodies natural and politic, though they may sometimes illustrate arguments, furnish no arguments of themselves." See R. Welcker, *Geschichte und Geschichtsverständnis bei Edmund Burke* (Bern, 1981), 58.

43. For an exposition of the logical features of the historist conception of historical change and for its implications, see my "Historicism: An Attempt at Synthesis," *History and Theory* 34, no. 2 (1995): 143–62, 168–74.

44. "One may well surmise that these [i.e., the administrative disasters resulting from Louis XIV's 'imperial overstretch'—as we would nowadays call it] have
produced the revolutionary movement. For as a consequence of the failure to
realize this intention (that had at the time been welcomed by everybody) all dominating doctrines and tendencies now changed not only with the will of later governments, but also against it"—needless to say, a perfect example of Ranke's pos-
tulate of *das Primat der Aussenpolitik*. See L. van Ranke, "Ursprung und Beginn
der Revolutionskriege 1791 und 1792," in Ranke, *Sämmtliche Werke* (Leipzig, Ger.,
1879), 54: 22, 23.

45. See my *History and Tropology: The Rise and Fall of Metaphor* (Berkeley,
Calif., 1994), 150 ff.

46. I should like to thank Jaap den Hollander for his invaluable advice for the
remaining part of my argument. My exposition here is deeply indebted to his
magisterial "Conservatisme en historisme," *Bijdragen en mededelingen betreffende
de geschiedenis der Nederlanden* 102 (1987): esp. 396 ff.

47. In fact, two other traditions should be taken into account as well for this
period. In the first place we should think of the rediscovery of Stoicism in the sixteenth century. Neo-Stoicism, with its emphasis on the *recta ratio* and on logical
argument, with its preference for deduction from first principles and with its affinities with natural philosophy can well be seen as a transitional phase between Aristotelian (or Thomist) natural law philosophy and its modernist competitor. In
fact, Grotius is often said to have been the first to present a system of modernist
natural law philosophy. But Grotius's argument is neo-Stoicist rather than modernist (as in Hobbes, Locke, and others).

Secondly, there is the tradition of *raison d'état* thinking, which in a mitigated
variant was especially influential in seventeenth- and eighteenth-century Germany.
This tradition easily mixed with Aristotelian practical philosophy—I shall venture
an explanation at the end of this chapter. Meinecke already observed the continuity between seventeenth-century *raison d'état* political theory and nineteenth-century
historism (see F. Meinecke, *Weltbürgertum und Nationalstaat* [Munich, 1919]). It is
to be regretted that he paid no attention to the variants of Aristotelianism in the period investigated by him: that would have provided him with additional arguments
for his main thesis.

Lastly, it should be observed to what extent textbooks on the history of political thought ordinarily present a caricature of the period between 1500 and 1800.
For most often only the modernist tradition is expounded in the textbooks, while
the other three remain unmentioned. Not only does this obstruct a correct understanding of the political thought of this period, but it also renders incomprehensible the transition from the eighteenth to the nineteenth century. Within accounts focusing only on the modernist tradition, the emergence of history-oriented
nineteenth-century political thought is something of an inexplicable miracle. However, this transition loses much of its mystery if we recognize that it resulted from a

shift in the relationship between the four traditions. Because the modernist tradition was, in the eyes of most theorists, thoroughly discredited by its involvement in the French Revolution, the other three reasserted themselves. And, indeed, most of nineteenth-century political thought can well be understood as a series of alliances of the other three traditions against modernist natural law philosophy.

48. Surely another example of such unexpected reemergence of political Aristotelianism is provided by contemporary so-called communitarianism (one may think of authors like Alasdair MacIntyre, Charles Taylor, Martha Nussbaum, Amitai Etzioni, and others). One wonders whether the communitarians, who so much like to present themselves as belonging to the politically progressive left, are sufficiently aware of the inherent (Aristotelian, Thomist, Burkean) conservatism of their argument.

More generally, the contemporary debate between the liberals or libertarians on the one hand and the communitarians on the other is, in fact, little more than a latter-day reenactment of the conflict between the Aristotelian and the modernist variant of natural law philosophy. And one cannot help thinking that a little more historical sophistication might render this debate more efficient and more to the point than it presently is. In any case, some historical knowledge might make it possible to avoid absurdities such as Richard Rorty's: Rorty seems to believe that his well-known attack on epistemology is the most appropriate theoretical background to the embrace of a Rawlsian political Cartesianism. In fact, this attack is fatal to all political Cartesianism. But, arguably, the progressivism that contemporary intellectuals never dare to question makes them oblivious of historical subtleties such as the intrinsic conservatism of all political Aristotelianism. *Nec lusisse pudet, sed non incidere ludum* ("One need not be ashamed of having played games, but one should if one did not know when to stop"), to quote Horace.

49. "What appeared to the generations after Burke as a turn to History, not to say as the discovery of History, was primarily a return to the traditional [i.e., Aristotelian] view of the essential limitations of theory as distinguished from practice or prudence." Strauss even believed that Burke's Aristotelianism contained "the most important part of his work." See L. Strauss, *Natural Right and History* (Chicago, 1953), 302–3.

50. Surely this is an echo of Aristotle. Thus Aristotle wrote:

> Let us remember that we should not disregard the experience of ages; in the multitude of years between these things, if they were good, they would certainly not have been unknown; for almost everything has been found out, although sometimes they are not put together; in other cases men do not use the knowledge which they have.

See Aristotle, *Politica*, 2.5.1264aff. for this apt "summary" of Burke's political thought.

51. Aristotle, *Nicomachean Ethics*, trans. and intro. David Ross (Oxford, 1991), 154.

52. Ibid., 1143b18–1144b5.

53. Its recommendations could be compared to recommendations to football players, like "Do your best," "Try to win," and so on—that is, very sensible recommendations, indispensable even, in the sense that one cannot play football if one does not know that one should try to win. But all real problems arise with the question of *how* to win. For a criticism of ethics as the foundation of political thought, see my "Against Ethics," the introduction to *Aesthetic Politics: Political Philosophy Beyond Fact and Value* (Stanford, Calif., 1997).

54. See Strauss, *Natural Right and History*, 311.

55. P. Lucas, "On Edmund Burke's Doctrine of Prescription; or, An Appeal from the New to the Old Lawyers," *Historical Journal* 11, no. 1 (1968): 58 ff.

56. E. Burke, "Abridgment of English History," in *The Works of Edmund Burke*, 7: 462–63. For a very similar statement about the general development of the laws of England, see E. Burke, "Fragment: An Essay Towards an History for the Laws of England," in *The Works of Edmund Burke*, 7: 476–78.

57. Burke, *Reflections on the Revolution in France*, 274–75.

58. When addressing the French revolutionaries, Burke writes, "You might, if you pleased, have profited of our example [of the Glorious Revolution], and have given to your recovered freedom a correspondent dignity." See ibid., 276.

59. Non-European countries, such as India, are a different affair.

60. In this context Kossmann's study of Dutch seventeenth-century political thought is instructive. For Kossmann demonstrates here that such a fusion or synthesis was already achieved in the Netherlands in the course of the seventeenth century, and he refers to this synthesis by the notion of *politica novantiqua*. Willem van der Muelen and Ulrich Huber (professor in Franeker) are presented by Kossmann as the main protagonists of this *politica novantiqua*. Since especially Huber was eagerly read and commented upon in eighteenth-century Germany, it is far from unthinkable that Dutch seventeenth-century political thought (whose originality was demonstrated recently in H. W. Blom, *Morality and Causality in Politics: The Rise of Naturalism in Dutch Seventeenth-Century Political Thought* [Ridderkerk, Neth., 1995]) was a major source of inspiration for eighteenth-century German political theorists. See E. H. Kossmann, *Politieke theorie in het zeventiende eeuwse Nederland* (Amsterdam, 1960).

61. As Wolff himself commented: the book was written so that "theory has continuously been interrelated with praxis." For this quote, see D. M. Meyring, *Politische Weltweisheit: Studien zur deutschen politische Philosophie des 18. Jahrhunderts* (Munich, 1965), 45.

62. "Around 1770 the Leibnizian/Wolffian philosophy completely dominated the Catholic universities of southern Germany and Wolffian natural law had completely replaced that of Pufendorf and Thomasius." See M. Thomann, "Christian Wolff," in M. Stolleis, *Staatsdenker im 17. and 18. Jahrhundert* (Frankfurt am Main, 1977), 265.

63. For an account of the political thought of a Dutch admirer of Wolff, see W. R. E. Velema, *Enlightenment and Conservatism in the Dutch Republic: The Political Thought of Elie Luzac* (Assen, Neth., 1993). Velema here follows the thesis already defended by Kossmann in 1966 that Luzac should be considered an "Enlightened conservative." For an elucidation of this striking oxymoron, see E. H. Kossmann, "Verlicht conservatisme: Over Elie Luzac," in Kossman, *Politieke theorie en geschiedenis* (Amsterdam, 1987), 234–49. Kossmann's (and Velema's) results are of interest here, for they strongly suggest that, in practice, this synthesis of Aristotelianism and modernist natural law will take the form of an "Enlightened conservatism." It might well be that Kossmann's oxymoron is also applicable to the mainstream of German eighteenth-century political thought.

64. Meyring, *Politische Weltweisheit,* 47.

65. Ibid., 79; see also the entry "Politik" in O. Brunner, W. Conze, and R. Koselleck, eds., *Lexikon der geschichtlichen Grundbegriffe,* vol. 4 (Stuttgart, 1979), esp. 831ff.

66. *Klugheitslehre* is now defined as "conceptions about how a prince may make himself and his country powerful." See Meyring, *Politische Weltweisheit,* 59.

67. The discipline that was developed in order to assist the state and its servants was "statistics" (literally, "knowledge of the *state*") and was characterized by Achenwall in the claim that "statistics is stationary history and history is developing statistics." See A. T. van Deursen, *Geschiedenis en toekomstverwachting* (Kampen, Neth., 1971), 9; and A. Seifert, "Staatenkunde: Eine neue Disziplin und ihr wissenschaftstheoretischer Ort," in N. Rassem and J. Stagl, eds., *Statistik und Staatsbeschreibung in der Neuzeit* (Paderborn, Ger., 1980).

68. See L. von Ranke, *Sämmtliche Werke,* vol. 24, *Abhandlungen und Versuche* (Leipzig, Ger., 1872), 288–89, for Ranke's comment on the relationship between history and politics.

69. For an exposition of this notion and of its role in the writing of history, see my *Denken over geschiedenis* (Groningen, 1986), 177–80.

70. Strauss, *Natural Right and History,* 295.

CHAPTER 3: *Freud as the Last Natural Law Theorist*

1. C. Barrows, *Distorting Mirrors: Vision of the Crowd in Late Nineteenth-Century France* (New Haven, Conn., 1981), 1.

2. Ibid.

3. E. and L. Freud, eds., *Letters of Sigmund Freud, 1873–1939,* trans. T. and J. Stern (London, 1961), 199. The other writings of Freud consulted for this chapter can be found in J. Strachey, trans. and ed., *The Standard Edition of the Complete Psychological Works of Sigmund Freud,* 23 vols. (London, 1953–74); hereafter *SE.*

4. G. Le Bon, *La Psychologie des foules* (1895; reprint, Paris, 1921), 84.

5. Ibid., 5.

6. A. Espinas, *Des Sociétés animales* (1877; reprint, Paris, 1935), 424.

7. Ibid., 413.

8. According to methodological individualism, only those explanations of human behavior are to be considered valid that can, in the end, be formulated in terms of the behavior of individual human beings, whereas the methodological holist is, in principle, prepared to accept also explanations that are either partly or integrally formulated in terms referring to collective human behavior. Put differently, methodological individualism is reductionist because it requires at all times a reduction to the behavior of individual human beings; methodological holism does not demand such a reduction under all circumstances.

A comparison with the sciences may be helpful here. Boyle's law relates the pressure, temperature, and volume of the gas in a chamber and is holistic from the perspective of the behavior of the individual gas molecules in the chamber; the kinetic theory of gas, however, can explain Boyle's law in terms of the behavior of these individual gas molecules. But this fact does not in any way reduce the explanatory power of Boyle's law—on the contrary, the kinetic theory of gas precisely demonstrates *why* it is valid. Hence, certainly something has been gained if we succeed in explaining a phenomenon in the manner satisfying the methodological individualist—but this is not necessarily a condition for all legitimate and reliable scientific explanation. So there is no reason to distrust holistic explanations because of the mere fact that they are holistic.

9. Le Bon, *Psychologie des foules*, 17.

10. Freud, "Group Psychology and the Analysis of the Ego," *SE*, 18: 69.

11. Le Bon, *Psychologie des foules*, 177.

12. Ibid., 179.

13. B. Groethuysen, *Origines de l'esprit bourgeois en France* (Paris, 1927), 168.

14. Ibid., 373.

15. Ibid., 236–80.

16. Ibid., ix.

17. Ibid., 184–85.

18. G. K. Chesterton, *Robert Louis Stevenson* (London, 1927), 244.

19. Ibid., 233. For an erudite and compelling exposition of Schopenhauer's influence on late-nineteenth-century pessimism, see J. Pierrot, *L'Imaginaire Décadent* (Paris, 1977), 61–103.

20. R. L. Stevenson, *The Strange Case of Dr. Jekyll and Mr. Hyde* (1886; reprint, New York, 1966), 47, 70.

21. Ibid., 57.

22. Ibid., 61.

23. Ibid., 58, 67.

24. E. von Hartmann, *Philosophie des Unbewussten*, 3 vols. (Leipzig, Ger., 1904). For a detailed, but not very imaginative account of the history of all conceptions of the subconscious since the end of the eighteenth century, see H. F. Ellenberg, *The Discovery of the Unconscious* (New York, 1970).

25. In my *Narrative Logic: A Semantic Analysis of the Historian's Language* (The Hague and Boston, 1983), I have tried to give a logical foundation to the historist's often somewhat impressionist manner of arguing this thesis.

26. P. Rieff, *Freud: The Mind of a Moralist* (New York, 1959), 212.

27. Freud, *Totem and Taboo, SE,* 22: 141–43.

28. For an elaboration of the insight that the collectivity may sometimes function as the best safeguard of the individual citizen's liberty, see my "Against Ethics," the introduction to *Aesthetic Politics: Political Philosophy Beyond Fact and Value* (Stanford, Calif., 1997).

29. Freud, *Totem and Taboo, SE,* 22: 67.

30. P. Roazen, *Freud: Political and Social Thought* (New York, 1968), 268–73.

31. Freud, *Beyond the Pleasure Principle, SE,* 18: 3–66.

32. Freud, "'Civilized' Sexual Morality and Modern Nervous Illness," *SE,* 9: 203.

33. Freud, *Civilization and Its Discontents, SE,* 21: 105.

34. "No doubt you were right; they are transmuting weakness into merit. . . . Impotence which cannot retaliate, into kindness; pusillanimity into humility; submission before those one hates into obedience to One of whom they say that he has commanded this submission—they call him God. The inoffensiveness of the weak, his cowardice, his ineluctable standing and waiting at doors, are being given honorific titles such as patience; to be unable to avenge oneself is called to be unwilling to avenge oneself—even forgiveness ('for they know not what they do—we alone know what they do.') Also there's some talk of loving one's enemy—accompanied by much sweat." See F. Nietzsche, *The Genealogy of Morals,* in Nietzsche, *"The Birth of Tragedy" and "The Genealogy of Morals,"* trans. F. Golffing (New York, 1956), 180–81.

35. Freud, *Civilization and Its Discontents, SE,* 21: 95–96.

36. Freud, a believer in science if ever there was one, places science outside the range of what may be affected by the vagaries of human psychology. In fact, this is quite strange if we recall that one of the main implications of Freud's conceptions is a "psychologization" of all of reality; there simply could not be a reality, as the subject matter of science, that is *not* closely bound up with our psychological condition in some way or other. But in opposition to this, the main strain in Freud's thinking about science is that science and only science may cure and safeguard us from neurosis and all the mental distress that civilization has inflicted upon the human psyche.

37. Marcuse's attempt to reconcile Freudian psychoanalysis to utopianism was therefore not very realistic. I do not wish to imply, however, that Marcuse would have been unaware of the problem involved in his enterprise. See H. Marcuse, *Eros and Civilization* (London, 1970), 24ff., and for a (negative) assessment of the book's plausibility, see S. Frosh, *The Politics of Psychoanalysis* (London, 1987), 150.

38. Rieff, *Freud,* 256.

39. Ibid., 244.

40. G. W. F. Hegel, *Lectures on the Philosophy of World History*, 4 vols.; vol. 1, *Reason in History*, trans. H. B. Nisbet (Cambridge, Eng., 1980), 49.

41. See Freud, *Moses and Monotheism*, *SE*, 23: 570 ff. A prototypical example of the repression of the murder of the father is the (hypothetical) murder of Moses by the Jewish people, which is discussed in *Moses and Monotheism*. According to Freud, the murder of Moses—a disciple of Akhnaton's solar religion—was repressed in the earlier phases of Jewish history. But finally, after having been latent for centuries, the repressed returned in the guise of the dogmatic hardening and radicalization that so much distinguishes the Jewish religion from others. See also ibid., 517 ff.

42. Rieff, *Freud*, 215.

43. Ibid., 218.

CHAPTER 4: *Representative Democracy*

1. C. Schmitt, *The Concept of the Political* (Chicago, 1997).

2. Q. Skinner, "Meaning and Understanding in the History of Ideas," *History and Theory* 8 (1969): 5–53.

3. M. Albert, *Capitalism Against Capitalism* (London, 1993).

4. Ibid., 18–19.

5. For a more in-depth discussion of these theories, see my *Historical Representation* (Stanford, Calif., 2001), chaps. 1 and 8.

6. Quoted in B. Manin, *The Principles of Representative Government* (Cambridge, Eng., 1997), 110.

7. Quoted in ibid., 115.

8. Quoted in ibid., 116.

9. J.-J. Rousseau, *Du Contrat social* (1762; reprint, Paris, 1962), chap. 15, 301–3.

10. E. Burke, "Speech at the Conclusion of the Poll," in *The Works of Edmund Burke*, 12 vols. (Boston, 1866), 2: 95–96. See Ankersmit, *Historical Representation*, chap. 10, for further comments on Burke's conception of political representation.

11. For a more detailed exposition of this argument, see my *Historical Representation*, chap. 1.

12. The fascination of American political philosophers for this kind of politically useless topics undoubtedly has much to do with the fact that for Americans the Constitution is sacrosanct to a degree that never fails to amaze the citizens of the democracies of continental Europe. Since a discussion of the state and of its constitution has thus, to all practical purposes, become impossible in the United States, the citizen could become so much the obvious focus of interest for American political philosophers. Though this is all too understandable within the context of American politics, one can only regret that European political philosophers have generally been so eager to join the American liberals, communitarians, and

republicans in this bizarre American prejudice with regard to what demands the political philosopher's attention.

13. See D. Anzieu, *The Skin Ego* (New Haven, Conn., 1989).

CHAPTER 5: *Political Style*

1. See, for example, N. Goodman, *Ways of Worldmaking* (Indianapolis, 1978).

2. C. Rosen, *The Romantic Generation* (London, 1996), 7 ff.

3. R. Barthes, "The Reality Effect," in T. Todorov, ed., *French Literary Theory Today* (Cambridge, Eng., 1982), 11–18.

4. M. Edelman, *Politics as Symbolic Action* (New York, 1971), 3.

5. J. E. Combs and D. Nimmo, *The Comedy of Democracy* (Westport, Conn., 1996), 28.

6. Edelman, *Politics as Symbolic Action*, 7.

7. Ibid., 4.

8. M. Edelman, *Constructing the Political Spectacle* (Chicago, 1988), 37. Alphonse de Lamartine already made this claim about what should be the political leader's guide. I owe this information to Professor C. A. Tamse.

9. For a further elucidation of this view of democracy, see my *Aesthetic Politics: Political Philosophy Beyond Fact and Value* (Stanford, Calif., 1997); and my *Exploraties: Politieke filosofie*, vol. 3, *Macht door representatie* (Kampen, Neth., 1997).

10. Here we may observe another difference between compromise and consensus: the kind of agreement achieved in consensus is, so to speak, without a point of view or perspective and for that very reason not dependent upon such an essentially *later* point of view as is developed in compromise.

11. Edelman, *Political Spectacle*, 19.

12. C. L. de Montesquieu, *L'Esprit des Lois* (Paris, 1973), 6.

13. Edelman, *Political Spectacle*, 19; emphasis mine.

14. For an inventory of Tocqueville's paradoxes and their significance for his conception of democracy, see my *Aesthetic Politics*, the last chapter.

15. For a further elucidation, see my *Aesthetic Politics*, chaps. 3 and 4 and my *Macht door representatie*, esp. 171–77.

16. A truly amazing argument to this effect was presented by Pascal. See my *Aesthetic Politics*, 245–54.

17. F. von Schiller, "Über naive und sentimentalische Dichtung," in Schiller, *Schillers Werke*, 12 vols. (Stuttgart, n.d.), 12: 110.

18. Ibid.

19. Ibid., 128.

20. Ibid., 118.

21. Ibid., 132.

22. Schiller's assessment of classical Greece—and I am thinking here specifically of how he contrasts Euripides with the older Aeschylus—is in complete

agreement with Hegel's justly famous characterization of "das Verderben der Griechischen Sittlichkeit," as presented in the latter's *Vorlesungen über die Philosophie der Weltgeschichte*, vol. 3; the pre-Socratic Greeks were still "naive," and only thanks to and only after Socrates could they become "sentimental," to put it in Schiller's terminology.

23. This is Schiller's own terminology; see Schiller, "Über naive und sentimentalische Dichtung," 118.

24. One cannot help being amazed by finding the unworldly Adrian VI in the same category as Caesar and Henry IV—obviously, we have to do here with two quite different conceptions of political naivete. Their political naivete gave them the directness of approach needed for an adequate solution of the political problems they had to solve. Ronald Reagan's dealings with "the empire of evil" is an illuminating contemporary example.

25. The exception to this rule would be "aesthetic political philosophy" as I defined this concept in my *Aesthetic Politics*.

26. Schiller, "Über naive und sentimentalische Dichtung," 119.

27. And insofar as ethics has an affinity with our conscience, with our inner moral convictions, and with what practical reason tells us that we should do, we may discern here the unbridgeable gap between the notions of ethics and of style. There could be no science of ethics for what ought to be the style of our behavior.

28. Schiller, "Über naive und sentimentalische Dichtung," 130.

29. "If the poet opposes nature and ideal in such a way that the representation of the former is predominant, I shall call him elegiac." See ibid., 138.

30. The idyll is seen by Schiller as a subvariant of elegy: it occurs when the natural is experienced as a *Gegenstand der Freude* ("object of joy").

31. Schiller, "Über naive und sentimentalische Dichtung," 133.

32. R. Hariman, *Political Style: The Artistry of Power* (Chicago, 1995), 13.

33. Ibid.

34. See, for example, H. Fenichel-Pitkin, *Fortune Is a Woman: Gender and Politics in the Thought of Niccolo Machiavelli* (Berkeley, Calif., 1987), 110–14.

35. Schiller, "Über naive und sentimentalische Dichtung," 136.

36. Ibid., 158.

37. For an account of the relevant aspects of the logic of representation and identity, see "Danto on Representation, Identity, and Indiscernibles," chapter 8 of my *Historical Representation* (Stanford, Calif., 2001).

38. Which has the important implication that to representation must be granted the same ontological status as things—that is, *not* that of reality. See, for example, my *History and Tropology: The Rise and Fall of Metaphor* (Berkeley, Calif., 1994), 90ff.

39. For this advantage of representation to true description, see my "The Representation of Experience," *Metaphilosophy* 31, nos. 1–2, special issue (2000): 148–69.

40. Combs and Nimmo, *Comedy of Democracy*, 16.

41. Ibid., 9 ff.

42. For a clarification of the idea that misconceptions of democracy belong to the set of conditions of its proper functioning, see my *Aesthetic Politics*, 186 ff.

43. P. C. Westerman, *The Disintegration of Natural Law Theory: Aquinas to Finnis* (New York, 1997), 32.

44. For a more detailed exposition of the unparalleled political creativity of democracy, see my *Macht door representatie*, 215 ff.

45. In which many aesthetic and stylistic elements may be present already; see, for example, W. J. Witteveen, "Enacting Law: Ritual Performances in Dutch Political Culture," in J. R. Lindgren and J. Knaak, eds., *Rituals and Semiotics* (New York, 1997), 193–222.

46. For a number of striking illustrations of this claim, see A. W. Robertson, *The Language of Democracy: Political Rhetoric in the United States and Britain, 1790–1900* (Ithaca, N.Y., and London, 1995). Robertson demonstrates in this book to what extent the evolution of Anglo-Saxon democracy during the period under investigation found its clearest expression in evolutions of political style and rhetoric.

CHAPTER 6: *Democracy as Antifoundationalism*

1. T. Hobbes, *Leviathan* (New York and London, 1970), 87.

2. There is the well-known old anecdote that Hobbes's mother had given birth to him when she saw the Spanish Armada approach the coast of Britain. The fright she felt at this spectacle, so the story continues, was somehow transmitted to the baby and this is said to explain Hobbes's later timorousness.

3. Hobbes, *Leviathan*, 89.

4. Ibid.

5. J. Rawls, *A Theory of Justice* (Cambridge, Mass., 1971), 121.

6. R. Rorty, "The Priority of Democracy to Philosophy," in Rorty, *Philosophical Papers*, vol. 1, *Objectivity, Relativism, and Truth* (Cambridge, Eng., 1991), 187. Rorty admits having been convinced of Rawls's foundationalism when he read *Theory of Justice* shortly after its publication. But Rawls's publication in the eighties made Rorty change his mind about this. It is more likely, however, that Rawls abandoned much of his former Kantianism in these later publications, and it might be wrong, therefore, to try to read Rawls's later and more attractive position into his *Theory of Justice*.

7. I. Shapiro, *Political Criticism* (Berkeley, Calif., 1992), 224 ff.

8. I. Kant, *Critique of Judgment*, trans. J. M. Bernard (New York, 1951), 150.

9. I. Berlin, "The Originality of Machiavelli," in Berlin, *Against the Current* (Oxford, 1981), 25–80.

10. It should be added, though, that despite the almost ritual condemnation of

what was considered Machiavelli's immoralism, seventeenth- and eighteenth-century political philosophers often remained remarkably close to him. Much of the most original seventeenth- and eighteenth-century political thought was clearly Machiavellist in argument and conclusion. See, for example, H. W. Blom, *Morality and Causality in Politics: The Rise of Naturalism in Dutch Seventeenth-Century Political Thought* (Ridderkerk, Neth., 1995). And, needless to say, there also is much Machiavellism in nineteenth-century political thought thanks to its strongly historist orientation. Perhaps Machiavelli truly became a *nomen nefandum* only in our own century, hence in the century of unprecedented political crime. Some deep truth is undoubtedly hidden beneath this paradox.

11. Berlin, "The Originality of Machiavelli," 45.

12. Ibid., 59.

13. This opposition between equality and freedom was also the central message in R. Nozick, *Anarchy, State, and Utopia* (Oxford, 1974). But where Nozick then opts for the foundationalist view to place freedom higher then equality, the Machiavellian attitude would be to avoid any such hierarchization of political values and to see, instead, the proper approach to political reality in an acceptance of the inevitable conflict between freedom and equality. This conflict, eliminated by Nozick out of a (foundationalist) desire for conceptual clarity, is precisely what most of politics is all about.

14. C. Schmitt, *Der Begriff des Politischen* (Hamburg, 1933), 42 ff.

15. See also my comment on Nozick in note 13.

16. See J. L. Talmon, *The Origins of Totalitarian Democracy* (London, 1952); K. R. Popper, *The Poverty of Historicism* (London, 1957); F. von Hayek, *The Counter-Revolution of Science: Studies on the Abuse of Reason* (Glencoe, Ill., 1952).

17. For the essentially monological character of ethical discourse, see Chapter 5.

18. Quoted in Rorty, "The Priority of Democracy to Philosophy," 180.

19. Quoted in ibid.

20. Ibid., 191–92. For a similar argument, see my *Aesthetic Politics: Political Philosophy Beyond Fact and Value* (Stanford, Calif., 1997), 252–53.

21. For this quote, see Rorty, "The Priority of Democracy to Philosophy," 179.

22. B. Pascal, *Pensées* (Paris, 1962), 23.

23. See Chapter 4, the section entitled "The Romantic Roots of Representative Democracy."

24. In Rorty's consideration of how to answer the kind of argument against liberal democracy that we may expect from people like Loyola and Nietzsche, he writes: "We have to insist that not every argument need to be met in terms of which it is presented. Accommodation and tolerance must stop short of a willingness to work within any vocabulary that one's interlocutor wishes to use, to take seriously any topic that he puts forward for discussion." See Rorty, "The Priority of Democracy to Philosophy," 190. But these are the worries of philosophers about how to conduct a meaningful philosophical debate with his weirder philosophical

opponents. However, from a political point of view "accomodation and tolerance" are simply all that is needed: let these people say what they wish to say, as long as they do not endanger public order by "fanatical" exaggeration.

CHAPTER 7: *The Network, the Expert*

1. For an introductory discussion of this issue, see W. C. Müller and V. Wright, eds., *The State in Western Europe: Retreat or Redefinition?* (Ilford, Eng., 1994). The editors of this collection conclude that recent stories about "the death of the nation-state" are greatly exaggerated:

> In attempting to explain the survival of the Western European nation-state in spite of (greatly exaggerated) crises we perhaps need to look more closely not only at its immense resources but also its infinite capacity for external and internal adaptability. Perhaps the dominant paradigm of the later 1990s may be less critical of the alleged inherent defects of the state and more sensitive to its unshakeable centrality and to its potential. (10–11)

2. Alan Milward recently argued that the European Community had originally been devised as an instrument to rescue the European nation-state: it was recognized that only unification would enable the European nations to successfully meet the challenges of the new world order that had come into being after 1945. The delegation of part of national sovereignty to the community was considered to be the only condition of the preservation of the nation-state, in the same way that cooperation with others may often prove to be the best way of preserving our own autonomy and independence from others. See A. Milward, *The European Rescue of the Nation-State* (London, 1994). Obviously, one's assessment of this thesis will determine whether European integration should be considered an attack on the European nation-state or its defense.

3. Amazingly, Guizot had already observed much the same 150 years ago. We are living, he wrote, in "an electric society where everything is propagated and immediately known to anybody, a society where millions of individuals of similar conditions and of similar opinions know all about each other's fate." And elsewhere:

> Power no longer rests with individuals nor with families; it has left its customary centers and has spread itself all over society; it circulates there with an amazing speed, hardly to be noticed on individual places, but all the more omnipresent for that. It has grafted itself on interests, on ideas, on public opinions that nobody can control and that nobody succeeds in representing so well that they will share their fate with that of the person representing them.

For this most penetrating and even profoundly prophetic insight, see P. Rosanvallon, *Le Moment Guizot* (Paris, 1985), 38–40.

4. J. M. Guéhenno, *La Fin de la démocratie* (Paris, 1993).

5. The challenge no longer is "to dominate a territory, but to have access to a network." See ibid., 25.

6. For an exposition of the Japanese paradigm of (political and economic) power, see my *Aesthetic Politics: Political Philosophy Beyond Fact and Value* (Stanford, Calif., 1997), 282–90.

7. Guéhenno, *La Fin de la démocratie*, 93 ff.

8. Ibid., 108. The similarity of Guéhenno's metaphor and those used by Guizot as presented in note 3 testifies, once again, to Guizot's prophetic talent.

9. One is reminded here of Mirabeau's statement that ten people who closely cooperate may make tremble hundreds of thousands of other people

10. Guéhenno, *La Fin de la démocratie*, 103.

11. J. Sachs, "Global Capitalism: Making It Work," *The Economist*, 12–18 September 1998, 21–26. In this article, Sachs argues that underdeveloped countries will have a fair chance of economic success only if states decide to restrict the financial network that sends around the globe thousands of billions of dollars a day. And it would only need the recognition of the appropriateness of Sachs's recommendations by the more influential nation-states to effect such a restriction.

12. Guéhenno, *La Fin de la démocratie*, 170.

13. A. G. Slama, *L'Angélisme Exterminateur: Essai sur l'ordre moral contemporain* (The destructiveness of moralism: Essay on the contemporary moral order) (Paris, 1993), chap. 4.

14. Ibid., chap. 5. See also my *Aesthetic Politics*, 186 ff.

15. Milgram did these experiments partly in an effort to understand what had happened in Nazi Germany.

16. Slama, *L'Angélisme Exterminateur*, 136 ff.

17. N. Machiavelli, *Discourses on Livy*, trans. H. C. Mansfield and N. Tarcov (Chicago, 1996); emphasis mine.

18. Ibid., 17.

19. Ibid., 18.

20. N. Machiavelli, *The Prince*, trans. George Bull (Harmondsworth, Eng., 1984), 30.

CHAPTER 8: *Compromise and Political Creativity*

1. See, for example, my *Narrative Logic: A Semantic Analysis of the Historian's Language* (The Hague and Boston, 1983), and my *History and Tropology: The Rise and Fall of Metaphor* (Berkeley, Calif., 1994). For a short synopsis of the views expounded in these books, see my "Reply to Professor Zagorin," *History and Theory* 29, no. 3 (1990): 275–97. See, more specifically, my *Historical Representation* (Stanford, Calif., 2001), chap. 1, and in the present volume, Chapter 4.

2. J. Rawls, *Political Liberalism* (New York, 1996), 134.

3. Ibid., 150–51; emphasis mine.

4. Ibid., 168.

5. Ibid., 147.

6. Ibid., 159.

7. G. A. den Hartogh, "Waarheid en consensus in de politieke filosofie van John Rawls," *Algemeen Nederlands tijdschrift voor wijsbegeerte* 84, no. 2 (1992): 93–121, 117.

8. Ibid.

9. I explicitly say here "what we have come to see as rights" because we should not forget that even these rights developed from what originally were mere compromises.

10. F. Fukuyama, *Trust: The Social Virtues and the Creation of Prosperity* (New York, 1995).

11. Quoted in M. P. Golding, "The Nature of Compromise: A Preliminary Inquiry," in J. R. Pennock and J. W. Chapman, eds., *Compromise in Ethics, Law, and Politics* (New York, 1979), 7.

12. In this context it is of interest to recall the findings of Robert Putnam in his much acclaimed *Making Democracy Work: Civic Traditions in Modern Italy* (Princeton, N.J., 1993). In those areas of Italy (especially the south) where civic traditions are least developed, compromise is distrusted: "To compromise with one's political opponents is dangerous because that normally leads to the betrayal of one's own side." On the other hand, "politicians in civic regions do not deny the reality of conflicting interests, but they are unafraid of creative compromise" (105; see also 115). The readiness to compromise is a sure sign of a mature political culture.

13. It is, in the present context, relevant to recall Hannah Arendt's most perceptive analysis of hypocrisy and its role in eighteenth-century political thought and during the French Revolution (when hypocrisy was considered, by Robespierre and his Jacobin followers, to be the major political vice, for which the guillotine was the only appropriate answer). According to Arendt, "What makes it so plausible to assume that hypocrisy is the vice of vices is that integrity can indeed exist under the cover of all other vices except this one. Only crime and the criminal, it is true, confront us with the perplexity of radical evil; but only the hypocrite is really rotten to the core." See H. Arendt, *On Revolution* (London, 1990), 103. This is precisely where the hypocrite differs from the person willing to compromise. For compromise, as opposed to consensus, does not require us to abandon our moral or political convictions and is therefore less a standing invitation to hypocrisy, as conceived by Arendt, than consensus.

14. M. Benjamin, *Splitting the Difference: Compromise and Integrity in Ethics and Politics* (Lawrence, Kans., 1990), 8, 46 ff.

15. Benjamin follows here the kind of view that was expounded by Nagel in several of his writings since his "The Fragmentation of Value," in T. Nagel, *Mortal Questions* (Cambridge, Eng., 1979).

16. See also my *Aesthetic Politics: Political Philosophy Beyond Fact and Value* (Stanford, Calif., 1997), chap. 3.

17. This has been the contribution of the doctrinary liberals who have done more than anybody else to introduce representative government in France. And in meditating what enabled them to do so, Guizot wrote:

> Some said: there is in the Revolution only crime and error and the *ancien régime* was right against it; others said: the Revolution has only sinned by its excesses; its principles were allright, but it pushed them too far; the Revolution has abused of its being in the right. The doctrinaire liberals rejected both these assertions; they refused both a return to the maxims of the *ancien régime* and the adhesion, if only speculative, to the principles of the Revolution. Compelled to both a defense and an attack on the Revolutions, they opted bravely, right from the start, for an intellectualist approach, they opposed principles to principles and appealed not only to experience, but to reason as well. It was to this mixture of philosophical elevation and political moderation, of rationalist respect of justice and of the contingencies of history, of both new doctrines and conservative doctrines, antirevolutionary without being retrograde, that the doctrinaire liberals owed both their significance and their name.

Quoted in Rosanvallon, *Le Moment Guizot*, 27. A more striking exemplification of compromise and of the political mentality presupposed by it will be hard to find.

18. J. H. Carens, "Compromises in Politics," in J. R. Pennock and J. W. Chapman, *Compromise in Ethics, Law, and Politics* (New York, 1979), 124.

19. No "new" political realities come into being, however, as long as compromise is restricted to the procedure of simple log-rolling, where one party abandons certain claims in exchange for the abandonment of certain claims by the other party. See Golding, "The Nature of Compromise," 14; and Carens, "Compromises in Politics," 127, 131, 135, 138.

20. Carens, "Compromises in Politics," 128; emphasis mine.

21. Such an (unlikely) coalition has ruled my own country, the Netherlands, since 1994, and does so quite successfully.

CHAPTER 9: *Respect*

1. J. Michelet, *Histoire de la Révolution Française* (Paris, 1952), intro. The "incommensurability" of justice and Christian love is expressed by Michelet as follows: "The Revolution continues Christianity but is also in contradiction with it. The Revolution is both the heir and the adversary of Christianity" (25).

2. See p. 190.

3. See chapter 4 of my *Aesthetic Politics: Political Philosophy Beyond Fact and Value* (Stanford, Calif., 1997), 170–76.

4. Held sees these as the "central premises" of pluralist (democratic) theory. Cf. D. Held, *Political Theory and the Modern State* (Cambridge, Eng., 1990), 61. See R. Dahl, *On Democracy* (New Haven, Conn., 1998); and Dahl, *Democracy and Its Critics* (New Haven, Conn., 1989).

5. Though I immediately concede that several theorists, both from the past and the present, most notably Rorty himself, have doubted the validity of the distinction. For Rorty, see R. Rorty, "Texts and Lumps," in Rorty, *Philosophical Papers*, vol. 1, *Objectivism, Relativism, and Truth* (Cambridge, Eng., 1991).

6. For a short summary of the relevant views, see my "Reply to Professor Zagorin," *History and Theory* 29, no. 3 (1990): 257–79.

7. B. Lang, *Act and Idea in the Nazi Genocide* (Chicago, 1990); Z. Bauman, *Modernity and the Holocaust* (London, 1989).

8. See Chapter 4.

9. See F. Meinecke, *Die Idee der Staatsräson in der neueren Geschichte* (Munich, 1976), esp. pp. 442–60.

10. In fact, to the extent that democratic politics should be associated with compromise rather than with *consensus*, democracy has even more affinity with *raison d'état* thinking than these other political systems.

11. Authoritative is G. G. Iggers, *The German Conception of History* (Middletown, Conn., 1968). For a debate about the political implications of historism, see the debate between Professor Iggers and me in *History and Theory* 36, no. 1 (1995): 3.

12. The freedom of movement demanded for historical perspectivism that was discussed a moment ago can best be analyzed in terms of historical experience. For the immediacy of historical experience, as described for example by Johan Huizinga, puts us outside the reach of all determinations of historical insight that are alien to its subject matter. In this way, the ultimate demise of the last epistemological remnants in historical thought may urge us to speak a new terminology, that is, the terminology of historical experience, where openness or freedom goes together with objectivity.

13. T. de Boer, "Elk mens Adam," in de Boer, *Tamara A.: Awater en andere verhalen over subjectiviteit* (Amsterdam, 1993), 110ff.

14. See, for example, N. G. Finkelstein and R. B. Birn, *A Nation on Trial: The Goldhagen Thesis and Historical Truth* (New York, 1998). See also D. J. Goldenhagen, *Hitler's Willing Executioners: Ordinary Germans and the Holocaust* (New York, 1996).

15. G. W. Leibniz, *The Monadology*, in Leibniz, *Philosophical Papers and Letters*, trans. and ed., Leroy E. Loemker (Dordrecht, Neth., 1969), §§ 57, 56.

16. See my *Narrative Logic: A Semantic Analysis of the Historian's Language* (The Hague and Boston, 1983), 140–97.

17. Leibniz, *Monadology*, § 60.

18. For a further elaboration of this view of the nature of political reality, see the argument in Chapter 5 about the *innere Stimme* of politics.

EPILOGUE

1. F. R. Ankersmit, *Historical Representation* (Stanford, Calif., 2001).
2. W. Welsch, *Unsere postmoderne Moderne* (Darmstadt, Ger., 1991).

INDEX

Achenwall, G., 30, 31
Aesthetic political philosophy, 134, 166, 212, 233, 234
Albert, M., 100, 101, 103
Anglo-Saxon versus Continental democracy, 100–104
Antifederalists, 109, 110, 111
Antifoundationalist political philosophy, 11, 12, 165; and democracy, 173–79
Arcana Imperii, 8, 23–28, 34, 35, 55
Aristotelianism, 56–59
Aristotle, 19, 32, 32, 247; and Burke 50–58; on *sophismata*, 23

Barrows, C., 61
Barthes, R., 137
Bell, D., 186, 187
Benjamin, M., 207
Berlin, Sir Isaiah, 167–69, 174, 178
Boer, Th. de, 223, 224
Bourgeoisie: Groethuysen on, 68–70
Bureaucracy, 47, 116, 117; departmental, 120–22
Burke, E., 8, 37–59, 206; and Aristotelianism, 39, 50–59; and constitutionalism, 54; compared to Gadamer, 38, 39; on history, 37, 44–50, 58, 59; on human nature, 37, 40; and natural law philosophy, 37, 47, 50–56, 59; on practical wisdom, 53, 54; on prejudice, 38, 39; on prescription, 53–55; on prudence, 52–55; on political representation, 111–13; on rights of man, 44–47;

on traditionalism 49; on wisdom and folly, 38–44

Cameralism, 57
Carens, J. H., 208, 209
Castiglione, B., 27
Chesterton, G. K., 70
'Classical' political theory, 138–42
Combs, J. E., 139, 157
Comedy, 155–57
Communitarianism, 165
Compromise, 11, 12, 96; as opposed to consensus, 142–44, 201–13; the creative potential of, 208–10; dangers of, 211; characteristic of representative democracy, 208
Conring, H., 29, 30
Consensus: as opposed to compromise, 96, 142–44, 201–13
Constitutionalism: Burke on, 54
Content: and form, 10, 11, 134, 135
Continental versus Anglo-Saxon democracy, 100–104, 106, 107
Creativity in politics: *see* political creativity

Dahl, R., 218
Danto, A. C., 109
Democracy, 9–11, 91–236; and antifoundationalism, 173–79; Anglo-Saxon and Continental, 100–104, 106, 107; as comic, 156, 157; and compromise (and consensus), 142–44; as

Cultural Memory | *in the Present*

The authorized representative in the EU for product safety and compliance is:
Mare Nostrum Group
B.V Doelen 72
4831 GR Breda
The Netherlands

www.ingramcontent.com/pod-product-compliance
Lightning Source LLC
Chambersburg PA
CBHW030348270326
41926CB00009B/1004